DIGITAL
VIDEO
AN INTRODUCTION

DIGITAL VIDEO

AN INTRODUCTION

TOM **ANG**

LONDON, NEW YORK, MUNICH, MELBOURNE, and DELHI

Contents

To Wendy

Project Editor Nicky Munro
Designer Jenisa Patel
Picture Research Carolyn Clerkin
DTP Designer Vania Cunha
Production Controller Maria Elia

Managing Art Editor Karen Self
Category Publisher Stephanie Jackson
Publishing Manager Linda Martin
Art Director Bryn Walls

Produced on behalf of Dorling Kindersley by
SANDS PUBLISHING SOLUTIONS
4 Jenner Way, Eccles,
Aylesford, Kent, UK ME20 7SQ
Project Editors David & Sylvia Tombesi-Walton
Project Art Editor Simon Murrell

First American Edition, 2006
Published in the United States by
DK Publishing, Inc.
375 Hudson Street
New York, New York 10014

05 06 07 08 09 10 9 8 7 6 5 4 3 2 1

Copyright © 2006 Dorling Kindersley
Text copyright © 2006 Tom Ang

A Cataloging-in-Publication record for this book is available from The Library of Congress.

ISBN 0 7566 1600 X

Color reproduction by GRB Editrice s.r.l., Italy
Printed and bound in Singapore by Star Standard

Discover more at www.dk.com

The material in this book has previously appeared in Dorling Kindersley's *Digital Video Handbook*.

Introduction

The extraordinary revolution that is digital video can turn your backyard into a movie studio, transform your study into an editing suite, and make you a director. Technically, it sounds simple enough. Instead of recording an image frame by frame on to film or tape, we convert moving images into a series of numbers. Yet this one change opens up the entire enterprise of moviemaking to anyone with a modern personal computer. Whereas the aspiring moviemaker once needed the support of a highly specialized industrial infrastructure, much of that is now redundant. Moviemakers— and that means you or me—can now go it alone: a single person can shoot broadcast-quality footage, record high-fidelity sound, and edit and postproduce it on their own and at home. And from there, to reach the rest of the Internet-connected world is only the click of a mouse away.

For us, the inconvenient and tiresome craft of editing film frame-by-frame is consigned to history's cutting room. Better still, the formerly very high cost of editing video is now almost vanishingly small. Even better, the once daunting scale of movie distribution—which used to need huge investments—can now be almost lost in the domestic budgets of any family able to afford an Internet connection, and feature-length movies can be reproduced for pennies.

While it is true that open access to technology is a seedbed for great moviemakers—the teenager who makes gory movies for fun grows up to be the architect of the *Lord of the Rings* trilogy—its significance to the majority of users is even greater. Incidentally, Peter Jackson could not possibly have shot three feature-length films simultaneously, as he did, without considerable help from digital technology.

Technology in the arts is nothing if it does not help you create new ways of seeing and telling, and today's digital video opens a world in which you can manipulate time, reach into your viewer's hearts, entertain or enthrall them, and even horrify or scare them. Above all, digital video gives you the power to create as never before.

In *Digital Video: An Introduction*, I share with you the thrilling, fast-expanding, and entertaining world of video and moviemaking. You can keep it simple, making vacation videos for your friends and family, you can make short movies for school projects or local groups, you can even take on more ambitious projects such as documentaries. Even if you know nothing about video, this book offers you all the key information you need to make a start, and gives you a firm foundation for your future as a moviemaker.

And the best thing is this: you will never have to put up with the movie mogul who declares "My indecision is final!" or the equally infamous "You have my definite maybe."

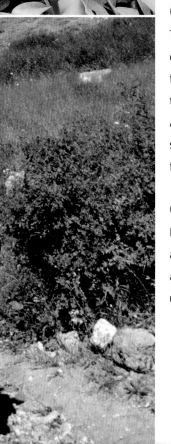

1
This is
digital video

Starting out

Digital video is a magical world in which almost anything goes. Here, the many aspects of digital video are explained, including the different levels of camera and the various formats, as well as how digital video does what it does. This is a road map for navigating your way through a new, creative environment.

Choosing equipment

The first steps toward selecting the right tools for the job are often tentative ones. Finding your way around the camera, familiarizing yourself with its features and learning how to use them are covered, as is the whole range of video accessories. Almost a book within a book, this chapter gives details of specific equipment as well as general information about the functions that you are likely to find most useful.

Computing necessities

Helpful tips on choosing computers and computing accessories are given, and there is a rundown of the different software available. The chapter rounds off with advice on how to set up an editing studio.

Digital video pathways

Digital video has added a host of possibilities to moviemaking that were once the province of the professional film studio. The key to this explosion in potential is the partnership between the relatively inexpensive digital video camera and the widespread availability of powerful personal computing. And the icing on this rich cake is the Internet. By adding two elements—movement and sound—to the still image, it is possible to go much further in digital video than in digital photography, in terms of creativity.

Sourcing material

Digital video can secure images from a range of sources. You can shoot new material directly with a digital video camera or work with still digital photographs. If you have old material on analog video tapes, you can convert this to digital. Footage from broadcasts can also be used, but be sure not to infringe on copyright (see p. 74). Sound can be sourced at the same time as video taping, or it may be added later, from music or sound-effects CDs, for example.

Digital camera
Many digital cameras can record short clips—30 seconds or longer—of video. You may not be able to zoom or focus during the clip.

Subject

Digital video camera
Modern cameras offer near-professional facilities in increasingly compact form, with good image quality. Ensure the camera is compatible with your computer before purchase.

Sound input
Sound may be recorded separately, either to be used as ambient background noise—or room tone—or for voice-overs, for example.

Analog video
Breathe new life into your analog video tapes by converting them into a digital form.

Video capture
Play your analog tapes through a video-capture device connected to your computer to compress and encode the video ready for editing.

Analog and digital technology

The development of video is intimately linked to advances in magnetic-tape technology. Images are recorded by varying the magnetic strength of minute portions of the tape. The principle is exactly the same as used in music cassette tapes. To reconstruct the signal on video playback, the variations of magnetic strength are read off, amplified, and used to alter the voltage of the electron guns at the back of a TV set.

With digital video, magnetic tape is still used (some cameras record directly on to DVD; *see p. 22*), but now the magnetic information is limited to just positive or negative. It is easier and more accurate to read positive or negative information, rather than measuring the strength of magnetism. However, this system can record much less information than analog tape. This is why compression is a vital element of the digital video process.

DVD
With DVD-mastering software, you can create DVDs complete with special audio tracks and extra features.

Domestic TV
A very convenient way to view your own videos is on the family TV screen. You can play them through your DVD player or direct from your computer or video camera.

Internet
Hundreds of hours of video clips are available for download. Equally, you can make your work available for others. You could also set up a web log so that a website is constantly updated with your recordings.

Processing in the computer
Images captured in your camera or downloaded can be worked on in your computer, allowing you to add titles and edit sound and vision.

Printer
You can print out individual frames from your video footage, but the quality will not be as high as with images taken with a digital camera.

The processing line

Making a digital video can be as straightforward as taking a digital photograph. You can simply point the camera and shoot footage to show events exactly as they happened, without editing or correction. Because you can "project" the results straight on to a television screen by connecting it to your video camera, you do not even need a computer. While this is effortless, it can result in dull viewing. Without planning your video, it is difficult to tell a story and the narrative will be rambling and difficult to follow. It will be the visual equivalent of sending a letter full of mistakes and mark-ups.

The importance of editing

When you record a movie digitally, you turn an analog process—the response of your camera sensor to changing light, color, and subject—into a digital form, as data that are recorded on to tape or disc. You also record the sounds of the scene at the same time. You might turn from one scene to another, perhaps wait for some development, then attempt to capture what happens next. In the process, you will sometimes catch the movement a little too early; at other times you may miss the start. The result can be a jumble of clips, with some that are successful and others that will have missed the moment you were hoping to capture.

Editing is the video equivalent of going through a stack of photographs and putting them in an album or an exhibition. It is important to realize that your movie does not have to show events in the order in which they actually happened—even documentary work does not have to respect the arrow of time. Video editing aims to make the best use of the material that you have recorded (*see Chapter 5, from p. 140*).

The rendering process

The next step in the process of turning your footage into a watchable movie is "rendering." This is the point at which your software program, having been instructed by you of your editing decisions, makes the transitions from scene to scene and turns your video footage into a movie. At the same time, frame by frame, all of the data is transformed into a standard format, such as QuickTime.

The rendering process can be extremely taxing on the computer, requiring a great deal of computing power, and it will produce a very large

Editing

The principle behind video editing is similar to that for forming meaningful and elegant sentences out of a jumble of words. Your raw video footage—like that of any moviemaker, beginner and experienced alike—may be in a random order, such as this sequence (*top right*) of a walk in Pisa, Italy. From the street, to indoors, and out again: there is no narrative. The edited sequence (*below right*), however, moves logically from street level to the first view of a cathedral, before stepping inside for a tour. In addition to simply reordering your footage, editing also gives you control over the pace and rhythm of the visual experience. For example, even if you shot only a few seconds of a detail, in editing you can hold the view for several seconds longer.

Unedited sequence

Edited sequence

file—possibly more than 1 GB for five minutes of video, for example. It is, therefore, important that your computer is running at its full potential, so shut down any programs you do not need.

From render to print

The term "print" is borrowed from the film industry, where it refers to making the final projection copies of a film from the edited master. In digital video, it is possible to print frames from your rendered movie on to paper. But more often you will want to "print" your movies on to CDs or DVDs. You can even upload your videos to a website so that they can be viewed online (*see pp. 176–7*).

If you create DVDs of your movies, you can add titles, chapters, and subtitles, just like those on a commercial DVD. This will enable viewers to jump to different parts and be treated to a professional movie experience (*see pp. 170–1*).

Simple editing
Software such as ImageMixer (*above*) may be bundled with your digital video camera. Although such applications are free, they are very capable: this one will organize albums of pictures, movies, and sound, as well as produce a basic VCD (video CD).

Nonlinear editing
Of all the learning curves in digital working, the one for nonlinear editing is perhaps the steepest. The terminology is confusing, the technical traps numerous, and the software can be daunting, as the screenshot above shows.

Video media

The variety and mutual incompatibilities of video media and formats may appear chaotic, but they reflect the course of technological development, as well as the competition between manufacturers. In addition, digital video has to work under the shadow of television broadcast standards that were adopted when the most stable time base was the alternating current of the electrical power supply. These standards resulted in oddities such as the American NTSC display rate of 30 fps (frames per second) actually being 29.97 fps. Although outdated, the standards still apply.

Medium and format

It is helpful to distinguish between the recording medium being used and the format being written to it. The medium is the physical device—tape, disc, or solid-state memory—that holds your video footage. The format is the way in which the information is coded and organized. In some cases, the format and the medium are effectively the same because only one format is written to the medium—an example is Hi8 tape, used only for analog video. On the other hand, MiniDV tape, for example, is used for the DV format but can also be used for the professional DVCam format. More blurring of boundaries will occur as solid-state memory—that is, without moving parts—is increasingly used to record MPEG-compressed movies as well as still images.

Consumer media

In the consumer arena, the emphasis is on the most compact form compatible with acceptable quality. Professional media are larger and more robust than consumer media, allowing rougher handling and higher tape speeds.

DV

Originally DVC (for Digital Video Cassette), DV is an international standard for consumer digital video created in 1993 by a group of electronics companies. Known as the DV consortium, the group now includes more than 60 companies. The group defined factors such as the way the image is compressed and cassette sizes. For example, DVC can carry more than 4 hours' worth of tape and measures 125 x 78 x 14.6 mm. The MiniDV cassette holds 1 hour of recording and measures 66 x 48 x 12.2 mm. In this book, we will be working almost wholly with the MiniDV cassette, since that is what most nonprofessionals use. The DV standard has given rise to two competing professional formats: DVCPro and DVCam.

MicroMV

The MicroMV cassette holds only 70 percent of the tape of MiniDV, yet it records a full hour by compressing the image in MPEG-2, the same format used for DVD movies. The small cassette allows for extremely compact cameras.

MiniDV
Running for 60 minutes in standard play, MiniDV tape (often simply DV) is similar in size to professional-format DV.

MicroMV
This is the smallest available medium, but limited numbers of new cameras use it. Its future may be limited.

Digital8
The digital version of Hi8 (*right*) offers good quality, but the fact that it is larger than DV makes it less popular.

Digital8

The Digital8 cassette format is something of a hybrid in that it combines digital video compression with Hi8 tapes. However, the tapes are run faster than normal: for PAL, a 90 minute tape will run only 60 minutes; for NTSC, it will run for just 45 minutes. Digital8 cameras are less expensive than their DV equivalents, but they are also larger. Image quality is equal to that of DV.

Hi8

This is a relatively modern analog format capable of recording up to 90 minutes of video on a single cassette. Hi8 cameras are less expensive than their digital equivalents. Clean transitions between scenes are possible and sound quality is acceptable, but the overall quality is lower than that of DV.

Solid-state devices

For some, even the diminutive MiniDV tapes are too large. A growing number of digital video cameras are incorporating solid-state memory. This means they have no moving parts, consume very low levels of current, and are extremely robust. The drawbacks of solid-state media are that they are limited in capacity and relatively costly. However, one advantage is that they can be reused thousands of times. Popular solutions are the SecureDigital, xD, and MemoryStick cards. In situations that require very small cameras (such as restricted spaces) and where limited filming times are acceptable, these are ideal.

Discs

Should you prefer a camera that is less compact than a MiniDV equivalent, you can benefit from using DVD (Digital Versatile Disc) as the video medium. This has the advantage that you can play the disc immediately on your DVD machine or DVD-equipped computer. However, spinning the disc and powering the laser will quickly run down your battery pack. Other media, such as MiniDisc and Super MiniDisc, may be used too, although there may be problems with compatibilities.

Why is digital better?

Digital video is preferable to analog video for the great majority of recording purposes. Some of the key reasons for this include:

- Resolution of digital video is about double that of VHS or 8 mm tape—that is, 500 lines instead of 250.
- Digital does not suffer color blur or noise to the same extent as tape, which is very susceptible to these errors because data can spread (cross-talk) on analog tape; digital offers far cleaner colors.
- Sound on digital video can equal that of CDs, which is vastly superior to VHS sound.

Hi8
This analog format is superior to VHS and uses a far smaller tape, but its quality is inferior to that of DV.

MemoryStick

SecureDigital

Solid-state devices
The future lies with devices such as these. New professional systems are tape-free, using large solid-state memory cards.

DVD
One advantage of writing to DVD, as some cameras do, is access to clips without using fast-forward or rewind.

How digital video works

All video images, during capture and display, are built up, or "drawn," in a scanning process. The image of a frame is built up line by line from, for instance, the top corner running across to the opposite side, then back again at a slight angle so that the whole screen is covered. For the next frame of video, the process is repeated: each frame is drawn in a sequence of scan lines.

Interlaced video

In the early days of television, the image was created by phosphors that glowed when hit by a beam of electrons; these phosphors only glowed (phosphoresced) for a very short time. It was found that the early scan lines of the image would start to fade before the last lines were drawn, leading to the top of the screen appearing darker than the lower.

The ingenious method of working around this problem is to draw the frame in two steps: the first line is drawn, the next is skipped, the third line is drawn, the fourth is skipped, the fifth is drawn, and so on. This takes half the time to draw than a full frame would because alternate lines are missed.

All the lines that were skipped—that is, all the even-numbered lines—are then drawn in between the existing lines. In this way, although the first lines are fading, it is not so apparent to

the viewer because only the early, odd-numbered lines are losing strength, while the early even-numbered lines in between still appear bright. This technique is known as interlacing, and each frame of the video is displayed as two interlaced semiframes.

With modern screens, rapid decay of phosphorescence is less of a problem, and with plasma and LCD screens it is not a problem at all. However, this system is so widely used that it is likely to be with us for quite a while longer.

Progressive-scan video

There is, however, a growing trend toward the progressive-scan image. This simply means that there is no interlacing and that each frame is drawn in its entirety in one pass.

For NTSC, which runs at 30 fps (frames per second), this is highly acceptable. In contrast, the slower frame rate of PAL/SECAM of 25 fps sometimes leads fast action to appear jerky and uneven, because each frame needs slightly longer to draw than it would if the video ran at 30 fps.

However, because the standard cinematographic frame rate is 24 fps and the PAL/SECAM frame rate is closest to it, that is the system that is being adopted as the preferred setting for achieving a filmic look (*see p. 76*).

Interlacing principles
An interlaced video frame is drawn by scanning first one set of lines (say, the red ones), and when the scan reaches the bottom it flies up to the top again—without writing to screen—o draw the next set (shown here in blue).

Odd lines
Here, the first, third, fifth, and other odd-numbered lines have been drawn in the frame of the dog relaxing. Along with the second interlaced frame (*near right*), which is made up of even-numbered lines, it forms the whole image (*far right*).

How video tape works

The roots of video tape go back to the origins of cinematographic film. The most practical form of "talkies"—movies with sound—were those in which the soundtrack was carried on the film together with the image frames. With the advent of video, not only was the sound encoded as magnetic data, but the images too. In digital video, the images are coded as changes in the polarities of patches on the magnetic tape—that is, as positives or negatives. Aside from the image, other data are needed to keep track of the image information and to enable correction of any errors (*see below*). Depending on the tape format, the subcode track may carry signals that control the head as well as carrying error-correction. The video tracks themselves may be subdivided and carry error-correction or timecode data—all of which is read off by the tape head.

Helican scan tape

When you load a video tape into a camera, the whirring and clicking you hear is a mechanism in the camera pulling out some tape and partly wrapping it around a drum that spins very rapidly. The drum leans at an angle and records a slanted track on the tape as it runs past: this method of recording means that more information can be accommodated than if the track went straight across the width. With NTSC, for example, 10 tracks cover a frame of video, with different parts used to hold audio and other data.

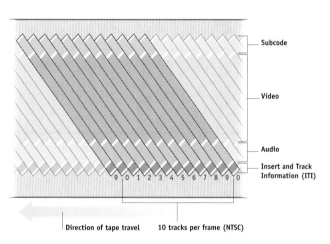

Subcode

Video

Audio

Insert and Track Information (ITI)

9 0 1 2 3 4 5 6 7 8 9 0

Direction of tape travel   10 tracks per frame (NTSC)

Even lines

The second half of the pair of interlaced frames shows all the lines of the image in between those in the first interlaced frame (*near left*). If the subject moves between these two frames, it can result in artifacts in the image.

Interlaced result

With a still subject, there is no real difference between a full interlaced pair of frames and a progressive-scan frame. However, with moving subjects, a progressive-scan frame looks more filmlike, making it increasingly the preferred mode.

Parts of a camera

For such a complex mass of electronics and precision machinery, modern video cameras are very easy to use, thanks to the functional separation of the parts of the camera and their controls. The controls themselves can be divided into those that are constantly in use—on/off, zoom, and playback controls, for example—and those less often used, such as setup, mode changing, and manual white balance. These less frequently needed controls may be assigned to buttons hidden under the LCD panel or to menus accessed from the LCD screen. As you gain in experience, you will prefer controls that are quickly accessed by pressing buttons, rather than the slower menu-based methods.

Accessory shoe

Dual-mode buttons

Battery latch

Filter attachment ring

Terminal cover

LCD cover

The left side
This is taken up largely by the LCD screen, but here you may also find dual-mode buttons, which do different jobs depending on whether you are in recording or playback mode.

Optics
Modern zoom lenses are masterpieces of miniaturization combined with superb image quality. Some camera models offer image stabilization, which reduces the effects of camera shake on the image.

Accessory shoe

A hot shoe or slot enables you to attach a separate microphone on a short boom or an extra light.

REC SEARCH · FOCUS · NIGHT MODE

CARD

EFFECTS   ON/OFF   OPEN

MultiMediaCard

DATA CODE   AE END

CARD MIX/□
SLIDE SHOW/
REC PAUSE

MENU

LCD screen
One of the greatest advances in digital video cameras is the LCD screen that is big enough to view comfortably and give instant feedback on the shoot. It may be rotated to view the image from various angles.

Controls
Many of the less frequently used controls, such as the digital effects, are tucked under the LCD screen. Some cameras may also conceal connectors here.

Zoom control

Tape/card switch

Mode control

Hand grip

Focus-assist lamp

Microphone

The right side
All modern cameras are right-handed, so you will find the grip for the camera on this side, together with the start/stop button and zoom controls.

Microphone
Many cameras carry a microphone. Those placed on the camera, as here, are more likely to pick up camera noise than one mounted on a boom held away from the camera.

Viewfinder
The electronic viewfinder may be movable to suit different viewing positions.

Thumb controls
The vital start/stop button is often given to the right-hand thumb. Check that its position is comfortable for your hand.

Battery access
On many cameras, the battery attaches to the back, but on some models it fits underneath. The latter is inconvenient for tripod work.

Boxed accessories

When you buy your digital video camera you will find, apart from the camera itself, several other items in the box. These vary from camera to camera and between manufacturers, but they usually include a battery, a battery charger/adapter, a power cable, audio and video cables, a SCART adapter, and a shoulder strap. You will also find an instruction manual or CD.

Battery

SCART adapter

Audio and video cable

Charger

Power cable

Shoulder strap

Digital zoom

Cameras offering fantastic zoom ranges—as much as 300x—rely on digital zooming. When the zoom effect given by the lenses themselves is exhausted, zooming can extend farther by enlarging the central portion of the image using digital techniques. The downside is that this results in rapidly decreasing image quality as the zoom effect increases. For more on zoom lenses, see p. 46 and pp. 58–9.

Closing in
Zooming in to capture the moving figure, quality is maintained with optical changes (*left to middle image*). But an extreme digital zoom (*right*) is gained at the loss of image quality.

Entry-level cameras

The inventors of television would be wide-eyed with wonder at the size and capabilities of even the lowest-cost and simplest digital video cameras on the market today. Except for the video-recording modes on mobile telephones, even the simplest models of video camera offer a great deal of fun, as well as easy operation not reliant on wading through tedious instruction manuals; at the same time, some can deliver a quality of recording that could have been accepted for broadcasting not so many years ago.

SP and LP

SP stands for "standard play" and LP for "long play," referring to the recording and playback tape speeds. Standard play offers the best balance between quality and length of recording (a higher speed could squeeze even more quality out of the tape, and this is exactly what professional versions of DV do). Long play, on the other hand, slows the tape speed—by varying amounts depending on the tape format—to give much longer recording and playback times. The drawback is that the quality suffers and tends to be adequate at best.

Small and compressed

The easiest way to make a small camera is to make the recording medium small: even the MiniDV tape cassette is relatively large compared to other media. The smallest cameras in this basic range use flash memory—that is, small cards of memory chips that have no moving parts. In fact, the latest professional cameras use flash memory too, and we can expect an increasing number of cameras to use this medium.

Small lenses—with limited aperture and restricted zoom ranges—also facilitate the manufacture of smaller, cheaper cameras. However, for much of your shooting, you will not need extremes of focal length.

With the smallest cameras, it is important to check that you can work the controls easily and handle the camera comfortably. Even for people with small hands, some cameras demand the manual dexterity of a neurosurgeon. In general, with small cameras you pay a premium for the miniaturization of the various parts. However, you are likely to gain more features and quality by purchasing a slightly larger camera rather than a similarly specified but much smaller competitor.

Ultra-compact
Cameras such as this can be so compact because they record directly to a memory card. The lens is fixed and zoom is digital. This model uses four AA batteries, connects directly to a TV, and can download to a PC.

Compact
This device is a little larger (and considerably thicker) than a credit card but incorporates an MP3 audio player, video camcorder, and digital stills camera. Video is recorded in MPEG-4 onto SD (SecureDigital) cards.

Tapeless
A growing class of MiniDV cameras records conveniently on to memory chip: this model offers a proper zoom lens of 10x and a fair-sized LCD screen. However, capable cameras such as this test the limits of their MPEG-4 format.

Light weight vs. sturdiness

Another factor to be aware of is that the entry-level models are generally made lightweight for undemanding and gentle use. They will not withstand serious bumps or shocks, nor will the mechanisms withstand the rigors of recording numerous tapes or being used extensively as a playback machine. In theory, cameras with solid-state memory should be very reliable, as well as being lighter in weight and more economical with batteries—these are three good reasons why they are becoming more popular.

Entry-level model

Models costing less than a basic computer offer ease of use and a fair range of features and are good value for money. This model has a 16x zoom and a swing-out LCD screen; it can also record stills images, but only to tape.

Viewfinder

Lens

Fill light

Microphone

To keep prices low, lenses offer limited zoom range supplemented by digital zoom.

Built-in microphones record from the camera position, so their usefulness is limited.

Versatile entry-level

Even some of the least costly modern DV camcorders offer features such as 16:9 format framing (letterbox). With a 10x zoom and bright LCD screen, and a 2-hour capacity standard battery, models such as this are ideal for an avid beginner.

Advanced entry-level

Cameras such as this are surprisingly well specified and offer excellent value for money. This model has a wide-ranging 24x zoom, webcam facility, remote and microphone handset, and DV output.

Image-stabiliized

It is possible to find well-specified, substantial cameras even in this class: this compact model offers a fast 10x zoom lens with image stabilization, an 800,000-pixel chip, a good range of controls, and a large LCD screen.

Intermediate cameras

For those who can afford them, intermediate-level digital video cameras present the best value for money. By offering more features and controls, these models give good-quality results. You can further increase the amount of features you get for your money by choosing a larger model, since smaller ones tend to be more expensive.

Cameras in this category are likely to offer zoom lenses with a good range; color viewfinders, both on a swing-out LCD and under the eyepiece; and digital-video in and out sockets. Some also have "luxury" additions such as image stabilization and transition effects. In addition, higher-resolution chips help improve the image quality. The top

Intermediate model
Semicompact upright designs offer a compromise between high quality—a 3-megapixel chip—and small size. Placing the majority of settings on the LCD touch-screen helps keep the camera compact.

A built-in light provides flash for stills work; you may be able to use it for videoing, too.

Modern zoom lenses keep compact by not extending with focal-length changes. Wide-angle is limited but can be improved with a converter lens.

The LCD screen can swivel forward and folds neatly away. On some cameras it is used to choose menu options.

Conventional design
With this type of camera, sensor resolutions reach 2 megapixels—as in this model—or higher, with a fast lens, image stabilizer, and video effects. These cameras are small but not compact and are very easy to use.

Direct-to-DVD
The intermediate category includes cameras that record directly onto DVD. All the usual digital video features are available, but the main selling point is the ability of these machines to play back as well as write DVDs.

cameras in this category include triple-sensor cameras: these use three relatively low-resolution chips to provide better color than a single chip.

Increasingly, intermediate cameras offer still-image capture, which means a memory-card slot will be provided. If you have a digital stills camera too, try to ensure that the cards used on both your cameras are compatible. Users of Sony cameras beware: old models use MemoryStick, whereas new ones use MemoryStick Pro. Card readers for MemoryStick may not read the Pro cards.

Ultraminiature cameras

Extremely small digital video cameras make their entrance in this category: some are so lightweight and small—easily fitting into a pocket—that you need a separate control to access their features. These models are convenient and good for snap-shooting, but check that you can work the controls comfortably before buying.

Holding steady

One of the main disadvantages of miniature video cameras is that they are difficult to hold steady—even breathing can cause movements. These movements may seem okay in the viewfinder, but they will soon frustrate you when seen on a TV screen. Consider this when choosing a camera.

Prosumer cameras

The term "prosumer" is derived from "professional consumer", which means a non-professional user who likes to use the best quality equipment without paying full professional prices. Cameras in this category offer superb results and, even thought they are not cheap, they cost a fraction of the price of broadcast quality cameras. The feature most typical of this type of camera is the use of triple sensor assemblies, one each for red, green, and blue. The improvement in image quality is significant and, to the perfectionist, essential.

Prosumer model
Compact and lightweight cameras such as this—using three sensors and equipped with a high-quality lens—are suitable for the non-professional user who requires superior images.

Dual function
Innovative designs are most likely to appear in this middle band of the market: this example offers both DV and stills recording without compromising either. It also supports four types of memory card, offering the user a range of options.

Triple-chip
In this category, you will find the least expensive triple-chip cameras, which provide good moving-image quality, especially if supported by image stabilization, and a high-quality lens. Still-image capture may suffer from the low-resolution chips.

Digital video accessories

There is a huge number of accessories available for the digital video enthusiast, and it would be easy to fill a room with all your equipment. For this reason, it is important to distinguish between the truly vital accessory and the attractive gimmick that is used once and forgotten forever.

Camera case

The first essential is a case that will protect your investment while at the same time being easy to use and appropriate to the conditions you work in. Unfortunately, the best protection is given by the heaviest cases, while the easiest to use offer the least protection. If all you video are family parties and vacations, you probably do not need a case that can survive being dropped down a mountainside or dipped in the sea. There is a lot to be said for a case that does not advertise the fact that it is carrying expensive equipment. In general, a padded case that can be carried easily over the shoulder is adequate for most needs.

A specialized waterproof housing is useful for a range of conditions. Besides the primary protection against water—to depths of 33 ft (10 m) or more—a waterproof housing can also protect the delicate parts of your camera from dust, sand, and debris.

Camera bag
Soft-sided, padded camera bags provide a good balance of light weight and fair protection for your equipment, but they are not dustproof.

Waterproof housing
Essentially tough plastic bags, waterproof cases are excellent protection against splashes and sand. Although costly, they are well worth the investment.

Delicacy of video mechanisms

The recording head of a digital video camera spins several thousand times per minute, in extremely close contact with the tape, which runs at nearly ⅘ in (19 mm) per second, laying data tracks narrower than a human hair. The gap between the recording head and the tape is precisely maintained and is equal to a small fraction of the thickness of a human hair. As a consequence of these fine tolerances, the smallest dust particle causes dropouts, or gaps, in data, which will show up as flecks of "snow" in the image. The recording mechanism is very delicate: always pay attention to any "Do not" labels on the equipment.

Battery charger
Portable battery chargers are an excellent reserve in the field, but they can be costly.

Alternative battery
It is possible to buy alternatives to manufacturers' power sources, such as the professional Lithium-Ion series from specialized manufacturer SWIT.

Hard case
Waterproof and dustproof cases from manufacturers such as Peli Products are the best, if bulkiest, way to protect your equipment.

Lens hood
This will protect your lens from both bumps and stray light.

Matte box
This bulky contraption serves a double purpose: it combines an effective and flexible lens hood with a carrier for filters.

Flare prevention

A lens hood is essential for protecting the lens from damage, and it also helps prevent flare (unwanted light reflecting into the optics). A matte box (*see below left*) provides even better protection, particularly if the zoom is not active. The sides of the box can be extended for maximum shielding for the focal length in use. Another approach is to use a card on a flexible arm, such as the Flarebuster: this mounts on the hot shoe or tripod and carries a flexible arm with a clip on the end, so that it can be positioned easily and stays in place.

Batteries

The efficiency and capacity of modern batteries are excellent examples of high technology. Those people who have been in the video business for very many years will remember having to transport their camera batteries on a little cart. Today's cameras, as well as other equipment, have very low power requirements. These two factors combined mean that batteries small enough to fit in your pocket will store enough power to last for hours. Some brands of battery tell you how much longer you can work before recharging.

Battery care

Follow these tips to achieve the optimum performance from your video camera batteries:
- Discharge the battery fully before recharging for the first two or three cycles. This improves the capacity and longevity of modern NiMH and Li-Ion batteries. Thereafter, you can recharge when the battery is only partially discharged.
- Always use the manufacturer's battery charger: another may look similar and even provide the same charging power, but it may lack electronics that monitor battery condition.
- Keep the battery's contacts clean: do not touch them, and use the cover whenever possible.
- Do not expose batteries to excessive heat or cold.

Filters

Placed over the lens to alter the image entering the camera, filters can be subtly tinted—to correct imbalances in colour temperature—or strongly colored or patterned.

The key technical issue is this: the more work you put into the image when shooting, the less work you need to do later. For example, if you achieve color balance with a filter, there will be no need to make white balance corrections in post-production. This helps maintain technical quality.

Plain or UV filters

Your expensive zoom lens, possibly the single most costly part of your camera, can be protected by using a plain glass or UV filter (strictly, minus-UV since they block UV). Keep it on at all times, but keep it clean—even on the inside, since dust trapped there will settle on the lens or filter.

Graduated filters

A common need is to darken a bright sky without making the foreground too dark. You need a filter that is strongly tinted at the top, fading to transparent at the bottom—a graduated filter. The shading may be neutral colored (gray) or tinted with blue to increase the coloring of the sky, for example. Graduated filters also come in various strengths to suit different scenes: strongly colored for high-contrast or bright scenes; weakly tinted for lower-contrast scenes.

Original

Original

With filter

With filter

Cutout filter

You can use a cutout to give shape to an otherwise formless shot. Here, the lines of a formal garden are softened and broken up by the filter. Cutout effects vary with lens aperture and zoom setting. Many cameras use aperture to control exposure, so you may have to experiment with the zoom to achieve the effect you want.

Graduated filter

The graduated, or "grad," filter is widely used to give color to a blank cloudy sky. However, it is easily overdone. Experiment with different strengths of filter. Here a tobacco-colored grad has been strongly applied with the lens set at its widest: with longer focal lengths, the effect is reduced.

Polarizing filters

Used primarily to reduce the effect of reflections in glass and water, polarizing filters are just as useful for increasing the intensity of colors where there are many shiny surfaces, such as plant leaves.

Special-effects filters

Starbursts, rainbow, and diffusion all come under the special-effects banner. They are occasionally useful, but overuse will reduce their impact.

Color-correcting filters

Filters with very soft color tints are often used by professional moviemakers to create subtle changes in the mood of lighting.

Working with filters

Just as filters affect your footage, your camera can also have an effect on the way filters behave.

- Turn off the automatic white balance, since it will negate the effect of any colored filters.
- Use graduated and special-effect filters sparingly.
- The appearance of an effect—especially with graduates—may vary with aperture. Check at the working aperture before committing to tape.
- The appearance of the effect may vary with zoom setting. Do not shoot without first checking.
- Check special-effects filters through the lens, not by holding them up to the eye.

Original

Original

With filter

With filter

Limited-field filter

Filters that look like varifocal spectacle lenses—with one part of a different strength than the other—can limit depth of field. This is valuable in digital video, which tends to give enormous depths of field. Here, the filter has been used to focus attention on the nearest flower, throwing the background out of focus.

Split-image filter

For fantasy or dream sequences, there is a place for filters that split or fragment a view. The filters are available with varying numbers of facets, like a cut and polished gemstone. They can thoroughly confuse the autofocus system, so set to manual focus. Here, the garden scene is broken into five repeating sections.

Tripods

Although they are cumbersome and can be awkward to carry around, tripods are vital in a wide range of shooting conditions to achieve a steady shot, which would be impossible to achieve with a handheld camera. It is entirely possible, and may even be necessary, to shoot a documentary or travelog without a tripod, but even the fastest-paced documentary could feature an interview with an expert; or a travelog may show the placid, lazy flow of a great river. It is sensible to be prepared for an unplanned shot. Paradoxically, it is not the static shot that benefits most from the stability of a tripod; a steady shot is most useful when recording movement.

Even the cheapest tripods come with pan and tilt heads to help you create smooth camera movements within static shots.

Pan head

The best way—some would say the only way—to obtain a steady movement that pans across the scene is to use a tripod equipped with a panning head, which rotates on a vertical axis around a large, smooth bearing. Buy the best you can afford, because precision machining of the parts of the head is critical for controlled movement. If you use very heavy equipment or you wish to pan with the zoom set to a very long focal length, you should consider using a fluid head—that is, one in which the bearings are separated by a lubricant at high pressure. Fluid heads are costly, but they provide a smooth, silky action that is second to none.

Fluid head
A fluid head has pan and tilt movements whose resistance can be adjusted to match the weight of the equipment for smooth operation. Markings enable you to position the head in the same place repeatedly.

Culmann 3150
For occasional use, an inexpensive but still relatively stable tripod is a good investment. This model has a simple center column with a locking screw and locking clips on the legs.

Gitzo G1027
Carbon-fiber tripods offer exceptional rigidity with relatively low weight. They are costly but highly reliable. This one weighs less than (1 lb 12 oz) 800 g and is only 17¾ in (45 cm) long.

Manfrotto 728B
Tripods offering four sections, a rising column, and built-in pan/tilt head are ideal for a wide range of work and situations. This model has a reversible column for very low level shots.

Tilt head

For tilting, or up-and-down movements, the rotation occurs about a horizontal axis: only when the axis is perfectly horizontal will the up-down movement run vertically. The best way to control movements, with both pan and tilt, is to use a handle attached to the head. The longer the handle, the greater your control.

Do not grip the handle tightly; guide it with your fingertips to give you accurate control over the camera movements. Pan and tilt heads for use with video cameras have a friction setting to alter resistance to movement. Set the friction for both so that the camera position is held but smooth movement is possible.

Spirit level

A built-in spirit level shows when the tripod is level on the left/right and forward/back axes. Usually set into the head or leg block, the spirit level contains a small bubble that centers on an inscribed circle or cross when the tripod is level.

Stable movement

Stability during movement, or steady camera work (steadycam), is a hallmark of professional videomaking. The simplest accessories use counterweights that hang below the camera on an arm. The camera is supported on a freely rotating "gimbal" and is held on a handle from below: this allows it to stay level, thereby dampening jerky, pitching movements.

Portable stabilizer
Handheld devices such as this keep the camera level and steady while following movement. The heavier they are, the more they reduce camera shake—but they soon tire your arms.

Linhof Profi 3
A good, durable tripod will give many years of service. This model rises from 10 in (25 cm) to over 6 ft (2 m), with variable leg spread. The column is adjustable to the weight being carried.

Manfrotto 5I5MVB
Supplied with a leg spreader as standard, heavy models of this design offer good stability and safety in the field. The center interface bowl accepts the spherical ball of a fluid or pan/tilt head.

Sachtler DA-75/2D ENG
Widely regarded as the finest of all tripods, a Sachtler is costly but will last a lifetime. This model has a quick-clamping system for its two-section legs and can carry a 45 lb (20 kg) camera.

Computing equipment

Digital video owes its existence and growth to powerful personal computers. However, it may seem strange that while a camera smaller than a paperback novel can capture and play back video, you will need a very powerful computer to work with the video on your desktop. This disparity is due to the computing demands of nonlinear editing (NLE)—that is, software that allows you to edit clips out of chronological order.

Data streams

Video produces very swollen streams of data that have to be processed at a constant rate to enable good-quality images and accurate editing. To cope with this, it is best to work with the latest and best-equipped personal computers you can afford. The hard disk and connectors should be of the fastest type available. Similarly, the data bus—the wires that carry data around the computer—should be as quick as possible. In addition, the system should have lots of spare capacity—both in terms of free Random Access Memory (RAM) and the amount of empty hard-disk space.

Windows users need Pentium III or equivalent processors working at 500 MHz or faster, with 512 MB of RAM, and operating with Windows 98SE or later. It is recommended that you run Windows XP; of the four versions available, the most suitable is the Media Center Edition, but the Home Edition is also highly capable.

Apple users will need PowerMac computers running G4 processors or later, with at least 512 MB of RAM, and running operating system OS10.3 or later. Apple pioneered the bundling of very capable software for video editing and DVD creation together with the computers, so that any modern machine can download videos, edit them, and burn them to DVD without the need for any additional software.

Hard disks

Both Windows and Apple Mac machines should be equipped with a hard-disk drive of at least 50 GB capacity (preferably as a second, built-in drive, in addition to the master drive). Your

High end
Very capable, but costly, the best Apple Mac computers, such as this model, are favored by many video professionals and are well supported by the specialized accessory and software industry. A dual-processor model is highly desirable.

Portable
Large laptop computers combine considerable computing power with portability. The price is relatively high, but the gain in convenience is considerable. This Apple model is popular with videomakers working on location.

Mid-range
This type of computer offers perhaps the best balance of capability with cost. A model from an industry leader, such as this one from Dell, is also more easily serviced, with extras such as memory upgrades being widely available.

Home computer
Even relatively inexpensive computers, such as this Sony model, can handle modest video-editing needs. Software provided with the camera is free, so simply connect your video camera to the computer to get started.

Dedicated video editing
A number of manufacturers assemble computers specially for video editing. This Poweroid model offers dual processors, the ability to run up to three monitors, massive storage capacities, and specialized video-editing cards at relatively low cost.

Compact home computer
Computers such as this model from Sony are highly versatile. They are able to provide computing and recording of broadcasts (for personal use only), as well as creation of DVDs and CDs: professional capabilities at domestic-machine costs.

machine should also offer a FireWire or i.Link port with the ability to capture DV. All machines will need a CD drive for installing software (some software applications install from a DVD, in which case you will need a DVD drive), together with a DVD writer for archiving material.

Your computer will need more than 360 MB of disk space for every hour of compressed video, rising to a vast 13 GB for every hour of rendered movie. Furthermore, the hard disk must be capable of sustaining data flows of at least 4 MB/sec to display movies smoothly—that is, without dropping any frames. The installation of NLE software can take up 500 MB—even more when help files, tutorials, and effects files are included. In addition, some software will demand large amounts of free space in order to process an edit list. If possible, you should install the system software on one disk, and store movies on a separate disk.

Laptop versatility
To experienced videographers, the most amazing development is the ability to edit video on a laptop computer. With NLE software installed, modern laptops allow full editing and output while working on location. The main problem is not technical but ergonomic: their small screens are quickly filled with the many windows required by NLE software. Like desktop machines, laptops need to be supported by an external hard-disk drive.

Should you upgrade?
It is tempting to upgrade an old computer to a faster processor by substituting the CPU (central processing unit) card for a new one. However, this is costly and often creates an unstable system through the mismatching of components. Furthermore, the bottleneck in video editing is usually in the moving of data around the computer, not at the central processor. It is better to put the money toward a new computer or a second monitor. Use the old one for low-level, office-type tasks or for burning DVDs.

Monitors

A powerful computer with the best software is nothing without a good-quality monitor to view your work and ample screen space for the many windows needed for video editing.

Identifying the different types

Flat-panel or Liquid Crystal Display (LCD) monitors provide the highest image quality in a compact and lightweight unit. Because each pixel is created by a single transistor controlling the brightness, the image is absolutely stable, unlike that of the Cathode Ray Tube (CRT) monitor. This makes it less tiring on the eyes and means it is possible to use a flat-screen for longer periods than a CRT. However, lower-quality flat-screen monitors have a limited viewing angle: if you are not looking squarely on to the screen, colors can vary significantly. This is not such a problem with CRT monitors. Furthermore, flat screens cost two or three times more than a CRT with a similar display area.

For video editing, irrespective of type of screen, the viewable screen size should be at least 17 in (43 cm) across the diagonal, with a resolution of at least 1,280 pixels in width.

For the best results, you should opt for a monitor that offers high pixel resolutions over one with a larger screen area.

Video cards

Designed to enhance the video experience, video cards can be slotted into a computer's motherboard to add new capabilities. The most basic types take over the job of controlling the monitor: they process the video signal, relieving the computer of that task. Thanks to the demands of computer gamers, powerful video cards can also benefit the digital videographer by making the computer and monitor more responsive.

Another type of card captures analog video for conversion to digital. It may be combined with a TV tuner for terrestrial broadcasts. This way, you can make digital recordings of broadcasts on your computer.

Heat sink for processor

Standard card connector

Digital and analog sockets

Radeon 9200
Modern video cards, such as this one, for accelerating the response times of computer monitors are fast and powerful. They were created to meet the demands of computer gamers.

Apple LCD
For a good design allied with superlative image quality, models from Apple are hard to beat, but the quality exacts a high price. There are no extras, such as built-in speakers, although USB ports are provided.

Formac LCD
As well as being highly functional, stylish models such as this are also becoming desirable objects in themselves. This one offers a 17 in (43 cm) antiglare screen and a two-port USB hub.

BenQ LCD
A mid-market LCD screen costs considerably more than an excellent CRT screen. However, this product is not only stylish, it also takes up little power and even less desk space. It is easy to move around and images are stable.

Using extra monitors

For the serious videomaker, there is no substitute for a "production monitor" on which to test effects and transitions. Glitches that may be barely visible on a computer monitor become apparent on a TV screen. Having a production monitor plugged in is more convenient than having to take a DVD to the player and screen in your living room.

A different use for an extra monitor is to enable the spreading of palettes and windows in your editing software between the two screens. This can greatly increase your productivity and can be more effective than upgrading an existing screen.

Monitor calibration

As viewers, we are tolerant of quite wide variations in color balance in the moving image. This is partly because of the low-quality color on domestic TV sets. However, because digital video cameras produce such superb color images, you really should work with a calibrated monitor.

Your screen may appear to give bright, crisp colors but, in fact, produce higher contrast and stronger colors than normal. You will naturally adjust the images so that they look right on your screen, but your video will then seem lacking in contrast and color if viewed on a screen that produces normal, less brilliant images.

If you are an Apple Mac user, the calibration process is free: you select it from the Preferences panel of OSX or the Control Panels of OS9. Windows users need the Gamma control panel that is provided with Adobe Photoshop. Better still, though, is a colorimeter, which matches the monitor's colors to a standard. The settings recommended for domestic television are gamma of 2.2 and a white point of 9,300 K.

Note that these comments do not apply to a field monitor used to assess images for broadcasting, which is set up to different standards. (*See also p. 175 on monitor calibration.*)

Colorvision Spyder
A hardware device such as the Colorvision Spyder offers a reasonably accurate means of calibrating your monitor. This process is automatic and the equipment is very easy to use.

KDS RAD7 LCD
This model has a 43 cm (17 in) flat screen and built-in speakers. With its combination of 1,280-pixel resolution and compact size, it is an ideal choice for video-editing work.

Formac Pronitron CRT
Large CRT displays offering a viewable screen of 22 in (56 cm) are large and heavy and produce a great deal of heat. But they cost less than smaller LCD screens and offer top-quality color reproduction.

LaCie CRT
Although they take up a lot of space, large CRT monitors, such as this 19 in (48 cm) model, offer the best value combination of excellent image quality—especially in color reproduction—and affordability.

Nonlinear editing software

Parallel with the development of digital video cameras has been an astounding growth in nonlinear editing (NLE) software. Arguably, one could not have prospered without healthy progress in the other. The result is that you can now edit and process video with very reasonably priced software. Even with professional software, the cost is a tenth of what it was in the first years of digital video.

Basic editing software

Some video-editing software is now available free of charge or is bundled with your computer's system software.

With Microsoft Windows XP, you obtain not only the Windows operating system but Windows Movie Maker. This offers basic editing functions, with a great deal of help for the beginner. A basic gallery of transitions and effects is available, as well as a titler for adding credits to your movie.

On the Apple platform, the outstanding software is iMovie. This application marked the arrival of NLE at the enthusiast's desktop. Suddenly, basic video editing could be fun and easy and need not cost a fortune—indeed, it was offered free with all Apple computers. It is possible to edit on the timeline; there is a large range of transitions and effects, supplemented by a growing number of commercially available plug-ins; and

titling effects are powerful and easy to control. Currently it is offered as part of a suite of software at prices that are effectively handling charges.

Intermediate editing software

The battle of NLE software producers is hardest fought at the intermediate level—and almost entirely for the benefit of the Windows user. Pinnacle Studio offers a good range of features with usability. Its wide range of import formats is attractive and integrates DVD authoring. The handling of music is versatile, with ability to add voice-over narration and background music. Other tools can correct sound and video problems, including stabilization (to correct camera shake) and noise reduction. Pinnacle Studio is able to capture and edit 16:9 widescreen format.

Roxio VideoWave offers asset control with a timeline editor supporting up to 14 tracks and in-place editing. It includes many transitions, titling, and effects and can customize DVD layout and create transitions synchronized to music.

For those working on Mac OS, Final Cut Express is the obvious choice for intermediate-level work, because it is currently the only full application available. It is much less costly than the full professional version, yet it will do just about everything even a serious amateur will want.

Adobe Premiere Pro
This basic software captures video and still images, and effects, transitions, and titles are easily applied. It offers integrated DVD authoring features and support for the 16:9 window.

Apple Final Cut Express
With its remarkably full specification for a mid-level application, Final Cut Express combines ease of use with near-professional power and flexibility. It can handle a wide range of media.

Sony Vegas Video
Vegas Video offers an integrated solution for digital sound and video, combining recording, mixing, and creation of Internet streaming content as well as of surround-sound effects.

Despite its versatility, it is easy to get started, and users of iMovie will have few difficulties becoming productive in a short time.

MacXware MediaEdit offers an interesting mix of features including the ability to create anaglyph movies for 3-D effects (visible using red/green shades over the eyes), a good picture-in-picture feature for this level, and high levels of Undo for reversing mistakes.

Professional editing software

For a long time, Adobe Premiere was the most popular NLE application for the desktop videomaker, in both Windows and Mac operating systems; it has even been used to edit Hollywood films. It has almost everything you could need but, although still a favorite in Windows, and certainly one of the most capable applications, it is no longer being upgraded for the Mac OS.

Avid Xpress DV is a very powerful editor, with all the features and functions needed by all but the most demanding professional, but is not easy to get started and is dongle-protected—that is, it needs a special USB attachment to work. It is by far the most costly of the desktop editors. The Pro version is even more expensive, but it offers a level of customization to different ways of working, and that flexibility is appreciated by the industry.

Selecting NLE software

More than any other kind of software, NLE programs should be chosen carefully with reference to the computing and other hardware that you use or intend to purchase. This is because video streaming and rendering place such high demands on computing systems that the many solutions involve software designed to work with specific video cards or compression hardware, and vice versa—some hardware works better with certain software than others. Here are some pointers to consider before you invest in costly software:

● Do you need to work in real time, i.e. do you need to see the results of your edits or transitions immediately and at normal frame speed? If so, ensure that the software provides real-time previews— usually in a compressed format—and that your equipment can work fast enough.

● Will you need to input analog video, or will you work solely in digital formats? If you intend to input analog, you will need format converters consisting of appropriate software plus digitizing devices.

● Before you commit to your purchase, confirm with the manufacturer's help center that the equipment you propose to use will be compatible with the software and your intended work.

MacXware MediaEdit Pro
MediaEdit Pro works more like a painting application. There is a choice of some 200 effects, filters, and transitions, and the user is able to design personal filters and effects.

Ulead VideoStudio
Support for beginners is offered here with Ulead's step-by-step guidance. More than 700 effects, video frames, and graphics are supplied. This is a wide-ranging and popular package.

Ulead MediaStudio Pro
This suite of applications offers MPEG capture with good real-time capabilities, video and sound editing, painting effects, and graphics. DVD authoring tools makes content creation easy.

DVD creation

One of the main problems of working with Digital Versatile Discs (DVDs) is knowing which format to use. For all the confusion, however, DVD holds the record for the fastest uptake in new recording technology. The key reason is that it is the most compact, least expensive, and most reliable way to present, distribute, and archive digital video movies.

DVD formats

A survey of the various DVD formats is the best way to ensure you do not use the wrong disc or buy an incorrect player. Physically, all DVDs are similar to CDs in size and form. The data are recorded as a spiral trail of microscopic pits and lands (level areas); a laser beam is shone at these points and the reflections are read off.

DVD-ROM: DVD-Read Only Memory is used to supply films, audio, or software to users. It comes in various forms with differing capacities and in single- or double-sided configurations. These discs cannot be written to by the user, but they can be used in DVD players or computers with DVD-ROM drives.

DVD-R: DVD-Recordable is the recordable version of DVD-ROM, and it is able to hold a nominal 4.7 GB per side (9.4 GB in total for a double-sided disc). These discs can be written

Burning a DVD
This screenshot of a basic DVD authoring program shows how you can set your movie within a stylish frame, complete with titles. Drag in or import your movie sequence, set chapters, and click Burn to create the disc—it is amazingly easy.

only once by the user, and they can be read in DVD players and computers equipped with DVD players. There are two types of DVD-R disc. To make many copies—for example, for distributing a film by duplicating from a master copy—you need the DVD-R For Authoring disc, which can then comply with the Cutting Master Format, when used with suitable software and recorders. For individual copies, use DVD-R For General discs. DVD-R can be used in DVD players.

DVD-RW: DVD-ReWritable is a rerecordable version of DVD-R that can be rewritten, it is

DVD writers
Modern desktop and even laptop computers incorporate DVD writers as standard. If you do not have one in your computer, it is easy to connect up an external drive, and it is likely to operate more rapidly than built-in writers.

DVDs
The variety in DVD formats extends from optical/electronic elements, to whether the disc is held in a caddy, as shown above, or whether they are plain, bare discs like CDs. Ensure you buy the correct type for your writer.

claimed, up to 1,000 times. The discs can be used in DVD players as well as in computers equipped with a DVD-ROM player.

DVD+RW: DVD+ReWritable (note the plus sign) is the most confusing format. It is a variant of DVD-RW but is designed to be easy to use and suitable for video as well as data. This new format may not play in older DVD players.

DVD+R: DVD+Recordable discs are similar to DVD-RW but they can be written only once, resulting in a disc that can be read in DVD players as well as in the DVD-ROM drive of a computer.

DVD-RAM: DVD-Random Access Memory is also rewritable and is used for computer data storage, with 2.6 GB or 4.7 GB capacities for single-sided discs. The downside is that they cannot be read by standard DVD players or computers with DVD-ROM drives. While their high capacities are appealing, the typically slow read and write speeds are not.

In summary, DVDs prerecorded with films are usually DVD-ROMs in the DVD-Video variant. DVD-RW or DVD+RW are the most convenient for archiving your completed movies. For general data archiving, DVD-RAM may be used.

DVD authoring software

There is a wide range of applications available to enable you to create, or author, a DVD—from professional authoring to the simplest DVD presentations—and they are improving all the time. Most DVD recorders come equipped with simple software that creates basic programs.

Software that comes with computer operating systems or is available at low cost includes Microsoft Movie Maker and Apple iDVD. These offer a fair degree of control but—most importantly—they also provide many presets and professionally created styles to help you make your discs. You do not have to worry about creating backgrounds, buttons, and windows because all are provided. However, even fully professional software applications, such as Apple DVD Studio, offer simple modes with many presets made for you. For further details, see pp. 170–3.

How DVD works

DVDs work like CDs, in that a series of tiny pits on a spiral track on a metallic surface reflect a tiny laser beam—but the resemblance ends there. DVDs space the tracks extremely tightly: just three-quarters of a millionth of a meter apart; if you could unwind the spiral it would be more than 7 miles (11 km) long. As a result, a vast amount of data can be placed on the disc. Furthermore, the data capacity can be doubled by using dual-layer technologies, in which the laser beam focuses on one or other layer at a time. By using both layers on both sides, it is possible to achieve capacities exceeding 9 GB per disc.

DVD mechanism
DVDs and CDs work through a close coordination between the mechanics of spinning a disc and the steady motion of the laser beam that reads the data. Correction for tiny errors in movement is a crucial part of the design.

Optoelectronics
The underside of a prerecorded disc, with its pits and lands, is shown here. The laser beam shines on to the disc, and the flickering reflections are read by the computer or DVD player.

Setting up a workroom

Initially, your digital video workroom can be very simple, consisting of just the desk at which you have installed your computer. But as you progress, your demands for equipment will grow. Videomaking spawns more technical gizmos and clutter than most pastimes, so it is a good idea to create a dedicated space in which you can work. It is also essential to be well organized, so that you can quickly find any tapes or cables that you may need.

The environment

The first and most basic requirement is often forgotten: it is the need for a darkened room with neutral-colored walls. Cinema was born in a dark room, and nothing has changed the fundamental need to work in one. A darkened room ensures that viewing conditions such as light levels are kept constant. And the neutrality of colors ensures that your eyes will not adapt over the course of a day to a strong ambient hue, adversely affecting the accuracy of any color corrections you make on screen. Even professionals have been caught out when they

decorated an NLE (nonlinear editing) studio as if it was a domestic setting, with warm-colored walls. The reasoning was that they should edit for a typical viewing environment. However, editors found that their images were getting colder—that is, more blue in overall tone—over the course of the day because their eyes had adapted to the ambient warm color.

It is also important to have a comfortable chair that supports your back and is set to the correct height. This is because once you begin editing you will find yourself getting drawn in for hours—if not days—at a time. For the same reason, it is best to edit on LCD screens (*see p. 32*) because they cause far less eyestrain than working with CRT screens. The fine labeling used in NLE software can easily cause eyestrain over a period of time.

It is also worth investing in tools that reduce strain on your "mouse hand," which will do most of the work: consider a graphics tablet or a mouse with multiple buttons. However, the best ergonomic aid—and it is free—is to use keyboard shortcuts whenever possible.

Lamp, turned away from monitors — CRT monitor — LCD monitor — Left speaker — Laptop — Removable drive — DVD burner — DV camera — DV tapes

The extras

Amateur moviemaking has come a long way since the days of cine film. With a typically equipped modern computer and monitor plus, of course, a digital video camera, you can shoot, edit, and disseminate complete digital movies. Some cameras can even capture broadcast transmissions that you can feed into the computer.

The first "extra" you should purchase for your workroom is additional hard disks: if these are installed internally, they will run faster and also save on desktop clutter (but they may also add to the heat and noise your computer makes).

Using a video tape recorder as the "acquire device"—that is, to run your video tape under the NLE software's control—is the best way to reduce wear and tear on your video camera's mechanisms. A second monitor is a useful extra since it increases the space available for the many palettes used by NLE software. Professionals will add a third: a CRT monitor to simulate the broadcast image. Another important monitoring device is a pair of loudspeakers—these are better than headphones, in terms of both accuracy and comfort.

●HINTS AND TIPS

"Safety first" is a good motto in the video workroom—not because the equipment is unsafe to use, but because a simple error in operation can threaten a project that has cost you much investment and effort.

● Work neatly and systematically: note down and label everything—all video tapes look the same until they are identified by labels and notes.

● Keep video tapes in their boxes to protect them from dust unless in use, and keep them away from drinks.

● Run video tapes through a machine once a year to keep them "aired"—this is said to increase their life span.

● Keep logs and actually write them up—you will save a lot of time when logging or looking for clips for stock purposes if you keep notes of every take.

● Give yourself a break. It is hard to stop in the middle of a creative flow, but you should have a stretch and walk around for a few minutes every hour. This will help in the prevention of errors.

● Back up your projects, preferably on some form of removable media. Store the backups in a different location from the studio. Use backup software that can be timed to work overnight.

Computer

A dream studio

You can achieve a great deal with just the central items of camera and computer, but relatively inexpensive extras such as high-quality monitor speakers will increase your enjoyment, as well as the quality of your work. And do not forget all the backup devices, such as a DVD burner. Existing equipment such as a VHS VCR can also be put to good use.

VHS tape archive

VCR

DVDs and CDs

Keyboard · Mouse · Analog converter · VHS tape · Right speaker

2
Camera and sound techniques

Camera techniques

Great shots will make your movies stand out from the crowd. This chapter discusses composition, framing, depth of field, camera angles, and camera movements. Quick-fix solutions to some of the most common problems associated with camera handling are provided.

Digital sound

Sound must not be forgotten in the quest for impressive images. The microphone techniques and effects detailed here will help ensure clear, clean audio, while the quick-fix page offers assistance with sound issues.

Look and transitions

The use of still images and the "film look" are almost essential in creative digital video work, and these are explored here. You will also see how to transfer video to your computer—either your own recordings or those from broadcasts. The quick-fix section on copyright will help you avoid potentially costly errors.

Mastering your camera

At first sight, a digital video camera appears to be dotted with myriad randomly scattered buttons and switches. This description would bring tears to the eyes of the designers who had spent weeks, if not months, pondering where to place the buttons, their size and shape, and how much pressure they need. The design is intended to be user-friendly, with all controls easily accessible. But what makes sense to an industrial designer may not suit your way of working.

An alternative to a proliferation of buttons is a menu-driven system using an LCD touch-screen, on which "virtual" buttons respond to a fingertip touch. However, with this system, you may find it difficult to locate a particular option or to work out the meaning of abbreviations such as SMTH INT REC or D-REC. Or you may find that, even after you become familiar with the menus, a feature you use very often is inconvenient to access.

It follows, then, that you should try out a camera before you buy it. But bear in mind that you need some familiarity with it to appreciate its merits. The logic of certain ergonomics may emerge only after a few hours of using the camera.

Outgrowing automation

The complicated nature of the controls helps ensure the majority of aspiring videographers stick to automatic controls, leaving the camera to get on with the work. But allowing the camera to make decisions has many disadvantages. In summary, they are:

● Autofocus systems cannot cope with fast-moving action in which things or people move across the frame between the camera and main subject. The camera will attempt to refocus on the passing object, and the focus on the main subject will be lost when it returns to view.

● Autoexposure systems rely on feedback loops that do not respond instantaneously: a move into a bright situation may start off overexposed then fade to correct exposure after a second or two. On the other hand, the autoexposure may try to respond to a passing change in light, when you want to keep the exposure steady throughout the take.

Zoom ring

Focus ring

Focus and zoom rings
These rings can control zoom and focus manually, but the inability to make settings by numbers will limit their usefulness.

● Auto white-balance controls may correct where you do not wish for a correction. You may wish to keep the orange color cast of an interior scene lit by tungsten lamps, but the camera will try to create a white balance that neutralizes these atmospheric hues.

● Automatic level or gain controls for the built-in microphone work well when there is a fairly constant level of sound. But in quiet moments, microphones will pick up all the background noise—the gain control will have been raised—only to distort when there is a loud sound.

● Automatic sensitivity in the camera compensates for low light levels by increasing the amplification of the signal—this creates a picture when almost nothing is visible to the naked eye, although the

ND FILTER   IRIS   FOCUS

Manual controls
Autofocus can be turned off on some cameras, but the feel of the lens will not match that of proper manual-focus lenses. In addition, the extensive depth of field given by small video chips means that focusing often produces hardly any visible effect.

Types of image stabilization

Recent advances in image-stabilization technology really do help ensure a stable image, free from high-frequency movements. But with some systems there is a price to pay. Those systems that jitter the sensor itself use up some of the sensor's capacity in order to provide the space needed to correct for movement. More effective are systems that provide optical stabilization by moving a group of lenses. This solution does not compromise picture resolution.

resulting image will be grainy. You may think that you have enough light to work with because the camera continues to show the monitor picture, but the image quality may be quite unacceptable.

In short, automatic features are a superb way to ensure that you have good results when you first start shooting. As you improve and become more ambitious, however, those same features will start to hold you back.

When selecting a camera for advanced use, therefore, ensure that there is not only a manual equivalent for every important function, but also that it is easy to set and adjust. Of course, such options are found only in more advanced cameras (such as the Panasonic AGDVC-18 or 100, Canon XL2, JVC HD1, Sony DSR-PD170).

Achieving a steady shot

Cameras that are easy to travel with because they are so lightweight are poor choices for shooting with for precisely the same reason. Having bought a compact camera, it is frustrating to find that you need to make it heavier, but that is exactly what professionals do: the extra weight gives stability, which helps deliver a steady picture.

For some videomakers, the best compromise is to use a monopod, perhaps in tandem with a shoulder brace. But simply reducing vertical movements will provide a visible improvement. Another method is to use a stabilizer, rather like a monopod, with a weight at the end. The pendulum weight steadies the camera when the rig is held at the center of gravity.

Hidden buttons
Buttons are often found under the LCD screen. Not all will be needed often, such as the zebra display, but an experienced camera operator will prefer easier access.

Audio display
A display of audio levels with timecode and status gives assurance to an experienced camera operator but may be confusing for the newcomer.

Audio controls
Controls on this video camera allow line levels for microphones to be controlled from the camera, together with balance between channels.

Quick fix Camera handling

Modern video technology is stable and reliable, and most problems are avoidable. Once you can identify how an error was caused—what you did or failed to do—it is easy to get it right next time.

Problem: Lens flare

Brilliant-white or colored, disk- or lozenge-shaped spots of light appear in the viewfinder or image, or the image floods with bright light. The image appears to be too light and the colors become weak. As you pan the camera, the flare spots move in the opposite direction.

Analysis

Bright sun or light sources enter the lens at an angle and reflect off the inside of the lens, filter, or inner camera parts. This causes veiling flare (or glare), degrading the image.

Solution

Even when the sun is not visible within the image, it can still cause flare. The best solution is to use a lens hood (see p. 35), but an additional shade may be needed to cast a shadow over the lens. Keep the sun to your back, and remove filters and other attachments. Sometimes lens flare can work in your favor if you are trying to capture a sense of heat and unbearable brightness.

Reflection
Bright sunlight has shone around the lens hood and flared into the picture. At the same time, a spot of water has picked up the sunlight to reflect a focused image into the lens. It may not be perfect, but it adds a sense of brightness and warmth.

Problem: Poor color balance

Images appear to be tinged with an overall color, such as orange or blue, in varying strengths. Attempts to correct the color later lead to poor results.

Analysis

The perceived color of an object can vary with the color of the illuminating light. In normal vision, the range of correction is very wide—wider than the capacity of electronic systems. In many situations, automatic color balance carried out by the camera is acceptable, but when it fails, it is seen in the image as strong color casts.

Solution

When shooting strongly colored scenes, make a manual white-balance reading. Select this option in your camera's Shooting or Setup menu and point the camera at a neutral target, such as a white wall. In extreme situations, you can help the camera by using a filter—for example, 80B (dark blue) for domestic light. Try supplementing available light by using video lights.

Problem...

...solution

Color correction
Under domestic lighting, everything turns cosy and warm in color balance, but skin tones become too red. A correction of white balance improves skin tones, and other colors—as in the curtain behind—are differentiated as a result.

Problem: Movement

When you examine images from a clip, they appear to be fuzzy, with multiple outlines. The defect appears even when the camera was set on a tripod.

Analysis

Motion blur in an image is caused by movement of either the subject or camera—or both. It is often due to the effective exposure time of the video camera not being brief enough to stop action in the way you expect to see with a still image. As a result, action moving across the screen appears unsharp when viewing a single frame.

Solution

When present, motion blur is likely to appear excessive when viewed as the first frame of a clip or when you extract a still from a movie clip. However, when the clip is played, the blur seems to disappear—lost in the general action or acceptable within the context of the scene. Therefore, motion blur does not need to be corrected.

Movement blur
A moment before the eagle owl launches herself off, everything within the frame is sharp. But her movements as she flies are too fast to capture sharply on video, as seen in the second shot.

Problem: Unsharpness

The subject of the image appears unsharp, with highlights appearing as large disks of light, and the outlines of objects are indistinct.

Analysis

Unsharpness due to poor focusing is caused either by a malfunction of the autofocus or by operator error. At times, the electronics accept an unsharp image as one that is focused, because they are confused by shooting through obstacles such as water or fences. Another cause may be the imaging of bright reflections or light sources.

Solution

If a focusing problem is persistent—that is, it occurs consistently with different situations, lens settings, and light levels—then you may need to have your camera serviced. If you cannot see the viewfinder to focus accurately, you may need to adjust the dioptre correction of the viewfinder. Allow time for the camera to focus before starting to record; this may take several seconds. Avoid focusing on light sources or rapidly moving objects.

Correct focus
Here, we want to focus on the fish, but the camera focuses on the bubbles because they are higher-contrast targets and therefore easier to focus on. In the second shot, without distraction of bubbles, the camera can focus on the fish.

Cinematic composition

The fixed size and shape of the "film window" may appear restrictive and prescriptive, offering you no opportunity to change the proportions or shape of the frame. In fact, the opposite is true. The film window is just that—a window. But it is one that you can move around and enlarge or reduce as you wish. Through movement—implied or actual—framing for movies is infinitely more flexible and versatile than for any other medium.

Through slow panning movements, you can imply a vast, open canvas. Using tight shots from close in, you can make the viewer feel a part of the action—a technique exploited in many martial arts and action movies. And there is nothing more emotionally involving than a close-up moving slowly over a face or body.

Visualizing the canvas

One approach is to visualize the canvas that you wish to work with, then use your camera's movements and zoom, together with any cuts you might need, to draw the canvas for your viewer. For example, suppose you want to show the large atrium of a modern building. The camera lens can take in only a small fraction of the view, even at its widest zoom setting. You must plan how to give a sense of the volume and the height of the ceiling.

A simple, horizontal pan is not only boring, it only shows one level. Instead, you could track someone walking across the space, then follow them as they take an elevator that rides up an exposed column to a high level, before zooming in on a small detail high in the ceiling. This sequence conveys both span and height in one continuous shot.

Creating strong images

Ideally, the image composition you should aspire to in the cinematic frame is as strong and coherent as in a still image or painting. But in a movie, the subject must have space in which to move. You can augment a strong visual impression with movement through panning or zooming.

Diagonal

A diagonal line, or one that could be drawn between principle elements, gives the most dynamism. A sweep across two axes appears to move faster and with more energy than a composition aligned solely with the horizontal or vertical.

Clean background

All objects—whether they feature elaborate or simple outlines—can benefit from being seen against an uncluttered background. Here, the lines of the rigging stand out against the plain sky and water.

Symmetrical

Where the elements of a composition are equally weighted and distributed, the psychological effects most naturally associated with it are stability, tranquillity, and calm. Symmetry can be found in natural scenes (*above*).

Center of interest

Lines leading to a specific point draws the viewer's attention. If you want to lead the eye to a center of interest, try doing it through the use of converging lines.

Framing action

Your video framing should take account of action that may take place a few moments into the take, so you should leave enough space around your subjects to capture their movements. A movement that starts outside of the frame and then appears inside can be disconcerting for the viewer, while one that starts in shot but ends out of shot can be frustrating to watch. In both instances, the problem is the lack of continuity. When you are working in a documentary or unscripted mode, or whenever you cannot fully predict which way your subject will turn, it is important to frame generously.

Composing for space

Unfortunately, the majority of amateur videomakers often leave too much space around their subject, frequently including many distracting elements. The trick, then, is to compose with generous amounts of space but without unnecessary distractions. At times, all that is required is to move slightly to one side or the other so that your subject obscures any unwanted background details in the scene.

Tracking movement

Another aspect of framing is the need to keep a subject in the middle of the frame while you are tracking its movement. Suppose you are following a bird in flight. You will find it difficult to keep the subject centered all the time. If you follow too

Allowing for movement
When videoing a pair of wallabies playing, you may be tempted to move in close. But the final frame illustrates a problem: if the subjects move suddenly in an unexpected direction, they may be cut off by the edge of the frame. Zooming out gives more space to the animals, but you lose some of the sense of involvement.

Tracking by hand
Some movements, such as a cormorant taking off (*above*), are easy to track. The hard part is keeping the bird centered. This inexpert example is partly a result of holding the camera by hand. Better results would have been achieved had the camera been mounted on a tripod and tracked with the pan/tilt arms.

Following the action
When the camera is zoomed tightly on to this ski school, the group fills the frame nicely (*above*). But what happens when they start to move off? You can start a clip with this framing, but zoom out to leave a bit more room when the skiers begin to fan out. They can then move into the space that you have allowed them (*right*). Hold the framing of the shot and let the ski group exit stage right, as it were. This will give you a timely cue to cut to another scene.

quickly, the bird will slip in the framing and could appear to be flying backward. Worse, if the framing is too tight, then the subject will appear to be bouncing around within the frame as you try to keep up. Even modest amounts of movement show up large on the screen. Someone walking along actually bobs up and down, so if their head is too close to the top edge of the frame, either it will be chopped off or you will have to move the camera up to keep them in shot.

If, instead, you show more around the subject, its movements relative to the frame are smaller and the viewer can see more of the background. You will then find it easier to keep the subject steady in the frame.

Expert framing can make or break your movie. Some of the key points to remember are:
- For smooth tracking of irregular movement, it is best to work with a tripod.
- Hold the camera away from your body if you are walking or tracking the subject—your arms will act as shock absorbers to cushion the impact of your footsteps.
- For unsupported tracking, heavier cameras give smoother movements. If you are using a lightweight camera, a camera stabilizer or shoulder pod will help.
- Try to give space in the frame for the subject to move into—that is, keep the subject to one side of the frame, rather than dead center.

Framing the shot

In moviemaking, perspective is far more than simply the point of view. It links a person's (or animal's) perceptions with their position, for it says, "This is what it looks like from here." Perspective puts the viewer in a position to experience, not merely to view.

That is why the approach of a hypodermic syringe as it advances toward the camera lens—as if pointing straight at the viewer—is so much more effective in expressing the fear of a soon-to-be-anesthetized dental patient than a side view of the syringe approaching. If you are showing a field that is full of flowers, try holding the camera down near ground level instead of viewing it from your usual height: the closeness—blurred and out of focus—to the leaves and petals can be far more involving than the usual vista.

Expanding on the principle

It follows, therefore, that videoing a scene such as a family picnic or wedding reception from the same position—even with the most clever panning and zooming effects—soon becomes rather dull. Instead, take the time to move in and out of the action. Watch a child's antics from the mother's position, but then cut and move around to watch the mother's reactions from the child's point of view. Watch an impromptu game of soccer from the side, then record from the goal so viewers can feel as though they are the goalkeeper. Or shoot a ballgame from afar, then get up close to the

ball just before it is kicked or picked up. In such a scenario as this, it is even okay to have an action coming into frame and going back out again because it is within the context of a game we all understand.

Long shot
A distant or long shot is one in which the audience can see the context and surroundings. Such a shot tends to be relaxed, leading the viewer's eye and mind to take in a general view.

Close-up
With modern zoom lenses you can home in to point out details. By then zooming back out, you can reveal to the viewer how this little detail fits into its surroundings.

Watching the crowds
Sometimes you simply need to let the scene organize itself before your eyes. Use your video camera to watch the crowds come and go. You can extract the best moments at the editing stage.

Taking it all in

From a vantage point offering such a fantastic view as this one in Dubrovnik, Croatia, you could spend the entire day bringing out its potential simply through different framings alone.

Take the time to explore the view fully. As the hours pass, the light and colors will change too. This will bring you further cinematic rewards, some of which you might expect and others you will not.

Wide close-up

The close-up wide-angle view is distorted but can be effective for a change of mood. Off-center framing (here of a photographer at work) allows for movement, making the viewer anticipate action.

Extreme close-up

Tight framing can create a sense of intensity for the viewer, especially if held for a long time. But when working unscripted, not knowing the subject's next move, it is easy to lose framing.

Depth of field

The term "depth of field" is used to define the measure of the extent of the scene lying in front of and behind the subject that also appears to be acceptably sharp or in focus. It is not as crucial a pictorial control in digital videomaking as it is in photography. Nonetheless, the skilled videographer should be aware of the importance of depth of field, which is essential for separating subjects and movements.

Movement and distance

Because a video consists of moving images, the photographic use of depth of field to depict space and distance is reduced in importance. Indeed, rather than showing distance, it can be used to keep the viewer in suspense. For example, we focus on a sleeping child's face while, blurred in the background, a menacing figure creeps up. As the figure moves closer, the threat seems imminent… until it comes into the field of view.

Now, seen sharply, the figure turns out to be the loving mother, coming to tend to her daughter. A close-up shows mother and child together.

Large aperture, long focal length

Because feature films are made on 35 mm or even larger formats, depth of field—even with wide-angle lenses—is very limited (*see also pp. 76–7*). Therefore, limited depth of field has become one of the hallmarks of the "film look." Digital video all too easily produces a large depth of field because the sensor chips are very small, so the lenses are relatively short—even at the longest zoom settings. The easiest way to decrease depth of field

Distant depth of field

Even with the zoom set to maximum shooting under an overcast sky (so that the lens aperture was at its widest), the depth of field is extensive. The reason is that the sensor chip is very small so that the longest focal length is still relatively short—and depth of field increases rapidly with decreasing focal length.

is to use long focal lengths as much as possible. To replicate the sleeping-child example, opposite, set up the camera about 6½ ft (2 m) away from the subject and use a long focal length to obtain a close-up of the face. Do not move close to the face to create the close-up.

Another method is to adjust the lens aperture, but, unfortunately, this option is not widely available on nonprofessional cameras. If you have a camera with variable lens aperture, you can decrease the depth of field by opening the aperture. Some semiprofessional cameras offer f/2 maximum apertures—this is worth considering if you want to create the film look.

Greater depth of field
At its widest setting, a digital video camera lens offers good depth of field even with subjects within reaching distance. The lens is focused on the wire but the lion is still acceptably sharp.

Setting focal lengths

On consumer cameras—and even on some prosumer models—setting the focal length is a matter of pushing a switch until you obtain the visual effect you require. For serious work, the ability to set a precise focal length is invaluable for ensuring continuity of image size and other settings. For this, you need a zoom controlled by a ring set around the lens and engraved with focal-length markings, rather than a rocker or sliding switch.

Focusing ring

Focusing scale

Zoom control

16x zoom
If you are serious about movie-making, there is no substitute for a top-of-the-line lens whose focus and zoom settings can be adjusted manually and repeated accurately, as with this lens on which focal length and distance settings are engraved.

Shallow depth of field
From the same viewing distance, but at a much longer focal length, it is evident that depth of field has decreased: the lion's face is sharp at the expense of the fencing, which is blurred.

Very shallow depth of field
With the zoom lens set at its longest setting and focused on the fence, the lion is thrown into an almost unrecognizable blur. This can be a powerful technique—called differential focusing—for exploiting the psychological effect of unfocused images.

Preparing for the shoot

So far, we have looked at composing a shot only from a static location (*see pp. 46–51*). However, to create a sense of dynamism and continuing action in the video, the shoot will benefit from the videographer moving around freely. This can be combined with panning and tracking (*see pp. 56–7*) and zooming (*see pp. 58–9*).

Needs for the shoot

Before you get to the shoot, consider your needs. This covers requirements of the shoot, ideally in the form of a shot list, as well as equipment (extra batteries, tapes, a tripod). Once at the shoot, you also need to be aware of everything that is going on, so that you can keep an eye on what may move into your frame and change your shot if necessary.

Shooting skills

When you come to record your footage, you need to combine your needs with your shooting skills to capture usable footage for your movie. You must also bear in mind the needs of the editing process. Once you are at the editing stage, you don't want to think, "Why didn't I shoot from *that* angle?"

The skills that you will need when recording your video footage are all fundamental to creating a coherent end product. They include:

● Ability to anticipate likely action. That is why wildlife cinematography is best done by experts in the animals being recorded; the same is also true for videoing sports.

● Rapid and precise focusing. This is important for unexpected changes in the action.

● A steady camera hand. The steadier your hand, the more usable footage you will have.

● Awareness of exposure consistency. Uneven exposure from one clip to another makes it impossible to achieve inconspicuous editing.

Improving your skills

Your shooting skills can be improved—to the benefit of your videomaking—through practice. A playful cat or dog is ideal for perfecting your anticipation skills, as is a trip to the zoo. Changes in focus can be practiced at the same time, or by trying to get close-ups at, say, a football game. A steady hand can be gained through relaxation of your body. Exposure awareness will come with increased use of your camera.

High-rise views

Looking steeply upward while you pass tall buildings is an effective way of conveying the massive scale of architecture—in this case, that of Hong Kong. Rapid changes of view are exaggerated by the perspective and aided by the movement.

Funicular ride

When location and situation are constantly changing, it is easy to gather a good variety of shots, but do not forget the small details. Observe your fellow travelers and the light and reflections around you. The movie is then about more than just the ride.

An overview

The view of Hong Kong's Peak is world-famous, having been used everywhere, from Jackie Chan movies to airline calendars, so there is little you can do to surprise an audience. It would be obvious to pan from one side to the other, or to zoom in on details. Fortunately, the overcast, foggy day forced a different approach, emphasizing the scale of tourists against the backdrop. Starting with the overview (*above*), we cut to views from the platform (*in the sequence below*) for a change of scale.

Shooting for variety

It is a good idea to shoot a scene from as many different angles as possible. This may call for both planning and anticipation. Planning your camera angles—that is, working with a sequence of perspective changes between normal, high, and low positions—is an important part of executing a shoot. A variety of camera angles creates changes in tension and pace even where there are no other changes in composition or lighting.

Variety when shooting also generates options in editing—it can be frustrating to find yourself short of footage once you enter the postproduction stage. And remember: the least expensive part of the entire exercise is digital video tape. You will also enjoy videoing much more if you move around and actively search for shots.

Camera height

It is natural to shoot from the most comfortable position—usually standing or from a tripod set to a little below head level. But shooting everything from the same height can cause your movie to become monotonous. Indeed, it may be appropriate for certain subjects to be shot from a lower or higher level. Videoing from above gives the viewer a sense of observation; this makes it an ideal way in which to set a scene, perhaps before cutting right in to the action.

It is always possible to shoot from a low level: simply crouch or lie down. This is almost always more dramatic when covering movement.

Involving the viewer
A group of children working off their energy makes a lively subject. It is easy to record from a distance, but getting into the action—holding the camera low—as well as following events from a greater distance is rewarding and fun.

The swivel screen

The swiveling or hinged LCD screen—present on the majority of consumer video cameras—has been a great invention for the videomaker. Since it can swing out to be adjusted to allow you to hold the camera at arm's length in any position, you can shoot low down, overhead, or to one side, and monitor your shooting in ways impossible with a viewfinder dependent on an eyepiece. So there is no excuse for not exploiting variety in perspective. Try practicing with making full use of the screen's movements so you become familiar with its possibilities.

DV camera with swivel screen

Think of the old cowboy movies in which the horses thunder past with their hooves just inches away from the camera. The immediacy of the action depends on a low camera position set close to the action.

By using a camera with a swiveling LCD screen, you can continue to monitor what you are shooting even with the camera at ground level. The trick is to keep the camera steady: keep the arms extended, firmly but not too tightly tensed, and try at all times to move smoothly and slowly. It can help to keep the neck strap as taut as possible against your neck.

Capturing fast-moving action
It can be tiring to follow all the action continually. Often it is better to hold a steady wide-angle view, such as here, and allow the action to move in and out of frame.

Visibility and safety

In the search for creative camera angles, consider the safety of yourself and those around you. People coming toward you may not see you if you are crouching. Being near to fast-moving vehicles is dangerous and increases exposure to splashes or stones being thrown up from the road. If you must have the shot, leave the camera on a tripod and move to a safe distance.

Following movement

There are three ways to follow moving action. Panning imitates a person's eyes following the action: it is a steady, rolling shot in which the distance between subject and camera changes. Tracking follows the path of a subject, moving in parallel and keeping at the same distance; for this, the camera needs to be on a mobile platform. Either of these movements may be combined with zooming, which can keep a subject at the same size by changing the field of view as it moves (see also pp. 58–9).

Zooming

A zoom is a change in field of view that makes it seem as though the camera is getting closer to or farther from the subject. When shooting, the zoom is a good way to move into the detail of a scene after starting with an overview. In the days of linear film editing, it provided a simple transition effect that anyone could do. And they did. As a result, zooming has become overused—and this overuse is a sure sign of a novice camera operator.

Stepping in and pulling out

The easiest way to distinguish yourself from a million other videographers is to step in, rather than zoom in. That is, instead of increasing the focal length in an unbroken sequence to zoom in, do it in large, distinct steps. This is more interesting for the viewer because it adds an element of surprise. Suppose you are videoing a carpenter

at work: you start with the scene-setting shot, then cut to a zoomed view of the tools hanging on the wall, perhaps with the worker just in view. Another cut takes you closer to the worker, showing their posture and the effort they are putting into their work. With the next cut, the viewer is zoomed right into the action—a close-up of the chisel cutting curling slivers of wood. You are trying to mimic a normal visual experience: you take in the scene, your eye is distracted by one thing, you look at something else, then you change your focus to get in close to what really interests you.

Zooming out

We can reverse the usual take on a scene by starting with a zoom into a detail (*right*). This leaves the audience wondering, "Where are we and what is going on?" In this shot, a very young and lonely kayaker could be in trouble in the middle of a huge lake. But a rapid pull back out of the scene puts her into context (*below*) and reveals that she is in no danger, after all.

Panning zoom
Zooming can be combined with panning, as shown in the sequence above. An establishing shot (*left*) shows the marina, before the second shot is achieved through a pan to the right while zooming in. For the final shot in the sequence there is no need for any more panning but the zoom continues, showing the moored vessel (*right*). Coordinating the speed of the pan with zoom action can be tricky, so do a practice run or two before shooting.

Whip zooming

Experienced camera operators favor the whip zoom, which is the fastest possible zooming. This technique simplifies the editing process, since the zoom movement can be either cut easily or used directly. However, whip zooming requires a manual zoom lever, which is generally found only on professional cameras. You can work around the lack of a zoom lever by first shooting a wide view—an example might be the quiet marina opposite. Next, stop shooting, zoom to a close view of a young kayaker on the water, and start taping again. When the sequence is cut together, the transition created makes it look as though you whip zoomed. You can follow the same unpredictable pattern when using the opposite movement, pulling out.

Combating camera shake

At the short focal-length settings of the zoom, handheld work is fine, since small movements are barely noticeable. But with increased focal length, camera shake is a bigger problem. It is always best to have a tripod with you, just in case.

Digital zoom

Modern digital video cameras offer zoom ranges from a modest 10x to a huge 880x. If the latter seems too good to be true, that is because it is. Most cameras offer true optical zoom of up to about 10x—that is, the longest focal length is 10 times longer than the shortest. The rest of the range is provided by digital processing: the digital zoom enlarges the central portion of the image. Quality drops rapidly, and beyond about twice the longest optical focal length, image quality is very poor.

Zoom comparisons
It is clear at a glance that the results from a digital zoom (*above right*) are markedly inferior to those from a true optical zoom (*above left*). At 120x, the image is 12 times enlarged from a zoom lens at its longest focal length (10x the shortest): 20x may produce acceptable quality, but much greater enlargements magnify image defects that were barely visible at 10x.

Camerawork continuity

The strength of a movie's narrative line depends on its continuity. This does not mean that every scene has to be connected, or that sudden breaks or jump cuts are never to be attempted; nor even that events should be shown in sequence, in the order in which they occurred. Indeed, there is a discernible fashion in filmmaking, encouraged by films such as *Pulp Fiction*, to place scenes out of chronological order. But continuity does mean that changes from one scene to another should move the action on, follow the logic of the story, and, above all, not distract the viewer. As an obvious example, if you were to show a man entering a car, then cut to a short sequence on the road before he exits the car, when he reemerges, he must be wearing the same clothes; if not, the lack of continuity will make the scene confusing for the viewer.

On the other hand, suppose you film a bride and bridesmaids entering a room and they close the door on you. In the next scene, the bride emerges from the door in different clothes. Here, the discontinuity makes sense: now she has changed for her journey—a symbolic shedding of the past—and it is not necessary to show any interim action.

Continuity should be maintained in two distinct areas. Screenplay continuity will be considered on pp. 194–9. In this section, we look at continuity in camerawork.

Focus and framing

Maintain your focus from one take to another, particularly when videoing people. If your focus is on the nearest eye, it should remain so even if the subject moves in the next take. And if you frame to contain the head and shoulders, change to a tighter view only for a specific reason—maybe to provide options in editing. When you return to your original framing, ensure you go back to the original focal length. Only extremely costly professional lenses have focal-length markings, so you will most likely need to use "markers" in the subject—for example, noting that the left frame is just beyond the right shoulder, or the right frame nearly touches the edge of a table just out of shot.

Color

Changes in white balance signal to the viewer a change in circumstances in line with the variation in lighting. It is okay for the white balance to shift to yellow-red when the action moves from outdoors into a building. But if the shift occurs for no obvious reason, the on-screen effect is unsettling. There is a common reason for the change. When you are filming someone on an overcast day, the white balance tends to be quite cool; but if the sun suddenly appears, there will be a change in color temperature and the scene will look warmer. Off-screen, the sun coming out is not visible, but the change in white balance will be, often accompanied by a slight rise in contrast. The lack of continuity here is an example of the principle of motivating the light (*see pp. 90–7*).

Exposure

You need to maintain an even exposure level between shots. This is difficult to achieve if you work in differing environments—moving from, for instance, an office to outdoors. The more carefully you shoot, the less exposure correction will be needed in postproduction, and the easier it will be to match takes so the edit points are less obvious. Poor exposure consistency is often a cause of poor color—so even if you match exposure across takes, color variations may still spoil continuity.

Light and contrast

Distinct from exposure and color control, you should also maintain the lighting style and the contrast when shooting different angles of the same scene. This is particularly important when you have to interrupt an interview shoot and reconvene at another date. Make precise notes of the lighting setup—where the light stands are positioned, height of lamp, light shaper used, and strength of light—so that you can reproduce the lighting conditions. Failure to do this will, at best, force the editor (or you) into an "A-mode" edit—working with scenes in the order they were shot. At worse, interview footage from different shoots

Color continuity

These dazzling jewelry displays appear white to the eye, but the large expanse of overcast lighting—weakly blue and dominant—causes the digital video to see them differently: the camera has rendered the displays strongly yellowed (*above left*). With a different angle (*right*), where most of the light is from the display, the camera responds with a whiter, compensating balance.

Exposure continuity

Deep in a souk in Marrakech, Morocco, the light is stunning and alluring—but it also presents a tremendous technical challenge. Here is evidence that the combination of camera operator and camera was not up to the task: the variations in exposure from one take (*above left*) to another (*right*) are evident and can only be corrected later in postproduction.

Light and contrast continuity

Color balance and contrast can be matched with filters and white-balance adjustments, and you can get away with small inconsistencies in perspective, but you cannot correct them all at the same time. Here, the biggest continuity problem is the soft light when the sun is not out, compared to the contrasty light and clearly defined forms when it is out.

Working with digital sound

Although the visual element of a movie tends to steal the limelight, it should not be forgotten that all great movies have a great soundtrack. And no film is truly silent; even so-called silent movies were originally presented with music, played by a pianist in the movie theater.

Unnoticed by all but hi-fi lovers, the digital revolution in sound recording is every bit as remarkable as it is in digital video and photography. It is simply not so dramatic or high profile, but it has brought true high-fidelity sound to the mall and the desktop, where it was previously the preserve of professional recording studios and those with large budgets. Nonetheless, sound is often the weak link in an amateur production. Good sound is vital to the success

of a movie, and it depends on parallel skills of discernment and technical competence, just as the visual side does.

The audio chain

Because digital video is a multimedia experience—combining vision with sound—running parallel to the imaging chain is the audio or sound chain.

The quality of sound recording should be appropriate to both the movie and the audience. A documentary on guitar playing obviously deserves the best quality possible, whereas it is less important for a compilation of police-car chases.

As with the imaging chain, the weakest link in the chain sets the ceiling on the quality attainable by the entire system. If in doubt, consult a sound

Camera mic
Most videomakers, especially when starting out, will use the camera microphone or connect their microphone directly to the video camera.

The source
It starts with the sounds emanating from a scene or environment. As with an image, you can choose to capture all of it—like a wide-angle view—with a microphone that records over a wide reach, or you can home in on particular sound sources—as with a telephoto view—cutting out peripheral sounds.

Mixing desk
Optionally, the microphone is connected to a mixing or routing device which balances or combines different sources before sending the resultant signal to the recording device.

Microphone
The sounds are converted by the microphone into electronic signals.

Cables
These carry the signals from the microphone to one of a number of possible destinations.

professional to ensure that you balance the quality of your cables with that of your microphone and that of the mixers, and so on.

Transparent sound

One reasons that developments in sound may not have been noticed is that a professional sound person wants his or her work to be "unnoticed." Sound is noticed only when it is poorly mixed, at the wrong level, or is inappropriate. A good soundtrack is simply an integral part of the whole experience. Just as with continuity, sound is noticed only when it is wrong and it distracts the audience.

Great sound is, therefore, transparent—its workings are not visible to the audience. Listen to a fight scene in a martial arts movie with your eyes closed: a good one sounds chaotic and unpredictable, like a real fight. A poorly made movie soundtrack sounds like a bunch of people randomly grunting and making whooshing noises while they kick punchbags. The transparent soundtrack is not noticed, it is enjoyed.

Computer
Together with the movie, the sound is next downloaded to a computer, where it can be mixed or combined with other soundtracks and edited along with the video clips. At the same time, the sound can be processed like any other digital file, to clean up noise and correct the levels so that they match from one edit to the next.

DVD writer
Once the soundtrack has been encoded together with the footage, it can be burned to a DVD. Once in this form, you can send copies out to family, friends, and people who contributed to the project.

Sound recorder
Some videomakers prefer to record their sound direct to DAT or MiniDisc. This process can also be done via wireless transmission.

Speakers or headphones
Finally, the DVD or other source of the movie is played, with the sound coming out through speakers or headphones.

Using a microphone

It goes almost without saying that the easiest way to use a microphone is also the way to obtain the least satisfactory results. But, as a solo operator—director of photography, producer, continuity, and gaffer all in one—you may have no choice. You will not be able to operate the camera and carry a microphone on a boom, so you will have to attach it to the camera. However, it is very disappointing to find that although you have shot a great sequence, you have recorded a distorted and noisy soundtrack.

The challenge is to get the best out of a camera-mounted microphone. This means placing the microphone as far away from the camera as possible, with a restricted or supercardioid acceptance, so that its sound recording is fairly directional. If your camera will accept a balanced line input, use a short gun-type microphone feeding a balanced line to the camera.

Hums and buzzes

The most common reason for poor sound is interference from other equipment causing clicks, hums, or buzzing noises. Clicks may be caused by poor-quality switches or damaged sockets. Hums and buzzing could be caused by anything from items of electrical equipment being placed too close together, to equipment such as generators in the street outside, or electrical cable being placed too close or parallel to sound cables: sound and electric cables should run at right angles to each other. Faulty cables or connectors can also cause a number of problems—from clipped or attenuated recordings, to interrupted sound and crackling.

It may seem straightforward to find and isolate these problems, but on location it can be very tricky indeed to track down and eliminate the source of interference. Only experience will help you diagnose the problem and find a suitable remedy quickly. But one thing is certain: if you do not fix the problem at the source, you will have even more problems during postproduction.

Another potential problem is the "third-man" effect. You can spend hours figuring out the positioning of microphones and levels to cut out background noise only to discover that the camera makes a noise too. Or that the addition of extra bodies or equipment changes the pattern of noise. The lesson here is that you should test for sound only when everything and everyone is in place.

Noisy backgrounds

When you are working in noisy environments, such as in a nightclub, near a busy street, or in a school playground, you have to confront two further problems. The first is auditory

On-camera sound
Sometimes—while covering a wedding, for example—there is no alternative to recording sound from the camera position. If there is a separate sound system being used—as here, the speaker is addressing to a large party outside—it may be possible to record that sound separately to be incorporated during editing. This cameraman has a microphone mounted above the camera lens on a short boom, and the box on top is a portable light.

Sound report
A well-trained recordist makes a sound report of every take captured on set, with notes of the slate number, conditions, quality, and duration. Such discipline is vital in a double-system recording, in which audio is recorded separately from video.

perspective—that is, how to ensure that the dominant sound stays close to the subject. Suppose you are filming a child unwrapping a candy in the playground and you want the sounds of the wrapper being torn. If you record from too far away—for example, from the camera position— the soundtrack captures the wrapper's sound only distantly, so it will be drowned out by the ambient noise, such as children shouting. The solution is to record close up, using a separate microphone.

The second problem is how to control levels between cuts, to avoid the soundtrack changing abruptly and unpleasantly. When taping in a school playground, you may stop recording just as a child's raised voise is suddenly heard above the general background noise. One solution is to ensure that a cut and its accompanying change of soundtrack mutually support each other. The classic cut is the closing door. As the door into school shuts, the sounds of the playground diminish. You can also use sound to convey emotional change, so that as the child becomes absorbed in enjoying her candy, the playground sounds recede. However, these solutions restrict the sequences you can make. Another solution is to record the background noise separately and add it to the edit as necessary. We will look at this option in more depth on the next page.

Balanced output

Microphones capable of good-quality capture will use balanced line inputs, whereas the majority of digital video cameras accept only unbalanced inputs. So if you wish to use a good microphone you need an adapter that takes balanced inputs and outputs a two-channel unbalanced signal. Sometimes called impedance-conversion boxes or routing devices, these adapters may also offer a preamplifier to boost the microphone signal, as well as some level controls.

Weight bonus
Impedance-conversion boxes are small enough to fit under a camera, using the tripod socket. On small cameras, this usefully adds to the bulk, facilitating a steadier shot.

Using a microphone continued

Sound effects

Given the ability of sound to reinforce a mood or emotion, one of the most effective ways of improving the impact of your video is by using sound effects. These can occur on screen or off, and can be naturally occurring at the time of shooting or recorded separately. The sounds could be recorded specially for the movie, and they could even be created through digital sound manipulation. It is easiest to record sound effects at the time of videoing, or close to it. For example, the sound of teacups clinking on china during a tea party is likely to be recorded together with conversation.

For the best possible sound effect, you may want the teacup-clinking sound to be recorded "clean"—that is, without any, or with reduced, ambient noise. This is known as recording a wild track—when the camera is not running at the same time as the sound. It is prudent to make as many recordings while on location as you can: the sound is then authentic, and you will not, for example, have to search for suitable teacups later.

Room tone

Nowhere is completely silent: even in the middle of the desert at night, the slightest breeze makes a singing in the sand. While trying to record exciting and beautiful sounds, it is also important to record room tone, or a buzz track—all the soft indistinguishable background noises that arise from life in the space, such as the distant and barely audible ticking of a clock or the rustle of leaves in the wind. You will need some of this for setting atmosphere and during sound editing because sudden noises such as a bird chirping or a dog barking cannot be simply erased—they must be replaced with room tone.

Foley sound

Recording foley sound—artificially made after filming, then edited to coincide with film action—is an art in itself. Seen, or rather heard, in almost every movie, but never noticed, it is custom-made sound to accompany perfectly the on-screen action—footsteps on a driveway, for example, or the jangle of a bunch of keys. Named after Jack Foley, a

Using a zeppelin
A microphone that is fully enclosed is the best—if the most cumbersome—method of recording ambient sound and that of the talent. Here, the recordist is taking both a monologue and the sound of the actor walking across the room. Zeppelins offer another advantage much appreciated by sound recordists: they give precious microphones excellent protection against the knocks of production.

sound engineer at Universal Studios in the 1930s, specialists in foley are called foley artists. They know just the right way to hit a saucepan to make the right clang, just how to walk on gravel so that it sounds like a detective creeping up to a window.

Simple effects like the amplified thumping of a heart, the unzipping of a jacket, and the crunch of tarmac as a car comes to a stop are all easily obtained, and using them is an effective way to give a professional dimension to your movie. For more elaborate sound effects—an explosion, police sirens, or a party, for example—"library sounds" can be purchased on CD.

Hard and soft effects

While sounds are always associated with action in the movie, that action can be off-screen (a scream in the darkness) or on-screen (someone stirring a cup of coffee). Off-screen sounds of, for instance, birdsong or falling rain represent extreme examples of a soft effect, one in which the timing does not have to be matched with any precision to the video. Any sound effects that need

to be timed to coincide with on-screen action is known as a hard effect—due to the fact that it is hard to synchronize the sound with the action.

It is helpful to recognize that synchronization means different things according to the action depicted. For instance, the clinking noise of a knife being placed on a plate should synchronize precisely with the action. But the startled look of an actor at the sound of a friend calling him should follow after a delay. A simultaneous response may make the viewer think that the call was expected. Thus, two completely contrasting readings turn on just a fraction of a second.

Locating the microphone
The sound recordist has instructed the microphone handler to try recording the sound from a variety of positions in order to discover the best recording perspective—that is, one that is analogous to the need to find the best visual perspective.

●HINTS AND TIPS

The following points will help you get the best out of your sound recordings:
- Whenever possible, do not mount the microphone on the camera.
- Remember that, unlike a camera, a microphone can "see" around corners.
- Monitor sound while it is recorded, if possible, using high-quality padded headphones.
- Cure problems such as hums and ambient noise before starting to record.
- If possible, rehearse for sound checks. Request silence from everybody on set and check for creaking floorboards, squeaking shoes, and ticking clocks.
- Turn off all cell telephones, watch alarms, and intercom sets.
- Keep sound reports. Note the time, data, content, situation, equipment used, and so on, during recording for future reference and also to help locate the right track quickly.
- Avoid hard sound effects—that is, those that need to be synchronized with on-screen action.
- Remember: mistimings of sound will cause misreadings of action.
- Ensure dialogue recordings—that is, anything involving voices—are correct at the time of the shoot. Errors can be extremely tricky to correct.
- There is no single right position for a microphone: try different positions and point it in different directions. Use different settings and even different types of microphone, depending on the soundtrack desired.

Using recorded music

Music is a most powerful way to create a specific mood, build tension, or close gracefully. And with so much great music in existence, there is sure to be something that would be perfect for your movie. Sometimes, the music can become as memorable as the film or more so. To many people, *Brief Encounter* is inseparable from Rachmaninov's second piano concerto, and even if you play *The Good, the Bad and the Ugly* with the sound off, you can still almost hear Ennio Morricone's haunting theme music. Certain movie genres are also defined by the type of soundtrack—rousing orchestral themes are typical of big-budget science fiction (*Star Wars*, for example), while the Danny Elfman scores for Tim Burton's films encapsulate perfectly the fairy-tale qualities of the stories.

So be bold—if you like a piece of music and it works well with your movie, use it. Even seemingly inappropriate music can be used successfully for comic effect: the love duet from Puccini's *La Bohème* for the meeting of two toddlers, perhaps? Or Wagner's *Ride of the Valkyries* playing over footage of the first outing in the new car? The combination of movie and music is so potent that it is wise to test the effect on a favored few before showing your work more publicly. You may think your choices are faultless, but you do not want viewers falling off their seats with derisive laughter. Beware that when you use commercially available music, you are infringing on copyright—in some legislations even if you do it solely for your own private use.

Commissioning music

With musicians of all persuasions enjoying wide access to digital sound samples and composing software, commissioning or composing your own movie music is now a viable option. You may be able to find a young composer who is willing to write for you in return for a small fee and a slice of any profits. By using electronic keyboards and sound synthesizers you can cancel out the need for a band or orchestra to play the music. And by commissioning it, you can ensure that the music perfectly fits the mood you wish to create. Better

Film soundtracks

Unlike on digital video, the soundtracks on film motion pictures are optical recordings. Audio recorded on tape is used to modulate the intensity of a beam of light that is focused on to the moving film, synchronized to the frames. The film is then chemically processed. On playback, a steady beam of light is shone through the soundtrack, which is now a row of light and dark patches. As the film moves across the light beam, the beam is modulated by the soundtrack. The variations are picked up by photocells, whose output activates a loudspeaker.

still, if the music is composed once the editing is complete or nearly completed, the length can be matched perfectly to the edits, meaning there is no need to trim or stretch prerecorded music to make it fit your movie.

If you choose to commission music, be clear about the rights you are obtaining for the work, but allow the composer to retain overall copyright so that he or she can use the work elsewhere.

Royalty-free tracks

It is possible to purchase CDs with hours of royalty-free music—which means you can use the music without any further payment. There may be some restrictions on high-profile use, such as for advertising jingles, but for the rest of us, these CDs provide a rich resource from which music can be used and elements may be extracted (to obtain the rhythm and beat, for example) and sampled for reconstruction. Music may be stored as MP3 files, giving many hours per CD, but higher-quality productions use CD-quality audio, meaning that less music can be held on each disc. For video work, MP3 quality is more than adequate.

Royalty-free CDs also offer a huge resource of sound effects—from forest atmospherics, to high-tech clicks and beeps and industrial noises. The sound quality of these is likely to be far superior to anything you could record yourself.

Quick fix Problems with sound

One of the challenges of digital video is that you need to master a number of different technical disciplines. Entire books have been published on sound recording alone. On this page, we cover some of the most common playback problems you are likely to encounter.

Problem	Analysis and solution
There is too much "noise" (background hiss), making it hard to hear the audio clearly.	You recorded at too low a level, so when you raised the volume for playback, you also raised the noise level (*see diagrams below*). Record at the highest level that does not distort, and lower the volume on playback to reduce noise.
Noise levels vary from take to take.	Your sound recordist was not paying close enough attention. This can be avoided by ensuring that the headphones used cut out all but recorded sound.
There is sudden unwanted sound, such as a dog barking or a door slamming.	This has to be dealt with in post-production. With the recording imported and on the video timeline, reduce the volume to zero on the soundtrack at the start of the noise and return it to normal afterward. Next, copy a clip of room tone of the same duration as the noise and lay it over the noise.
Sounds that can be heard in stereo cannot be heard when played back in mono.	The signals are out of phase. Somewhere in the system, wires were literally crossed, possibly where adapter jacks were used. Always check all of your cables carefully.
There is too much echo in the room, and it interferes with the clarity of voices.	The microphone is too far from the people speaking, so it is also recording too much room tone, creating an echo effect. Place it as close to your subjects as possible, without it appearing in shot, or use clip-on microphones.

Getting sound levels right

All recording will contain noise. The strategy is to separate the audio level from the noise level as far as possible.

The first diagram illustrates that, when the audio level is recorded as high as the system will take it without introducing distortion, on playback the audio level is reduced, which also reduces the noise.

If the audio level is set too low, the sound is recorded together with the noise. When raised to proper playback levels, the noise level is amplified too.

If the audio level is recorded too high, loud noises and very high frequencies are lost and not regained on playback: notice the flattened peaks of the waves.

Recording

Noise level   Audio signal
High level recording without distortion

Low audio signal

Recorded too high: cut-offs and distortion

Playback

Low noise: undistorted audio signal

High noise: interferes with audio signal

Low noise but distorted audio signal

Transitional methods

Many video enthusiasts have very large collections of VHS tapes of family vacations, birthdays, and parties, and these take up a lot of shelf space. In the past, you may not have considered attempting to edit the footage since it would be a difficult and costly exercise. Now you have access to digital video, that has all changed. Not only can you edit your vacation tapes at long last, but you can also archive the footage in a compact form—the DVD.

Analog to digital

Analog capture is the video equivalent of scanning old photographs to work on them on a computer. Old video content, typically VHS tape, can be easily converted by playing the tape in your VHS recorder through a box that codes the signal in a digital format.

Another source of footage could be an old analog camcorder producing composite or S-Video outputs. This kind of equipment is supported by software such as Windows XP provided the output is fed into the computer through a compatible device such as those available from Pinnacle or Viewcast. The range starts with small devices—such as the Viewcast Osprey-50, Eskape MyCapture or MyVideo, or the Dazzle DVC-90—that interface between the video source and the computer's USB input.

PROS AND CONS

The advantages of DVD over VHS are that it:
- Is more compact and holds more material.
- Is more durable.
- Offers better image quality.
- Offers random access.
- Can be navigated easily through chapters that are used to subdivide the movie.
- Can be viewed on a computer; most modern computers come with DVD palyers already installed.
- Can be programmed with interactive features and extra material running parallel with the film.
- Takes up less room on your shelf.

More powerful solutions, although a little more costly, are expansion cards installed in the circuit boards inside the computer. These deliver higher quality (and therefore larger pictures) and improved speeds of operation. It is not necessary to buy special software, since Movie Maker, which is bundled with Windows XP, will capture from these devices, as will the Mac equivalent iMovie.

If possible, choose S-Video over composite: its image quality is superior because of the separation of signals. However, cards accepting S-Video may be more costly.

Viewcast Osprey-50
This tiny device takes a composite or S-Video input and outputs to a USB video-capture device for those encoding situations that require the convenience of portability on a laptop.

Eskape MyCapture II
This USB device supports all three principal formats, capturing 320 x 240 pixels at 30 fps with NTSC or 384 x 288 at 25 fps with PAL/SECAM using compression.

Eye TV
Desktop boxes such as this allow you to watch broadcast TV on your computer, also enabling you to record broadcasts to a hard disk for later viewing.

Capturing broadcasts

Another major source of analog video signals—though not for long if governments in the northern hemisphere have their way—is terrestrial broadcasts from TV stations. There are many desktop units that will tune in to a TV station using either their own antenna or a TV antenna, decode the signal, and pass down a digital stream to the computer. This means you can store TV programs on your computer to watch at any time. Not surprisingly, this solution is rapidly replacing the cumbersome VHS tape machine for many enthusiasts.

The TV programs you record will then be in MPEG form, which makes them accessible to your editing software. However, do be careful not to breach the copyrights of the owners of the programs; this applies equally to public-broadcast services as it does to commercial stations.

Legality of recording broadcasts

In the majority of countries, it is legal to record television broadcasts for your own private use. However, you should check with your own local legal advisers if you are in any doubt, and certainly if you intend to show your recordings to anyone besides your immediate family within your own home. Note that in some legislations,

Synchronization problems

When you capture analog video together with the soundtrack, the two tracks may drift out of synchronization so that the closing of a door or somebody speaking is not heard at the same time as it is seen to occur. Prevention is far easier than cure: to minimize problems, devote all your computer's resources to the task of capture by shutting down all other programs.

such as the European Union, if you use the recordings for some future commercial purpose—to research plot lines for a feature film, for example—you enter a gray area of law and may be expected to pay some license fees. Furthermore, if you show the recording to a group of people that is not made up of immediate family, some legislations may consider that you are projecting to the public and so require the payment of license fees. Finally, if it is illegal in your country to receive a particular broadcast—for instance, from a certain satellite or cable station—then you can be sure it is also illegal to record such a broadcast.

Media Center PCs

Microsoft has set up a standard for PC hardware and software called Media Center PC. Machines that comply with the standard offer, among many other features, a tuner to accept TV signals from satellite, antenna, or cable sources, as well as a hardware encoder to capture TV signals to be saved to the computer. In addition, there are video outputs allowing the viewing of results on a TV screen as well as audio in and out sockets. All of this is run through Windows XP Media Center software, which combines the operating system with a number of applications, including those for editing video and authoring DVDs.

Home Media Center
Following in the footsteps of Apple Mac computers, which have long been able to handle multimedia, modern Windows machines now offer integrated multimedia facilities.

Using still images

Sometimes, you may want to incorporate a still image into your movie. When faced with using a still image, many videomakers allow the camera to roam all over the image; this is not the same as animating the print (*see Stop-frame animation, opposite*). The roaming is intended to imitate the way one might inspect a picture: first to pan or look over the picture, then to zoom in to a detail that catches the eye—just like starting with an establishing shot, then moving in.

More often that not, the image is likely to be a photograph, but you could also use a painting, a book, or a map. This technique, when used with a map, can be used to show the course of a journey, while many movies of fairy tales begin with the opening of a big book, with the camera moving into the picture on the first page.

Maintaining quality
A zoom-in from a full-resolution image is still captured at video resolution, but since it involves an interpolation down from a large file, rather than interpolating up from a small file, image quality is far superior. This is the kind of result delivered by proper pan-and-zoom software.

Using a rostrum camera
In the past, this roaming effect was achieved by using an instrument called a rostrum camera, a mounted camera pointing at a freely movable stage, on which a print was mounted. The camera was set to film as the print was moved around with one hand and the zoom operated with the other. Indeed, this may still be the simplest way to liven up video of a photograph if you do not

Pan and zoom made easy
If you shot a still picture but no video footage of this landscape, for example, you can still incorporate it into your vacation movie, using pan and zoom. You might start at the top of the image, with a zoom into the hotel (*above, top left*).

Image quality is rather poor, even for digital video, but a rapid movement will make it less noticeable. Then zoom out, taking in more of the video-resolution image—the image quality will steadily improve (*above, bottom left*)—and pan from the top left corner toward the

center of the image. In the final shot (*above right*), the end of the pan-and-zoom effect, the image quality is highly satisfactory because it is based on a high-resolution photograph. Do not hold this view for long or it will become evident that the palm fronds are not moving.

want to use editing software to achieve the same end, although it is probably easier to keep the image stationary and move the camera.

Mount your picture on a wall or table and set the camera up to point at it. Rehearse the movements across the image, as well as the timing, and ensure the lighting is flat and even across the field of view of the lens. You could also try using different zoom settings or zooming in as you move. Practice until you are happy with the movements before you start to record them. You can crop out jerky movements or slow down playback to make the shot smoother.

Using pan and zoom

The NLE software equivalent of the rostrum camera is pan and zoom, sometimes also called the Ken Burns Effect (after a documentary filmmaker who makes extensive use of photographs). The effect digitally simulates the panning and zooming movements after video has been shot. It does so by progressively cropping to a small portion of the image to imitate a zoom or moving across the view in successive frames for a pan. This is a similar concept to digital zooming.

The problem with working on a digital video image is that it relies on interpolation—the calculating and insertion of new pixels to fill gaps

Using specialized software
The Moving Picture utility simplifies and greatly powers pan-and-zoom effects with its ability to work on high-resolution images. You can also rotate the cropping area as you move it. At each turning point, you set a key frame: intermediate frames are calculated between key frames.

in the enlarged image—with the result that image quality of any zoomed-in area can be poor. For best results, you need software such as Moving Picture from StageTools, which can be used as a plug-in to NLE software or as a stand-alone application. Moving Picture allows you to load an image as large as 8,000 pixels square: you can pan around and zoom into it while retaining high quality.

Simplifying the task
This simple but effective NLE dialog box allows you to set the start point, end point, and the speed of the pan-and-zoom effect, as well as the level of zooming out or in. With zoomed-in views, it is possible to click on the image, dragging it to choose the cropping position.

Stop-frame animation

A variant of using photographs in a movie is to string together single shots and play them back at normal speed. This is applied to models made of clay (but Lego and similar toys are also popular). To shoot, for instance, an arm moving, the model's arm is moved a fraction of an inch, then a single frame is shot. After another small movement, another frame is shot. To speed up the movement, several frames could be shot of each new position. When played back at full speed, the arm appears to move normally. The technique calls for meticulous planning, infinite patience, and great model-making skills. The art reached its peak in Russian and East European cinema of the late 1990s.

Quick fix Copyright and rights

While you keep your moviemaking to yourself, creating digital videos for the entertainment of immediate family, you are not likely to encounter copyright or other rights problems. But as soon as you show your work publicly—and that can be as informal as at a club or wedding party—your work enters another realm, one strewn with traps for the unwary. Copyright and other rights may not seem important while you are developing an idea, but if it takes off, failure to attend to these matters can kill off the project.

Problem

The lens sees all as it sweeps around a room. Recording contemporary life will often include shots of call phones, magazines, and books, for example, all of which are protected by trademark and copyright. How do we know which need clearance or permission to use?

Analysis

If trademarked or copyrighted material, such as a magazine cover, is merely decorative, there is no need for clearance for an "incidental inclusion"—one in which it could be any magazine. But if the item, such as a certain type of cell phone, is featured as something that a character's life revolves around, then you need to seek advice. In particular, beware if any disparaging view is taken of the object—for example, your hero's life is threatened because it is unreliable.

Solution

If any branded object features prominently, seek legal advice. You may be able to obtain sponsorship through product placement. Otherwise, disguise the object.

Product usage
In a documentary movie, a product that is featured will not attract the attention of lawyers unless you make critical or disparaging remarks about the product—for example, if you say it was the cause of an accident. In works of fiction, prominent placement of a product calls for legal advice.

Problem

You plan to hire a photographer to take production stills for your movie, and you want to be sure you can use the shots both for publicity and in the movie.

Analysis

The issue is whether the work of the production photographer falls under the concept of "work for hire," where this is recognized in legislation. Since the team creating a movie is so large and many people make a creative contribution, the norm is to view all contributions as "work for hire" and belonging to the movie as a whole.

Solution

When you commission a freelancer to work on a movie, be explicit about the rights they have over the work they produce for you. If you want to use stills within the movie, you may allow the photographer to retain the copyright but obtain exclusive license to use pictures within the movie without further payment. If the stills are crucial to the story, the photographer may ask for more money.

Movie stills
A gesture by an actor between takes catches the eye of the editor, and he wants to use it in the movie. To do so, the producer will have to pay the photographer for the rights unless the photographer was commissioned on a "work-for-hire" basis.

Problem

While recording a documentary, you will probably feature numerous people. Some people say it is essential to obtain model releases; others say it is not necessary and that is it impossible anyway.

Analysis

There is no definitive answer because it is conditional on (a) which country you are videoing in; (b) what you are recording for; (c) what you will say or imply in the finished movie; (d) whether the people depicted have been paid in any way to be in the movie; and (e) how you intend to use the movie. Broadly speaking, documentary work shot in public spaces does not need releases, but you need to be careful if you are being critical about anyone, and especially careful if that person is not in the public eye—that is, not normally subject to public scrutiny. However, even in a public space, people may have certain rights of privacy that may be breached by your videotaping.

Solution

It is not safe to rely on common sense. If in doubt, seek advice. In general, while it is ethically dubious, the farther you shoot from the point at which the movie will be

viewed, the safer you are from legal action. But in these days of global mobility, it is unwise to rely on such evasions. If the documentary will be used commercially, particularly for promotion or advertising, there is no question: pay fees for models' and actors' releases.

Right to privacy
In a documentary on fishing ports around the world, you record someone watching harbor activity. In Morocco, you may get into trouble for

not first asking permission, if you broadcast the finished movie. In France, if you do not ask first, you will liable for breach of privacy whether you broadcast or not.

Problem

What you have recorded has been seen and photographed by millions of tourists over the years, so how can anyone have any rights over it?

Analysis

What is in public view and easily accessed by the public is almost always owned by someone, and that person is likely to have property rights over any depiction of the object. If you simply feature the object in passing, that is an incidental inclusion and an exception to breach of copyright. But if it features in a big way, perhaps being digitally altered for the movie, then you could be in trouble. For instance, a sculpture very similar to one in the National Cathedral in Washington was featured in the film *The Devil's Advocate*, during which it was animated to become an evil, writhing mass. That scene had to be cut under threat of an injunction preventing distribution.

Solution

If in doubt, seek advice and permission, even if you create a model based on an existing original, and particularly if you give it a meaning other than its original one.

Association
If you feature this sculpture from an Italian cathedral in a movie and two lovers identify

with it, there may be no problem. But if you associate it with something sacrilegious or heretical, there may be.

Achieving the "film look"

As digital video becomes more popular, it is being discovered by people with a more critical eye and some with more traditional tastes. To them, video looks hard-edged, lacking in subtlety, with a tendency to burn out highlights—that is, lose detail in a glare of white. Film is the standard by which video is judged, and it is usually found wanting.

What is the "film look"?

The "film look" comprises a collection of disparate features. First, film is shot with entire frames at 24 fps (frames per second). Second, and more importantly, at its best, film tonality is smooth, colors are rich, and, above all, film handles a wide lighting or dynamic range. Part of the perceived difference in color quality between film and video is due to video's more limited exposure latitude compared to that of film—its tendency to burn out highlights with little provocation.

Another feature of film is that the apparent depth of field can be very small compared to that of digital video—that is, it is very easy to throw the background out of focus when shooting film, particularly 35 mm. The reason is that film uses formats that are much larger than the tiny sensors of digital video cameras, and larger formats call for lenses of longer focal length. Depth of field

reduces rapidly with increase in focal length. Digital video cameras use short focal-length lenses, which inherently offer extensive depth of field.

Imitating film

Video that aspires to the film look aims to imitate these features. The most obvious technical feature to imitate is film's frame rate of 24 fps. A number

Diffusion filter

The easiest method of simulating something like a film look is to use a diffusion filter over the lens. Technically, this is a low-pass filter: it lets through soft detail but does not pass jagged, hard-edged fine detail. If you use an auxiliary lens for wide-angle or telephoto effects, you will need diffusion filters over these lenses.

Matte box for filter and hood

Diffusion, or softening, filter

Original

Anti-aliasing
Jagged edges, or aliasing, is a natural consequence of the low number of pixels used by the video format to record information. It is exaggerated by the sharpening filters used in the image processing. The result is a harshness of subject outline that is

Film effect

typical of video. A softening filter—simulated here with a blur filter—blends details together and softens, or anti-aliases, the edges. In a still photograph it looks too soft, but that softness is acceptable in a movie.

of modern prosumer-grade cameras are able to capture entire frames, at a rate of 24 or 25 fps. This may be called the progressive-scan mode, shown as 24P or 25P, depending on frame rate. While a film frame rate of 24 fps gives smooth movement on a movie screen, 24 fps or 25 fps on video may not deliver smooth movement on a TV screen. Progressive-scan mode is best when you need to take stills frames from moving-image clips or when you wish to transfer video to film.

Lighting can help disguise that you are working with digital video: by using very soft lighting you can avoid burned-out highlights. Professional-level cameras display warnings—a zebra pattern or flashing areas on the image—to indicate overexposed parts of the frame (*see p. 174*).

Limited depth of field is far harder to simulate. If your camera allows you to set aperture manually, you should first set the largest aperture (smallest f/number) that you can. In bright conditions, you may need to use a neutral-density film to obtain correct exposure. Try to frame as much as possible using a longer focal-length setting, or ensure the background is as far away as possible. But these measures are of no help with wide-angle views. Ultimately, the only way to reduce depth of field is to use a camera with a larger sensor.

Low contrast
No light is too low in contrast for video—even on the dullest of days (as in this detail), the bright side of the shiny surfaces of these gilt Bodhisattva statues in Hong Kong are rendered white on video. On film, there would be golden color in the bright areas.

Original

Film effect

Color correction
Another way to improve the look of your video is to process it in a nonlinear editing (NLE) software program, all of which provide some—if only basic—color correction. On the overcast day on which this footage was recorded, colors were lacking in bite and vigor (*above left*). This was corrected with the help of the Color Corrector function in the NLE package (*above right*). Plug-in "film-look" filters may be obtained for professional NLE applications.

3
Understanding and using light

Properties of light

An understanding of light and its properties is essential for anyone working in video. This chapter considers the many characteristics of light, such as quality, direction, color, and quantity. The effect that lighting has on mood is explored, and there is an in-depth look at lighting setups. Quick-fix solutions are provided for exposure problems.

Controlling light

Through the control of light, you can create a different feel for each of your movies, or even a unique look that is all your own and is common to all your work. Extensive illustrations and lighting diagrams lay the foundation for perfecting your camera lighting technique. Learn by practicing the lighting ideas shown here, then try experimenting to come up with your own solutions. The quick-fix section on lighting problems will help you avoid some of the most common pitfalls.

Capturing light

By using a range of different lighting techniques, you can endow your video movies with a sense of time and place, imply a mood or feeling, and even create a visual style. All of this adds to your ability to communicate a story.

Awareness of light

Like a photographer, a great videographer is at all times aware of the light. Everyone is familiar with the feeling when a large cloud suddenly obscures a bright sun: it is chilling and it alters one's mood. But what of the quieter changes during the course of a day or between seasons? Or the change of light as you move between the rooms of a house?

The quality of light

Diffused, or soft, light is recognizable from the effect it has on the scenes we view. It manifests itself in weak, blur-edged, or nonexistent shadows. From this, we know that the light is being scattered in all directions, with no concentration in any one direction. This is the product of a large source—maybe a cloudy sky.

In contrast, if we see sharp shadows with a great difference between the lightest and darkest areas, clearly delineated forms and intense colors, then we deduce that the light is concentrated into one main direction. This is the product of light seemingly from a small source, such as a spotlight.

Shifting exposure

A setting sun can help create a romantic wedding portrait. But when the sun is directly in front of the camera, it can affect the exposure reading and render the foreground too dark. Compensate for this by increasing the exposure (*see pp. 86–7*).

Exploiting soft light

In this shot of young cheetahs playing under a cloudy Kenyan sky, the only visible shadow is under the deepest hole of the old tree. The soft light of the overcast day is ideal for bringing out the texture of the cheetahs' fur and its delicate hues.

Diffusing light

A thin veil of high cloud (*above*) softens the fierce Mediterranean sun but without eliminating shadows. This is ideal lighting for the intricate stonework of this building in Pisa, Italy.

Using sidelight

In this scene, the strong directional light from the side means that every turn of the deer's head presents a different pattern of light and shade. Just keep shooting to capture great variety.

Lighting styles

One of the most direct ways to impart a visual style in your movies is through lighting. By using one quality of light consistently, you can give a very strong indication of your intentions. Think of the predominantly spooky lighting from below in *The Blair Witch Project* as well as in many other horror movies. Many musicals and comedies make use of even and steady lighting, which indicates a lightness of content and meaning. In contrast, fantasy and adventure movies make much use of dramatic sidelighting—look at *The Third Man*, *Terminator 2*, and *Blade Runner*.

Direction of light

In moviemaking, the direction of lighting contributes more than simply an artistic effect. It can dictate the whole direction of movement and gives powerful—if indirect—clues about narrative continuity. Broadly speaking, there are three sets of light direction: above or below, in front or behind, and left or right.

Before considering these sets, think about your instinctive understanding of light. The sun—the source of natural light—always shines from above or from one side, seldom from below. The light's elevation, strength, and direction offer information about the season, time of day, and direction of travel. Any light created by humans originally came from the ground in the form of small camp fires, and lighting from below often casts spooky, unnatural-looking shadows.

Above or below

Lighting from above emulates the light from the sun, and so tends to look the most natural, whereas lighting from below, with its unnatural connotations, is often used to indicate the unknown. In between, horizontal light, from just above or just below head height, can signify domestic lighting and the safety of home.

In front or behind

Our instinct is to position ourselves with the sun behind us, since that affords the best view of anything coming toward us. A subject lit from the front (that is, with the light coming from behind the camera position) appears the least threatening and most comforting because it displays the greatest clarity and detail.

In contrast, a subject lit from behind appears in silhouette; and this black form, displaying no detail, could appear threatening. However, if the light from behind is very bright, the subject is surrounded by a halo of light, suggesting innocence or goodness.

Left or right

During the course of action in a scene or series of scenes, the "handedness" of light—whether it comes from the right or the left—tells the viewer about the direction in which the action takes place.

Suppose your protagonist sets off hopefully with the sun to his right but soon runs into trouble. If he flees with the sun to his left, the viewer subconsciously knows he is running back home. Or suppose you are recording a conversation between two people: if you shoot

Overhead light

With light from above, this scene appears bright and sunny. However, the contrast is too harsh for the video sensors, causing the highlights to be too bright and to burn out (*above*). To avoid this, reduce the dynamic range by filling in the shadows with reflectors or lights (*left*).

over the shoulder of one with the light coming from the left, then you cut to shoot over the shoulder of the other, there should be a corresponding flip-over of light direction—the light should appear to come from the right. If not, it may be that no one notices, but it can be unsettling to the viewer, if only subconsciously.

If you shoot continuously, you will not make such an error, but you may, for instance, take a break then sit your subjects back in different positions because the camera is already set up. Then you will create a continuity problem (*see pp. 60–1*).

Backlight
Found keeping themselves entertained at an Italian family gathering, these boys have left behind a brightly lit world, in which nothing can be seen despite the light. A generous exposure for the foreground brings out the details in the boys.

Even lighting
Broad, even lighting indoors is an artifice created by the needs and limitations of videotape and broadcast TV. Houses, in fact, are lit in different ways, with some areas darker than others.

In real life, even lighting can convey overcast skies, a dull day, with a sense of the daily urban grind and the unwholesome atmosphere of the city.

However, even lighting remains the type that is kindest to video—one in which neither shadows nor highlights have to struggle to be recorded. It has been said that no light is too soft for video, and even lighting delivers an abundance of softness.

Even light
Usually bathed in brilliant sun, this wall in Marrakech offers a promising backdrop for the comings and goings in the street. In harsh light, the high contrast would degrade the color in the image. Here, on a dull day, the wall is lit perfectly.

Sidelight
With strong floodlight from the left, the curves of the guitar and sculptural forms of the musician's hands are captured perfectly. The reflective surface occasionally threw light into the lens when the musician moved with the flow of the music.

Color of light

A great deal of expertise and expense is devoted to the control of color in traditional filmmaking. Light sources have to be filtered carefully with colored gels in order to ensure accurate color balance and, even then, further corrections are made when the final edit is printed out for distribution. With digital video, the need for consistent color and accuracy is as great as ever, but electronics can do much of the work. White balance is the process of compensating for the color temperature of a light source to ensure accurate color recording.

Color quality

Digital video cameras make automatic white-balance adjustments for the prevailing color of the illuminating light. The intention is to ensure that neutral colors, such as whites or grays, are truly neutral; it is then assumed that other colors will be more or less accurately recorded. Thus, we want white walls in a room to appear white when illuminated by afternoon daylight as well as in the evening light. White-balance correction in digital video happens almost as a direct consequence of the way in which colors are sampled then encoded in the video signal, but the system can be confused if it is unsure about a true neutral color, so you may need to help the camera.

Shifting hues

When shooting from a lift in a shopping mall in Hong Kong, the camera was correctly set to the color balance for the incandescent lights, to give a neutral cast and generate accurate colors. But as the lift ascended into the daylight, the color balance was not automatically adjusted. This led to the overall heavy blue cast and caused the red taxis to appear magenta.

Achieving the right color balance

Under the incandescent lamps of a restaurant, the white china setting looks distinctly yellowish (*below*). But a full correction (*bottom*) renders the red table too dark. A partial correction (*right*) strikes the right balance, providing a more satisfactory image.

Gray-card calibration

The best way to ensure that the camera is measuring a neutral color for white-balance correction is simply to present it with a known neutral color. Cards printed with a standard midtone gray, can be bought at low cost. First set the camera to "manual," or "hold," then show the card to the camera and set the white balance.

The calibration method varies slightly between video cameras, so check the procedure in your instruction booklet.

Color temperature

Color, or the quality of light that gives the impression of hues, does not have a temperature. But the temperature of an incandescent light source is related to the color of the light it emits: the hotter it is, the cooler or bluer the light; while lower temperatures produce red or yellowish light.

Color temperature is measured in Kelvin (K; where 0 K is absolute zero): 5,000 K is taken as the color temperature of domestic lights; 6,500 K is that of tungsten halogen lamps; 9,300 K is a typical daylight color temperature.

Quantities of light

Digital video cameras, almost universally, operate on automatic exposure control. As with white balance, exposure control is almost a direct consequence of the way in which the video signal is processed. The amount of light reaching the video sensor—that is, the exposure—is controlled both by the shutter time (or the electronic equivalent) and the lens aperture used, both set automatically. In addition, the sensor itself may adjust its sensitivity to the incoming light, also automatically. Unlike digital photography, there is a limit to how long the shutter time can be, for it must fit into the frame rate of the video (for example, 30 frames per second), and of course it needs to be as short as possible in order to capture movement without blur.

Controlling exposure

Most of the time, you will not need to worry about exposure control. While the camera takes care of every setting, the viewfinder or LCD screen displays the video signal that is being recorded, so you have constant feedback on the accuracy of the exposure control.

But no system could get it right in every instance. For example, your subject may be a small target—a face or a flower, perhaps—surrounded by large areas of darkness. Automatic systems are likely to overexpose the image, burning out your subject. Or you may be following a figure moving from light to disappear into shade, and the last thing you want is for the camera to boost exposure when the shot moves into shadow.

To counter this problem, your camera may offer a function called spot metering or memory hold. Using this system, you select a point in the scene as the basis for the shot. Beware that some cameras will hold the exposure until you cancel the setting, while others will revert to normal automatic function at the end of the clip. Ensure that you are familiar with the way your camera works.

Dynamic range

When encountering dynamic range that is too wide, you must decide which tones to leave, which to lose. Here, I judged the tones of the hawk to be more important than the blue skies.

Shifting autoexposure

This sequence shows how autoexposure responds to changing light. The camera correctly exposes the close-up of a red-leaved tree in New Zealand, but as we tilt upward, the bright sky causes a reduction in exposure. Once the exposure corrects for the sky, the tree becomes nearly black.

Photography workshop
The brightness of the light box in this dim library caused an auto-exposure setting that resulted in the underexposure of everything

but the light box. But when the light box was partially covered, the exposure system registered the change and, due to a reduction in the luminance range, was able to shift the exposure (you can

watch this take place in the video camera's viewfinder) until it provided a good exposure overall. Notice that the image color also improves during the process.

Working in low light
Another problem is lack of light, making the image too dark. If the camera has tried to give sufficient exposure—by increasing sensitivity—the usual option is to supplement the light (*see pp. 92–7*). This may be impossible or undesirable—for example, if you do not wish to disturb your subject.

Some cameras allow you to switch to "black light," or infrared (IR), sensing. This may use a supplementary IR source or rely on available IR from the subject—all warm-blooded animals and working machinery emit IR—and will enable you to record in total darkness. However, the resulting images will be black and white and rather grainy.

Video exposure

Exposure in a video camera means the same as in photography: the amount of light reaching the sensor assembly depends on the combination of exposure time and the lens aperture (the setting that controls how much light passes through the lens). However, in video, the need to deliver up to 30 frames per second limits the longest shutter time. Modern video cameras add a further control, to vary the sensitivity or gain of the sensor chip. In low light, sensitivity is increased; in bright conditions, sensitivity is reduced.

Quick fix Exposure control

Diffused or soft light is generally easy to expose for: either the camera or you must be very accurate. Hard or contrasty light is trickier. The difference between light and dark may be more than the video sensor can cope with. You must decide which exposure is best. Compromise is necessary, since a perfect exposure is impossible.

Problem: Tracking changes

Exposure changes as you track a subject from one part of the scene to another, so the subject is sometimes too dark, and at other times too light.

Analysis

The autoexposure system is continually measuring and responding to changing lighting conditions, attempting to deliver correct exposure. If your subject moves into shadow, it will overcompensate, lightening the image, unaware that you are prepared to let the captured image go dark.

Solution

Set the camera to manual exposure, autoexposure memory hold, or spot-meter mode. These variously named functions all have the same effect, allowing

Tracking changes
The camera renders the beginning of the clip at the correct exposure. Although this should have been held or memorized for the rest of the take, it was not (as in the details above). The dark background dominates, resulting in overexposure.

you to set an exposure that is maintained throughout the take. This means you must decide on the single exposure to suit all, which may be something of a compromise. It is preferable, in general, to allow a subject to become too dark when entering shadow rather than allowing it to become too light when moving into the light.

Problem: Near-total absence of light

Sometimes, there is so little light that it is hard to see anything at all, but you still wish to shoot—at a party, for example—and adding light will disturb the subject.

Analysis

There may be little or no visible light, but any scene with live subjects will emit infrared (IR) light, so you need to use a camera that will record using IR light.

Solution

All digital video sensors are sensitive to infrared, but most have a filter permanently mounted to prevent infrared from affecting normal taping. Some cameras, however, allow the filter to be slipped aside when a night-shot or IR mode is set. This mode cannot record in color but can register images in near-total darkness. A supplementary IR lamp may improve illumination; it is not visible to humans or to many animals.

No light
In a lift with minimal light, the night-shot mode comes into its own, enabling a scene to be recorded where it would otherwise be impossible. The cost, however, is a very noisy (grainy) image in black and white only—but it is much better than nothing at all.

Problem: Backlighting

The subject appears unnaturally dark against a correctly exposed background. Attempts to correct this allow the subject to appear correctly exposed, but it then lies against an unnaturally bright, overexposed background.

Analysis

The subject receives more light from behind it than it does from in front: the main light source faces the camera, so the main subject area lies in shadow. As a result, there is a very wide luminance range between the subject and the background—far too extensive for the sensor to encompass.

Solution

Using camera exposure controls is only a partial solution because you will not find it possible to select an exposure that does justice to both subject and background. One option is to use supplementary light from the camera side to increase lighting on the subject. This reduces the luminance range to help fit

in with the sensor's range. Another option is to use a graduated filter that is darker in its top half and transparent in the bottom half (*see p. 26*).

Problem…

Scene contrasts
Against a bright hazy sky, the foreground detail is underexposed, yet the sky is not correctly exposed either. A correct exposure for the sky would make the foreground black. Alternatively, if we expose the foreground correctly, we can leave the sky a bright white.

…solution

Using lights

In the early days of moviemaking, extra lighting was essential when shooting indoors. The increased sensitivity of film, along with the miniaturization of film formats, however, has steadily liberated camera operation—in terms of both handling and the amount of additional lighting needed.

Nonetheless, few things can magically transform a location into a space full of romance, mystery, or paranoia better than a carefully positioned light. Using extra lights to improve the look of your videos is a sign of a serious videomaker. You can get by using only the light that is available but, aside from being restrictive, that may prevent the discovery of unconsidered creative possibilities.

The downside of supplementary lights, aside from the extra work they cause, is the need for a power source: you either have to work within reach of an outlet or carry a heavy battery around. The trick is to use as few lights as possible and the smallest, yet reasonably powerful, units.

Motivation of the light

If there is one trade secret in movie lighting, it is simply that every light should be "motivated." This means that every light or light source visible to the viewer should appear as an element of the scene, a natural part of it.

A face in the dark becomes suddenly visible when a beam of light rakes across it; then it quickly falls into shadows. This is achieved by someone swinging a lamp across the actor's face, but what viewers see are the beams from a car turning a corner. Lighting a face with a flashlight is a crude option, but when the script says that it is the only light available, as in *The Blair Witch Project*, clumsy lighting becomes a cult-film signature.

Motivation, furthermore, means that the angle of the light, its intensity, its relation to the visible action, and its color must also appear a natural part of the scene. This applies especially to the main light, since it is out of shot. Other lights in shot—the table lamp, the light from a corridor, or a candle—provide their own motivation.

Camera-mounted light

The worst possible place from which to light a scene is a lamp attached to the camera. The light is frontal, flat, and it is very difficult to match its brightness to the surroundings. Of course, in many situations, such as working in documentary mode in challenging conditions, a camera-mounted lamp will be the only option. However, minimal reliance on such a lamp is recommended, unless it provides exactly the lighting effect you want.

Basic outfit

The most minimal lighting outfit is a lamp mounted on the camera. But for stationary and more considered work, you need lamps mounted on lightweight stands. The basic lighting kit includes:
- 1 focusing flood
- 1 flood
- 2 stands
- 1 set of barn doors
- Diffusers and gels.

This kit will be useful for head shots, interviews, or supplementary room lighting. It can be costly to put together a more professional outfit, but aim to add another focusing flood, a soft-box, and a way to adjust the brightness of the lamps.

The Dogme approach

Dogme is a cinematic movement that started in Denmark in 1995, celebrating character and real life. One aspect of this is the use of no supplementary lighting at all—only natural light. This stylistic decision is one of the ten rules gathered under the "Vow of Chastity," which eschews all technological intervention such as special effects, separate recording of sound (wild track) from film, and even the mounting of the camera on a tripod. Whatever its philosophical contradictions, one great advantage of the Dogme approach is clear: setting up takes hardly any time at all. *Italian for Beginners* by Lone Scherfig, Dogme's first female director, is a fine example of the style and is recommended viewing.

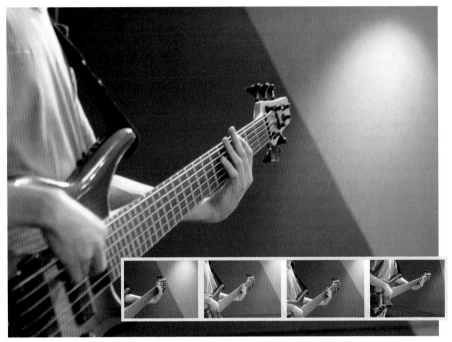

Additional lighting

In some situations—for example, when videoing in a recording studio—lighting possibilities will be limited. In this example, it was not possible to change the main lighting on the bass guitar, but a spotlight aimed at the wall from an angle added a lively supplementary circle of light. The motivation for the light here is very simple: it is there to create a decorative visual effect by adding variety to the background.

Bright and breezy

With soft, open light at high levels, the gobo window (see p. 97) in the background is reduced in intensity, shadows are not heavy, and overall contrast is low. This is not the light for depicting high drama or intense situations, but it suggests summertime and fresh breezes through an open window.

Dramatic effect

This lighting, with its hard key from the side and gobo window in the background, is not meant to be cheerful. Through its heavy shadows and high contrast, it suggests a serious scenario. Since it is easy to make the lighting too high in contrast for digital video, record a test clip before shooting the whole scene.

Lighting setups

For video work, the basic lighting setup is three-point lighting: a key lamp providing the main illumination; a fill, which reduces the shadows; and a backlight, which separates the subject from the background. This may seem formulaic, but it is the product of countless attempts to find better alternatives. Even when exploiting ambient light only, Dogme-style, you can see that the director of photography has positioned the subject in such a way that he or she is, in effect, lit from three directions. Any variation usually indicates a special or changing situation because, for example, part of the person blends into the background or details are lost in the shadows. Three-point lighting may be said to be emotionally neutral, which makes it a good starting point for moviemakers.

Setting up

Planning ahead is essential for lighting technicians. It affords you the opportunity to establish clearly the look and lighting you want, as well as the positions of the lights to achieve that look. This will then save you time on set. Planning will also help ensure that you place your lamps in the most suitable positions without having to shift furniture or find yourself bumping into immovable objects

such as a chandelier or wardrobe. When building lights for a scene that incorporates movement, such as walking across a room, ensure that the light coverage is sufficient to span the whole movement without a change in brightness—unless, of course, that is what the director intends.

A methodical working practice is also vital. You are dealing with potentially dangerous equipment, so ensure cables are not tangled and that lights are set up safely and out of the way of the cast and crew.

Building the lights

When examining the following lighting sequences, it is important to understand that there is no fixed right or wrong about any lighting setup. Strong, glaring light in the face with harsh shadows on the wall are appropriate for certain work—thrillers or horror films, for example—but inappropriate for others, such as love stories or Merchant Ivory-type period pieces. By the same token, balanced lighting with no deep shadows and in which everything can be seen clearly is the hallmark of soap operas and made-for-TV movies. You may be able to build tension under such lighting, but you and your actors will have to work hard because the lighting does not add to the emotion of the scene.

Dynamic range

While cine film can work with a contrast range (strictly, a luminance ratio) of about 96:1 (a difference between shadow and highlight of nearly 7 lens stops), consumer-grade digital video is restricted to about 30:1 (a range of under 5 stops) and often less. This far

narrower latitude means that lighting for video must be softer—that is, it must offer a small luminance ratio to avoid burned-out, or "hot," highlights. In practice, this may call for the extensive use of diffusing screens, as well as the filling in of shadows using reflectors.

Range of sensor

This set of images represents the dynamic range that you can expect to be able to record with a typical CCD sensor on digital video cameras—ranging from –2 stops underexposed to +2 stops over. The safe range runs from 2 stops under correct

exposure to 2 stops over: in this range, color is recorded with some detail. In this relatively high-contrast image, notice how the bright patch to the model's left retains its brilliance almost no matter what exposure you set.

One of the joys of moviemaking is that you work with a multidimensional event: not just the composition of the shot, not just the dialog and sound, nor just the lighting. Every element fits together so that, just as the soundtrack is at its best when not noticed, the lighting, too, is best when it is part of the action. Many scenes in *Chicago Cab* (by Mary Cybulski and John Tintori) feature people being driven around in a taxi. Yet, as the street lights recede past the taxi's windows (from a back-projected movie), the lighting on the actors is, inaccurately, unvarying. The majority of viewers will not notice this artificiality, but still the discrepancy will be subliminally jarring.

Key

Subject

Camera

Camera with light

Subject

Reflector

Spotlight, wide beam

Spotlight, narrow beam

From the side

Side key light
A single floodlight with a relatively narrow beam or with the lamp placed close to the subject causes several problems. The light is harsh on skin tones, the shadow thrown by the subject is dense and distracting, while the unevenness of the lighting is undesirable. The motivation for the light is poor, being clearly an unnatural setup.

From the front

Front lighting
Lighting from the front, such as that from a lamp mounted on the camera, can give acceptable results if there is no other way to light and carry the camera at the same time. It is best to keep the subject away from a wall so that their shadow does not appear in frame. Shoot from just below eye level, otherwise the lamp will throw heavy eye shadows.

Lighting setups continued

Flexible shade

Lights off-center but facing the camera can throw flare into the image: even if you cannot see the lamp, its light may hit the insides of the lens hood and bounce into the lens. Once in the lens, light can be reflected backward and forward until it hits the sensor. One solution to this is to position a small shade to hide the light: the shade is attached to the camera by a flexible arm, which is then fastened to the camera's hot-shoe or tripod socket. The shade may be replaced by a reflector or used to hold other accessories (see Flare prevention, p. 25).

Flood- and spotlights

The flood and the spot are the building blocks of lighting for video. Pointed directly at the subject, the lamps produce a hard lighting, with clearly delineated dark shadows. Their illumination can be softened by shining them through diffusing materials or bouncing them off a reflective sheet or wall. Changing the focus of a lens built into the lamp varies the angle of light from a wide, or flood, to a narrow, or spot, light. For the same lamp setting, a spotlight concentrates the light into a brighter spot compared to the weaker light of a flood, giving you two brightness controls.

Single flood 1

Single flood: poor shadows
With a single light, you can obtain strong shadows, both on the subject and thrown away from her. But you can work with this if, for example, you have a large room in the background with secondary sources of light such as a window. However, here the shadow of the nose is not very pleasing to the eye.

Single flood 2

Single flood: improved shadows
Only small shifts in the position of the light or subject's head can significantly improve the shadow on the face. Here we have the standard arrangement. The end result is that the shadow of the tip of the nose just avoids the shadow of the side of the face.

Defining floods and spots

The wide beam (*left*) from this floodlight shows a clean, circular, and even distribution of light, with a rapid falloff at the edges exhibiting little color fringing: this is a high-quality light source.

The spot beam (*right*) is far more intense but also exhibits a very clean and clear-cut profile that is perfectly circular, making it ideal for limiting the light to exactly where it is wanted.

Bounced light 1

Bounced key lighting

The only way to obtain a soft light suitable for skin tone on digital video is to ensure the light source offers a very large area compared to the area being lit. If you do not have a soft-box to diffuse the light, then bounce or reflect the light from a suitable surface. Here, the white walls of the room are perfect for bouncing the key light.

Bounced light 2

Key and fill lighting

The fun begins when you start using two lights. In this view, the shadows are shown deliberately so you can assess the relative strengths of the lamps—here bounced off reflectors. In this set-up they are almost equal: the lighting is flat, with just a hint of shadow since one lamp is slightly closer to the subject. Flat lighting is best for creating the "film look."

Lighting setups continued

Balance through exposure

The combination of lighting with exposure control creates a powerful team that touches every aspect of the image—from its emotional content, through color accuracy, to composition. Exposure control is not solely about making the correct camera settings; it is about shaping the image to meet your artistic ends. For example, you can turn a threatening silhouette into a light-filled angelic vision simply by altering exposure and making no other changes.

Balancing the exposure

With an exposure set between the bright background and the dark foreground, the framing effect of the window is very strong and the profile of the subject is emphasized. This is the right exposure if you want to emphasize shape and form over detail. A higher exposure, optimized for the face, throws the background into overwhite. This is right for showing facial details.

Key lighting 1

Key lighting and a weaker fill
You can see from the shadows as well as the light on the face that the lamp to the model's right is brighter—it is the key light. The lamp on the other side is weaker, so it does not wholly fill the shadow side with light, but it enables a lot of detail to be retained. Position the model a little farther away from the wall for the shadows to fall out of shot.

Key lighting 2

Key lighting and a stronger fill
As you adjust the strength of one light against another, the less bright light may become the brighter one. It is then seen as the key light, reversing the direction of the lighting. This is a good way to concentrate the viewer's attention on your subject's best side.

Using gobos

An inexpensive way to create variety in your lighting effects is to cast different shadows on to the background. Gobos (or "cukies") are cut out of metal or heat-resistant material in various patterns to cast shadows of trees, window frames, or abstract shapes (*see right*). They are relatively inexpensive, even those professionally cut with a laser. You can cut out your own, but for safety reasons, ensure you use nonflammable materials such as sheet metal. Shadows can be projected as sharp, hard outlines. For this, you need to set up the projector spotlight so that the gobo slots between the lamp and a projector lens, which can focus an image of the gobo on to the background. For a softer effect, place the gobo in front of a lamp or spot.

A selection of lighting gobos

Key lighting 3

Spot key lighting with fill and underexposure

Modern luminaires are highly flexible and can be used for nonstandard setups. Here, instead of a broad key light, the lamp has been focused to a narrow spot that accentuates the face while shadow detail is maintained. An exposure for the bright areas helps give the lighting more character.

Key lighting 4

Key lighting with fill and back lighting

By adding a third light, you can add to the illumination on the model, but you will need lights that can be easily controlled. A backlight placed behind and to one side of the subject—to provide a glancing beam that just touches on the neck and shoulders—can add interesting highlights, but make sure you do not overdo it.

Quick fix Lighting problems

The main problem with digital video is its limited dynamic range—that is, how much light between darkness and brightness it can manage. With that comes an associated problem of reduced exposure latitude: setting the correct exposure is a finely balanced thing. Here are some simple ways to handle difficult light, plus a lighting technique for compositing.

Problem

Outdoor high contrast due to direct sunlight is impossible to control. Exposure can be difficult, too.

Analysis

Direct rays of the sun are not diffused, but they travel nearly parallel to each other. The result is fierce highlights with very dark shadows. But if you look closely at the shadow side, you will see that there is also some light and that all of that light is diffused.

Solution

Use the diffused light in the shadows, and shoot in the shadow side as much as possible, especially with people. Try to fill the frame with your subject's face or body so

Outdoor lighting
In the full summer sun of Croatia, a pretty girl caught my eye. With no available shade, there was only one way to record a brief portrait: use her to hide the sun and shoot in her shadow. Her face seemed too dark, but the result was surprisingly good.

that there is not too much brightness in the background. Note that any brightness in the image is likely to fall outside of legal broadcast limits.

Problem

It is too dark to shoot and you can hardly see anything at all; still, you would like to capture the moment if possible. But you do not want to add any lights, since that will spoil the mood or alert those being taped.

Analysis

Lack of light used to spell the end of your videoing or filming options—you had to bring your own lighting to compensate or not shoot at all. With modern digital video cameras, however, what little light there is needs to be amplified a very great deal before an image can be recorded.

Solution

Modern image processors can register low light levels and correspondingly increase sensitivity to amazing levels. In fact, some cameras can tape in total darkness, with a bit of help from an infrared (IR) lamp. Modern cameras are able to record something in almost any circumstance. The downside is that the image will be very grainy: full of noise and artifacts. Remember, though, that image characteristics, even excessive grain, can be exploited for some movie projects, especially those in the thriller and horror genres.

Mood lighting
In a dark restaurant, it was hard to see the food, let alone try to record. Yet I did achieve a result: it is poor in color, very grainy, and unsharp, but it is a movie. Note that the moving image appears more acceptable than a stills frame from it.

Problem

You need to shoot some footage in order to prepare it for later compositing with images from another video.

Analysis

The action in front needs to be lit with a color that is easily separated from, in particular, skin tones.

Blue-screen shot
This musician is videoed against a blue background—a ready-made blue screen.

This is easily removed by a mask during compositing, and footage of stage equipment can be placed behind him.

Solution

You need to light the action as blue screen (also called green screen, chromakey, or color keying). Hang an appropriately colored screen behind the person you are shooting, and ensure that the lighting on the person does not fall on the blue screen. Blue or green screens are most commonly used because they are opposite colors to skin tones, making it easy for NLE software to pick out all the color and substitute the other footage. (Of course, if your subject is a mechanic wearing a blue overall, for example, you choose a red chromakey.) Note that MiniDV is not a good format for this process: the sharp, aliased edges of images tend to create jagged composites—evident on the image on the right. A blurring filter may help improve keying, since it softens image boundaries.

Composited shot
Here, the blue has been masked off and replaced by footage of the audio console.

Note that care was taken to ensure that the light on the musician's face matches that on the console.

Problem

To the eye, the lighting is very effective—a strongly backlit subject against a dark background. But the video camera does not see it that way.

objects. In addition, the exposure should be set so that the brightest whites are not too white. In this situation, that would make the shadowed areas very dark, losing much of the color and detail.

Analysis

The range of brightness to darkness that a video camera can record comfortably—its dynamic range—is very limited. Although you expect problems in strong sunlight (see opposite), you may not expect them indoors, but it is easy for the scene luminance range to be excessive. Also, video standards do not tolerate the recording of superwhite—overbright white areas—such as paper.

Solution

If you are able, you need to use reflectors and diffusers: in this example (right), a diffuser over the window lighting the musician would help. White objects such as he piece of paper can be replaced with darker colored

Window lighting
The direct light from the window falling on the paper would give problems to any

recording medium. While it nicely lights up the face and neck, it must be made less white in postproduction.

4

Digital video projects

Inspiration

Sometimes it can be difficult to know what project to undertake or, indeed, how to start it if you do know. This chapter is full of ideas for your next video, as well as tips to help you bring your vision to the screen.

Transferable knowledge

Any movie is the sum of its parts, and those parts can be put together in myriad ways to create wildly differing works. Through extensive illustrations of key frames, you will see one way in which each of these projects could be shot and edited. Simple techniques that avoid the need for elaborate equipment and costly sets are also revealed.

Hints and tips

The dozens of hints and tips within these pages will save you time and effort in your moviemaking pursuits. You will increase both the satisfaction you feel in making your videos and the satisfaction of the viewer.

The main approaches

Once you have some experience in using your camera and have perhaps invested in a few accessories, you are equipped to create movies—theoretically, at least. There are two main ways to approach making digital video movies.

One school of thought says you have no chance of making a successful, interesting, engaging movie unless you plan it to the last detail. This means writing a script or screenplay.

The opposing philosophy admits that a bit of planning has its place, but says that overscripted moviemaking interferes with creativity and runs against the flow of life and chance; the scripted movie is art in a straitjacket. This is the "shoot-and-run" or "run-and-gun" approach.

In fact, there is much to be said for both—each suits a different kind of movie. Make your choice based on your budget and the time available.

Following the screenplay

A full screenplay should enable anyone to make an entire movie without further instruction. But even the most detailed shooting script cannot describe camera movements and framing with precision. The script is a map by which anyone involved in the moviemaking process can navigate their way. It can be as detailed as you want to make it, giving timings, camera movements coordinated with dialog, and actor's actions. This approach is suited to a short video movie—perhaps the story of two strangers meeting, spending some time together, then going their separate ways.

Alternatively, the script can be more like a shot list—a set of notes and headings that ensures all the key subjects and locations are shot. This is best suited to documentary-style work such as a friend's wedding or a "once-in-a-lifetime" trip. In both cases, you must ensure nothing is missed that you will later regret omitting. For more detail on this way of working, see pp. 180–1.

Another advantage of a shot list, even for run-and-gun shooting, is in identifying potential problems. You may know you need a wide shot to set the scene but feel that a panorama would be dull and clichéd; instead you could opt to start with a detail, then zoom out to reveal the scene.

Scripted clips
The script called for typical views of everyday beach life, and that is exactly what was shot. The variety within the clips informs us that the camera operator knew exactly what was needed for the movie and went after it.

● **HINTS AND TIPS**

When working to a script, do not feel bound by it, but bear these points in mind:
● Read and reread the script as you shoot: you will not remember everything.
● If you feel inspired, vary from the script provided it does not upset your schedule.
● Remember: the cost of tape is minuscule—shoot more than you think you will need.

A SIMPLE SCRIPT	
Synopsis: To show the importance of safety awareness on beach vacations.	
Title: *Beach Aid* script p. 1	
VIDEO	**AUDIO**
Close-ups of feet splashing through water. Pull out to show groups walking to the beach. Children playing, dragging beach toys with them. More groups coming on to beach. Glimpse of parking lot behind trees. Track walking groups past sand dunes.	Splashing water. Excited voices and children's laughter.
Zoom to long view of people already on beach, playing in waves. Short clips showing different activities. People running around, sitting, reading, sunbathing, eating. Pets also.	Sound of waves, distant voices.
Lifeguards taking it easy, chatting, and drinking soft drinks.	Distant whimpering sound from child, partly obscured by sounds of sea. Cries from seagulls.

An audio-visual (AV) script (*above*) helps you plan, anticipate, and structure the shoot. Arranged as about two minutes of screen time per page, the script can also help you later, speeding up the editing process.

Shoot first, edit later

The unscripted approach is how we all start with moviemaking. We walk out of the door, camera in hand, ready to shoot whatever comes into view. It is also, combined with forward planning, the natural mode of the documentary-maker. With experience, you can record effectively; but initially, less planning means more work later.

It is advisable to shoot more than you need when using a script, but it is essential to shoot a huge amount more than you think you will need when working unscripted. Try to anticipate what you will need for the editing stage later.

●HINTS AND TIPS

Unscripted work can be mentally tiring, since you must remember to shoot all the footage you need.
● Shoot from as many angles and positions as possible to give you more options when editing.
● Shoot at different focal lengths and distances from the subject.
● If possible, have someone compile a shot list as you work, so you know what you have recorded—this is especially useful for scenes you did not expect to tape.
● Take at least two more tapes with you than you think you will need.
● Take at least two spare fully charged batteries.

Unscripted clips
An unscripted visit to gardens produced this medley of shots without any order or logic. If you end up with clips of wildly varying lengths, you will create a lot of hard work at the editing stage when trying to balance the importance of each element.

New baby

The arrival of the first baby in a family is often not only a cause for celebration but also for the purchase of the family's first video camera. The subject is a source of joy, wonder, and love. Changes will take place almost by the hour, and the video enables so much of the experience—once edited, of course—to be recalled for years to come.

Storytelling

With a subject that is so easily accessible, the problem is not what to record, but what not to record. Even so, a common error when videoing a baby is to make each take rather short; this causes the movie to jump too rapidly from one scene to another. A video of a baby will be more enjoyable if it tells a story rather than showing a random string of events.

While a day-in-the-life narrative is obvious, it is none the worse for that. You could start, for example, with a view of the room, taking in all the "new baby" greeting cards, before revealing the small movements inside a bassinet that signal a little person beginning to wake up. Make the audience do a little work, by asking themselves the significance of the movements; then reward them with the solution as the baby gazes up at the mobile above the bed and the story begins.

A video of a baby is likely to be full of the baby—just as any viewers would expect. So make them wait for it, make them wish to see the baby. Start with something different, perhaps the greeting cards and gifts that announce the subject.

Focusing on the baby is, of course, very rewarding for the parents, but an infant's growing awareness of her new world is endlessly fascinating to anyone. The parents may make embarrassing cooing noises, but these should be recorded, too.

While babies are small, relatively still, and largely unaware of the camera, you can film extreme close-ups without limitation. Make good use of this opportunity, because it does not last for long. The results are almost always worthwhile.

●HINTS AND TIPS

These tips will help make your baby video a pleasure to watch, as well as the envy of all other parents.

● For variety (and veracity), record all aspects baby life as well as changing moods.

● Hold the camera still: when your child becomes more mobile, use a wider angle to allow movement in and out of the frame.

● Get in close: your subject is very small.

● Use contrasts to express your feelings about the baby's vulnerability, small size, and delicacy.

● Do not use extra lighting or video in direct sunlight, since the baby's delicate skin tones will be lost.

② Small movements of the crib can be used to indicate the baby's awakening. Tantalize further by cutting to something unexpected, such as the mobile positioned over the bed, before panning down to show the baby.

③ Before your viewers have a chance to get bored, try cutting to another aspect of the change in life for the parents. The contrast in size and form between adult and baby is always a source of fascination.

⑥ It is easy to miss the day-to-day and the prosaic in your moviemaking; it may seem that no one would be interested in the mundane details. But even the simple act of putting the baby to bed is rich with symbolism and signs of love, and it can be visually rewarding. Here, we allow a very limited color palette of whites, with flesh tones in soft light, to create a sense of calm and peace. The movements of the mother's hands contrast with the stillness of the infant. Keep the camera steady throughout the scene.

Birthday party

The key to shooting a good party video is the lighting. Everything else is there in abundance: happy faces, festive decorations, and cooperative subjects. Unfortunately, lighting is also the very thing you are likely to have least control over when recording a party for posterity.

Checking the location

If possible, survey the site before the event. Try to time the reconnaissance trip (or "recce") for the same time that the party is due to take place. If outdoors, check the positions next to a wall that will be out of direct sunlight.

Finding frames

As part of your survey, look out for archways or verandah details—such architectural features can be used to help frame people. You may also be able to shoot through a window from outdoors, providing another interesting compositional device. Best of all, though, is to try to get high up for a good bird's-eye view. If possible, construct a platform that raises you above the action; a stepladder secured to the ground makes a usable solution—but make sure no children climb on it while you are not using it.

Considering extra lighting

See if there is any way you can add extra lights without spoiling the atmosphere. If the party is during the day, draw open any curtains and raise blinds. Spotlights or desk lamps (ideally those with low-voltage tungsten halogen bulbs) can boost the lighting without spoiling the mood, since they offer local lighting effects without increasing the overall light levels.

The best option is to video parties taking place outdoors on a day with diffused light. Most people pray for sunshine, while videographers tend to be the only partygoers who are pleased when the sun does not make an appearance.

Set the scene with a close-up of the treats and decorations that turn the house into a party palace. This will start the video in an engaging way, with a wild track of excited background noise. Then pull back for an establishing shot, showing the location.

I noticed a smaller child moving with less assurance and saw an opportunity for a change of pace. By intercutting close-ups of the baby with the faster activity of the older children, you can make the movie more interesting to watch.

● POINTS TO CONSIDER

It can be difficult to stay focused when videoing a party. Bearing these points in mind should help.
● When taping little people, shoot at their height as well as at yours. A tripod may make this easier.
● Take part in the fun when you can: you will appear less of a outsider and more a guest with a camera.
● Keep shooting or pretending to. If you constantly stop and start, you will draw attention to yourself.
● Keep on the job: sitting with the grown-ups is a sure way to miss half the shots you need.
● Do not speak or laugh while filming: this is difficult advice to follow when you are in the party mood.

2

Cut to a different location and another establishing shot to show the main areas where the action will take place. Here, we are in the backyard. After starting with a wide shot, you can zoom in to focus on the activity in the distance.

3

It is not necessary to cover the arrival of every guest in detail, so cut right to the party action. This offers an interesting contrast with the preparty footage, and at the same time gives an immediate sense of the party atmosphere.

5

Once the guests are having fun, they will soon forget about the camera. This medium-shot sequence tracks the children as they chase after bubbles. Do not follow too tightly: children move very quickly, so give them plenty of room in the frame. If you swing backward and forward all the time, it can be disconcerting for the viewer and make it difficult to follow what is going on. The relatively small digital video sensors help record activity by giving a good depth of field.

Birthday party continued

6

Do not follow any action for too long. After the frenetic bubble-chasing scene, the face-painting offers a chance to slow things down. An extreme close-up with a relatively short focal length takes the viewer right into the action.

7

The party game of Pass the Parcel offers a new angle with a potentially amusing soundtrack. The danger here is to allow the movie to dwell too long on the subject. This is a chance to hone your editing skills, picking out only the very best moments.

10

Next, we cut back to the party games, this time demonstrating how they are seldom fun for those who are not involved, especially towards the end of a game. Here a sturdy piñata resists destruction with the result that some of the guests have become bored, leaving only the more determined to carry on. This sequence shows how important it is to keep shooting whatever happens. It is easy enough to edit out – or not even load – any parts of the movie that you do not need.

8

A cut here reveals an surprise spectator. In fact, the family cat was watching a bird, not the game. But by intercutting the games clips with the attentive cat, you can make it seem as though she is transfixed by the amusements.

9

Or maybe the cat has her eye on the dog, which is accompanying the grown-ups as they arrange the furniture for the next game. Cross-references between the cat and the dog can help create a narrative continuity and structure.

11

The eventual destruction of the piñata leads to a scramble for the goodies. Get in close to capture the activity and the excited voices of the children. You might also record the comments of the watching adults as a counterpoint to the frenetic scene.

12

The birthday cake is an almost universal symbol of good wishes on birthdays, so it cannot be missed. Prepare for this element of the party by consulting with whomever is organizing everything, so that you are ready and in a good position for taping.

13

Always try to give every guest some time on screen. You can ensure that everyone is accounted for by devoting some time to each person in turn, perhaps asking them to perform a party piece or say a few words for the camera.

14

I had intended to finish the video with the birthday girl asleep, exhausted from the party. But as I grabbed some last-minute footage of the now-broken piñata swinging in the breeze, one of the guests ran past and into the distance. Perfect. Fade to black.

Natural history

Movies featuring the landscape, plants, or animals require sustained shots that move smoothly and steadily. Dramatic editing is not usually called for unless, for example, you have the rare fortune to capture a predator attacking prey.

Telling the story

Most nature videos tend to be fairly sedate. The difficulty, then, is in holding the viewer's interest. We are all familiar with the whispered voice-over narration telling us fascinating details about nature and wildlife, but this is usually added later so as not to obscure atmospheric sounds. If you do not wish to add a voice-over track, you must instead move the video along with your footage first, and with the editing second.

We start with a scene-setting wide-angle view: the establishing shot. The bright sun and blue sky are very attractive but restricted by trees on each side. Instead of the anticipated pan across the scenery, we present an unexpected shot.

Getting the low-down

An effective way of involving the viewer is to present unusual angles or perspectives. The easiest is the low-down, or crouching, position, taking the camera down to ground level. This is especially rewarding for environment or natural-history work: the unusual perspective immediately grabs attention. The swivel LCD screen on the majority of DV cameras gives you an advantage even over the best professional camcorders.

Now we move to a different location—a pool a little farther down the stream, and we could either snap-cut or cross-dissolve to this scene. The pool is full of young trout, and the sound establishes a link between the stream and the pool.

We can whip zoom (zoom in as quickly as possible) to show more detail of our main subject. Now we can identify the trout easily. But while the fish's movements are a pleasure to watch, the light is not very attractive, so we quickly move on.

2

As we show more of the stream, we can allow the audio levels to rise, to capture the sound of the stream and prepare for the next cut. Ideally, we would move closer to the water, which will bring the audio level up naturally.

3

Because the trees restrict any sideways panoramic movement, we tilt down from the sky to take in more and more of the grasses swaying in the wind. After a pause to admire the movement, the view moves down toward the stream.

6

In direct contrast with the flat lighting of the previous clip, we now shoot a scene that is full of gorgeous lighting, brought to life with several trout coming and going. For a transition, we could try a zoom-out combined with a cross-dissolve. This footage is the perfect backdrop for some voice-over narration revealing some facts about the stream and its importance to the local wildlife community. The gentle splashing of the water, which can be recorded wild, should also be audible.

Vacation

The modern vacation is incomplete without either a stills camera or a video camera slung over one shoulder. But recording your trip is not only about creating a way to remember the experience; it can also be part of the experience—one that helps enrich your travels, deepen your understanding of a place, and increase interaction with other peoples and cultures. At the same time, though, be aware of the impact that videoing may have on others vacationing with you and around you.

It does little for one's moviemaking inspiration for your friends to say, "Put that camera away." Unlike in photography, in which the camera is up to your eyes for a relatively brief period of time, a video camera may appear to be semipermanently fixed to your face.

Preparing yourself

It may seem that the easiest approach to the vacation-trip video is simply to pick up the camera whenever the inspiration strikes. The trouble is that you then stand a good chance of returning home with a series of unrelated clips lacking vital continuity links. So plan your video before you travel. Research visual material, and try to imagine how to record and connect your scenes.

Planning and mapping

Planning your video before you travel can be part of the fun of preparation. You can research visual material, try to imagine in your mind's eye how to record a scene—how to join a railroad station with a city view, or how to relate a close-up of an orchid to a sunny beach view, for example. You can start to work out what kind of movie you want—something straightforward (traveled there, did that, did this, went home)—or whether to try something more ambitious.

On a recent trip to Tuscany, Italy, we did all the usual things, such as sightseeing in Pisa and Florence. Our video of the trip is presented as a day in the life of a tourist. We start with a shot of a railroad station and life there.

Our wipe from the boy on the phone leads us on to a busy bridge in Pisa with life going on, much animated movement, and the passing by of pretty girls and good-looking boys. We pull back slightly to take in a little more of the bridge and slow

We then pan down the platform of the railroad station before settling on a shot of a stylish public telephone. We zoom in on the phone and hold the shot for a second. Just after that pause, a figure walks into the frame.

We pull back to reveal more of our telephone user just as he makes a call. We hear nothing of his conversation because of the ambient noise of the station. As we record, a nonstop train rushes past. The blur of this gives us a wipe to the next scene.

From the bridge sequence we dissolve into a (near) match shot of the columns on the famous Leaning Tower. We then pull back to reveal more of the tower but are careful not to hold the shot too long. Long shots of static objects quickly become boring.

down the action by giving the cyclist more space in which to move. When we edited the video, we saw a similarity between railings in this sequence and the columns of the Leaning Tower of Pisa; this gave us an idea for a dissolve.

●HINTS AND TIPS

This is a list of things to consider for your videomaking vacation. Think about them in advance, since they may mean obtaining permits and extra equipment.

● Find out if you need permission to video anywhere (cathedrals, museums, airports) and how much it costs.

● Ensure your battery charger will work in the countries you are visiting,

● Prepare a shot list; this is a note of the minimum video footage you need in order to make your movie.

● Pack a spare battery or batteries, as well as lots of video tapes to cover every eventuality.

Vacation continued

6

From the bridge, we straight-cut to a scene showing some of the things that tourists get up to. These girls are posing for photographer friends who are lining them up against the Leaning Tower behind them.

7

The activity of the girls gives us a cue to observe a little of the local life. Here, some dogs wait patiently while their owners discuss plans for the evening. A good camera microphone will pick up much of what you yourself can hear.

10

A scene such as this, showing a shuttered building with colorful window boxes, calls for a straightforward panning movement. The shot was set up on a tripod so it could be slow and, above all, steady, allowing viewers time to savor the details.

11

We cross-dissolve (*see p. 157*) from the yellow buildings of the previous scene to the golden light of a summer evening. Hold this steady and avoid the temptation to zoom in—this would be distracting when all the viewer wants is to enjoy the view.

12

Next, we cut to a riverside scene of two friends sharing a beautiful evening moment. The street is fairly quiet now, with only the occasional passer-by. At the edge of the frame, a local takes a break on her way from the shop.

13

Just as I zoomed in for a closer shot of the riverside friends, one of them lifted her shirt to scratch an itch. Fortuitous moments such as this add a point of human interest to the movie where there may otherwise have been none.

8

9

Another straight cut to this cat helps suggest that it is watching the dogs with interest. In fact, the two scenes were shot at different times and in separate locations but the viewer need not know this. That is the power of video and editing.

If a location is brimming with beautiful shots and bright colors—such as this hotel wall—the delightful problem is what to do with them all. You can simply hold these shots still for just 2 or 3 seconds, as if presenting a series of photographs.

14

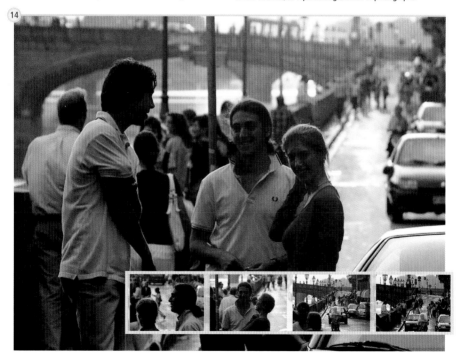

We dissolve to a close-up sequence of friends sharing a joke. Unfortunately, they are aware of the camera and seem a little self-conscious. Still, that did not stop them from enjoying themselves and having fun. This sequence can be allowed

to run on into a fade to black. About midway through the sequence you may consider taking down the volume of the scene as you bring in your choice of music to end the movie. Once you have faded out, you can add end titles if you wish.

Quick fix Permits and access

The moviemaker of infinite sagacity and resource is not easily put off when told "You can't film there." A legal, permissible way around any obstacle can usually be found. Here, we consider strategies appropriate to different obstacles. The crucial point to remember and never betray is: honesty is all. Never give an assurance you have no intention of keeping. Do not be tempted to lie or pretend to be anything other than who you are to obtain an advantage. You do a disservice to yourself and other moviemakers.

Problem

You are recording in what you consider a public space, and a uniformed person tells you to stop.

Analysis

You may not be in a public space. An area open to the public—such as a shopping mall—may be privately owned or run. As soon as you appear to be a professional—using large cameras or tripods—you are likely to be asked to move on. In addition, use of tripods will be regarded as a safety risk since someone could trip over an extended leg.

Public space
Practitioners of t'ai chi may not mind you taping them if they are in an open park, but if you look professional and may be doing it for profit, their attitudes may change. For extended recording, obtain consent first: you may also gain their cooperation.

Solution

Do not look so professional. Use small cameras and work handheld. If you need a large camera or a tripod, obtain a permit. Permission is likely to be given if you say you are taping for private purposes, promise to work safely, and offer a copy of the finished movie to the location owner.

Problem

You are prevented from reaching a good vantage point for videoing by an obstacle such as fence or railing.

Analysis

Fencing and railings are often raised to keep out people as well as prying eyes. At times, though, such obstacles are simply an inconvenience. Assuming that the obstacles were not erected precisely to prevent people from taking pictures and, most importantly, you do not breach any laws in so doing, then you have to find an alternative choice of shot. You may even find a better viewpoint.

Blocked viewpoint
A grand house is protected by railings that prevent a clear view of its façade. So shoot it anyway, but explore other possibilities too. Beyond the railings, for example, is a pond in which the sky is reflected, with a quiet fountain. This is just as interesting as the building and could easily have been overlooked.

Solution

You can try to make use of the obstacles in the shoot: perhaps it says something about the mind-set of the owner. Or, see if you can take artistic advantage of the patterns in the railings. Obstacles can force you to find a more creative approach. Alternatively, you can extend the reach of the camera: with modern digital video cameras

it is possible to tape from a camera at the end of a boom or monopod: of course, this is very unsteady and a method of last resort; a better option would be to use a mini camera crane. You will need a video feed from the camera to a monitor to see what you are recording.

Problem

You wish to enter an area or zone restricted to the public at an event or in an official or commercial establishment. Behind-the-scenes activity of a film gala, dressing rooms of a fashion show, high-security areas, and the locker room of a big game, for example, are all difficult to access.

Analysis

You have no rights and no bargaining power. This is going to take planning, effort, time, and probably a good dose of luck, too. Do not expect quick results. Regular or annual events can prove slightly easier because then you have time on your side.

Solution

The key is finding something that you can offer in return for the permits or cooperation. Find out if there is anything that the planners need that you can help them with, and the door will swing open. So the trick is to make an attractive offer. This may take time and planning and, ideally, someone senior on the inside who can put in a good word for you. Try shooting your video from public spaces and presenting it to the organizers to show how

Cramped shooting
Shooting a documentary about a big movie production is a glamorous prospect, but you may not be welcome simply because there is almost never enough space for all the crew, equipment, props, and actors to fit in anybody else. Your chances may increase if you are prepared to work alone, with just a handheld camera.

much better it could be with increased access. Once you gain a meeting, show your other video work—your style may be just what they need for a promotional video. Build a reputation for being reliable, safe, and professional—you never know who might give you a reference.

Problem

You have shot some great footage on your travels or vacation, and you want to use it commercially. You are not sure of your rights, nor those of the people you taped.

Analysis

Very many people the world over—some in surprisingly remote parts—are aware of model-release rights: they know that they have a right to profit from your commercial exploitation of representations of themselves. So you must be very careful and not make any assumptions if you wish to exploit your movie commercially—for example, in royalty-free footage.

Model release
You taped a rugged sailor while on a trip to Dubrovnik. You think nothing more of it until your agent shows it to an art director who would like to use it in a TV advertisement. If you do not have a signed model release you need to weigh up the risks—and perhaps put aside a fund in case a claim is made against you for unauthorized use.

Solution

Ask your subjects to sign model releases to allow you to use your movie in any way you wish. To ensure the release (essentially a contract) is valid, it is best to pay the subjects a fee. Most people will agree since they feel they are getting something for having done nothing.

Carnivals and parades

Public events such as street carnivals can provide lively video footage, but because there is so much going on that feels exciting at the time the temptation is to simply stay put, point the camera at the parade and let the action unfold in front of you. But a movie that makes it too easy for the viewers is not very interesting to watch. The challenge lies in recording engaging footage that truly captures the atmosphere and the imagination.

Create a story

Narrate the event in a roundabout way. A parade can make for dull viewing if that is all you show, so try to use it as a background, a context, for a people-watching exercise, recording the audience instead. Present the subject of your video by implication, through oblique references and details. The clothes people are wearing and the background noise and music will make it clear what the event is about, but do include a few inserts of parade floats and carnival performers.

Capture the atmosphere

Remember that the sounds of a carnival can be every bit as colorful as what you see. Record as much as you can, and try to reveal the spirit of the event in sound

Archive the original

You may not know until later quite how important your work will be. Abraham Zapruder used his cine camera to film the US president on a visit to Dallas. The date was November 22, 1963. Little did Zapruder know that his shaky footage of Kennedy's assassination would be the most intensely analyzed and debated piece of film in history.

So shoot and keep shooting, and always hold on to the footage. Tape is inexpensive and MiniDV takes up little space, so there is no excuse for reusing it when it contains documentary material.

This footage is of a parade through central London. There is often a lot of waiting around before a big event gets under way, so try to capture some of the anticipation. Here, a child is kept amused and content with a snack.

In order to work in a good variety of shots, you should use the whole range of your zoom. At the long focal length or telephoto end—as in this shot—you can crop easily to detail, but it is hard to keep the camera steady. If possible, use a tripod.

How do you end your movie? People walking into the distance, perhaps; sounds reducing to silence? On my way home, I noticed the leaves that had been crushed into the road by the parade. Along with the arrow, they seemed ideal for signaling the end.

2

Change perspective with your zoom lens. With extreme close-ups, try to pick up snatches of conversation; with wider views, general crowd noise. You may have to hold on shots of crowds for a few seconds before catching signs of excitement.

3

Once you feel that you have enough crowd footage, change the pace and cut to the parade itself. There will be lots to choose from, so select the most colorful and amusing participants. Being selective is editing before you edit.

5

The soundtrack is an important consideration. Here, the subject is not only colorful, but it also provides some cheery music, so it is worth including. Allow the music to continue even if the movie changes to show a different subject.

6

Where you have the support of sounds from an obvious source—such as the brass band—you can indulge in simple visual abstractions, such as reflections from the instruments. Hold the shot and let the action enter and leave the frame.

8

But then I threw in a surprise by adding the firework display that lit up the night sky a few hours after the parade finished. Since the actual fireworks images did not work well, a number of clips were superimposed during editing to "improve" the effect.

●HINTS AND TIPS

The considerations to bear in mind when shooting a public event such as a parade tend to concern issues of planning, personal security, and red tape.

- Obtain passes or letters of permission in advance.
- Dress smartly—this will help you when dealing with officialdom—but try not to stand out from the crowd too much.
- Check out or walk the route or ground in advance.
- Look at the weather forecast for the day, and wear appropriate clothing and footwear.
- Stay aware of your surroundings to avoid pickpockets and surprise movements of crowds.

Wedding

Videoing a wedding can be a stressful experience. It is a task for which you have the burdens of a professional and very few of the advantages. You have to get it right first time—you cannot rehearse or rerun, nor can you give much direction. And you will also be expected to produce high-quality work without the benefit of lots of experience or the authority to call the shots.

Thinking ahead

Always check out the various venues in advance: for the ceremony, official registrations, and the party or reception afterward, not forgetting the transitions from one to the other. Your goal is not to simply record an event—anyone can do that—but to produce something that people will enjoy again and again. For that, it is essential to keep the action flowing, just like a good feature film. Aside from the possibility of a shocking speech, you do not have the benefit of being able to surprise the viewer with twists in the tale; after all, we know what is going to happen to the hero and heroine.

Plan the movie and the types of shot you want to capture before the day. This enables you to be in place in advance, ready to shoot a lead-in—for example, an empty passageway before the bride bursts in, with her dress lighting up the space.

Look for an interesting or unusual angle on the usual head shots and unavoidable portraits. In this clip, I caught the bridegroom keeping his guests entertained while they all waited nervously for the bride's entrance.

There will usually be decorations and balloons that help to create a festive atmosphere—all part of the event and usually forgotten. The happy couple will be pleased to be reminded in your movie of how their wedding venue was decorated.

Use a wide-angle adapter to capture a view of guests listening to the speeches. Be aware, however, that it causes barrel distortion—that is, straight lines tend to bow outward. This effect can be disturbing to the viewer, so use it sparingly.

Cultural variety

As your reputation grows, you may be asked to video weddings from cultures that you know little about. If you are not familiar with the wedding protocols, you should spend time with family members or the person performing the ceremony in order to learn the order of events and the key points that need to be recorded—there may be a literal "tying of the knot" that is central to the service, for example. Also, find out whether there are any sacred moments that you should not tape or any areas where you should not walk.

Once you have recorded the obligatory ceremonial entrance of the bride, your work as a creative camera operator starts. Details of the bouquet and dress are more interesting than shots of the guests looking on, smiling.

The tiniest moments are easy to miss unless you are taping all the time. Keep your eyes open, and look around you even as you video. By doing just that, I caught sight of the marriage certificate seconds before it was safely pocketed.

For crucial rituals within the ceremony—and these will vary according to local culture—find yourself a suitable position in good time and start videoing before the main action commences. Here, the anticipatory recording has captured

a delightful moment of amused complicity between the couple before the cake-cutting itself. The latter proceeded with accompanying camera flashes, but without any drama or interest—the best moment had already taken place.

Wedding continued

Capturing the vital shots

Weddings cannot be repeated, so it is essential that you remember to record everyone important—each and every relative, especially the parents from both sides—and every major part of the day. This becomes more of a challenge toward the end of the celebrations, when it may be difficult to keep shooting at all, so start early.

It may help to have an assistant with you, whose job it is to keep notes of what you have covered and what remains to be shot. Failing that, make a checklist in advance of the big day, and cross off items as you go.

One trick you can try is to watch what the official wedding photographer does—here organizing the bride's portrait—then avoid it. For one reason, he may appreciate your keeping out of the way. For another, why repeat what the professional is doing?

As the videomaker, you must start recording before the main action really starts, so as to give a sense of casual observation. Here, what seemed like an unpromising grouping became a sequence to cherish, since it led up to the moment when these close friends expressed their feelings toward each other in a group hug. For such sequences, it is very helpful to work with a tripod, particularly if it is late in the day and you are getting tired and perhaps even a little unsteady.

8

No wedding anywhere in the world is complete without an embarrassing relative narrating a tall tale to a captive audience. Keep your eyes open for such an opportunity and keep the camera rolling—you can always shorten it at the editing stage.

● HINTS AND TIPS

It is easy to get caught up in the excitement and bustle of a wedding. However, certain important factors must be taken into consideration, before and during the event.

● Take ample spare batteries and lots of tapes.

● Remember that the camera will record everything, including any comments you make about the bride's dress, so be discreet.

● A tripod is essential if you are planning on directing formal group shots.

● Do not get in the way of the official photographer: he or she has a difficult job to do.

10

A wedding is the ultimate chance for people to flaunt their style. You can shoot simple portraits and edit them together as a gallery of the fashions of the day. No clever camera work is needed: just hold the shot for as long as possible and edit it later.

11

Intersperse the standard, formal shots with some more unusual moments. Once they are edited, they offer opportunities to vary the pace and provide an element of unpredictability that helps keep the viewer's interest.

12

As the celebrations and festivities progress, you may entertain increasingly experimental and adventurous camera angles. There is no harm in experimentation, but try to keep the camera steady, and slow down all movements.

13

Intimate moments are very much on public display during the celebrations, but they may not be so welcome in a movie that will be watched in many years' time. Use some oblique or more abstract shots along with the obvious choices.

Promoting a cause

Video is an ideal medium for promoting a cause that you support. You can easily distribute copies as DVDs or VCDs (*see pp. 170–3*) or place it on a website devoted to the campaign.

Engaging the emotions

When you are caught up with the importance of an issue, it is easy to forget that a stranger seeing your movie may know nothing about it. Therefore, you need first to engage their emotions and then tell them about the cause. The needs of the campaign must not override the need to tell a story. In this example, a campaign to raise money for a bird sanctuary in Africa is presented through a visit to a falconry center. The story aims to explain the connection while presenting an attractive subject.

Enthusiasm and anticipation

One of the most difficult things in videomaking for campaign work is knowing when to become involved. It is hard to recapture the atmosphere of excitement when one first gets fired up to change the world for the better. As a videomaker working in documentary mode, you need to anticipate—and plan for—the longer term: you may not know the future importance of people, events, or what is being said, so try to record all that you can.

HINTS AND TIPS

Having a good cause to fight for and promote does not absolve you from the need to produce a video that is interesting and watchable in its own right. You should try to:
- Present information in the form of a short story.
- Reveal facts methodically at a sensible pace, rather than in rapid succession.
- Show contact details or a website address at the end of the video.
- Hand out leaflets or fact sheets whenever the movie is shown, using photographs from the shoot or stills images from the video as illustrations.

Work on the assumption that not every viewer will know from the outset what the video is about. Start with something a little mysterious to arouse curiosity. Here, we used silhouettes against the sky and the sounds of birdcalls and flapping wings.

Make the viewer feel involved by closing in on a little action. A cut to an inquisitive visitor handling an owl and asking questions about the campaign allows the narrator to reveal more about the center and its work.

Through the use of some attention-grabbing active footage, you can relax a little with the narration and allow the viewer to consider the information that has been shared. Let the movie speak for itself for a while.

2

A good way to impart initial information is through an expert. Here, a bird handler is explaining the work of the falconry center and preservation of birds, including a rare eagle in Gambia. She is talking to visitors on a weekend trip to the center.

3

Remember not to bore the viewer with the same talking head for too long. We cut to the visitors while the bird handler continues. This can be a voice-over—in this case, mixed with sounds from the birds in the falconry center to create atmosphere.

5

While the visitor and bird handler continue their discussion, we cut to a close-up of a falcon to create some visual diversity. This is also a good time to introduce a new voice to reduce the likelihood of monotony setting in.

6

Next, reveal who the new voice belongs to. It is important to show that your protagonists care about their cause. This bird handler shows the closeness of his relationship with his charges. Now may also be a good time for a change in the narrative.

8

End the active sequence with a suitable clip—here the bird landing on the bird handler's glove—and include some narration to draw the movie to a close. Strong imagery will stay in the mind long after the words are forgotten.

9

Finally, cut to a shot that obviously marks the end or coming to an end. A clear sky area is perfect for displaying acknowledgments and contact details for the campaign: the words can be displayed over the last frozen frame.

Portrait of a place

You may fall in love with a place, whether a beautiful vacation destination, somewhere you call "home," or where you met someone special. How would you capture some of that excitement in a movie? What are the best ways to convey the character of a place? This is a different exercise from videoing a straightforward vacation trip (*see pp. 112–5*) because you are concentrating on the character of the place, rather than the enjoyable time you had there.

Shooting all you can

Making a portrait of a place is classic "run and gun" videomaking: you will not know what to shoot until you see it. At times you will miss shots that you would have caught had you known more, but this exercise will really open your eyes and make you a more observant videographer.

The beauty of DV is that the amount you shoot is limited only by your budget and the number of hours in the day. Even if you video constantly during daylight hours, the cost in tapes—perhaps half a dozen cassettes—is minuscule compared to the cost of cine film.

Be considerate to family or friends traveling with you. Although this is not a traditional vacation video, try to involve them whenever possible.

The visual essay

A portrait of a place offers as good a structure for shooting as any. At the editing stage, you can turn the essay structure upside down and inside out if you wish, but at least you will have the basic materials to work with. The classic approach helps ensure you shoot constructively.

Overview sequences give viewers a sense of where you are taking them by providing a context and creating a mood. Are we in a mountainous region or a desert? Are we in bright sunshine or surrounded by somber shadows? Is this going to be fun and lighthearted or a serious documentary?

Panoramic vistas are a good general introduction to a place, especially one with breathtaking views. You could start by videoing the landscape around your base location to create an establishing shot before revealing other aspects of the area.

Signposts and arrows are invaluable "B-roll" material. When used in close-up, they are especially useful for masking errors in continuity, as well as for creating changes in the movie's tone or narrative direction.

Video and environment

Being observant and attentive is a firm foundation for videoing, but you should be aware of the impact of your shooting on your environment and yourself. Including footage of the view as your flight comes in to land may be difficult, for example, because your camera generates electronic noise that could upset sensitive equipment on aircraft computers. Or your recording could lead you to become distracted so that you neglect to watch where you going. An important rule is to stay attentive to everything around you.

2

3

Remember to pan slowly: while videoing, the correct panning speed usually feels too slow, but you must impart a sense of affection for this location. Avoid zooming slowly from an overview to a detail—instead, jump closer in several distinct steps.

Activity clips show what goes on in a place and focus on people going about their business, living their lives. Not everything that is depicted on video must be on the move: stillness and relaxation also contribute to the variety of pace and tension.

5

A particular scene may not seem important or relevant at the time, but you might want to video it anyway. When I first spotted a skier stopping to pick up her cell phone calls at the top of a mountain, I thought it was an unusual sight. Later I realized that people were doing it all the time; indeed, the most skilled skiers were able to answer calls without even interrupting their downhill run. If you can pick up what they are saying, it may be that they are talking about how much they love this place too.

Portrait of a place continued

6

7

A big part of life at a ski resort is dealing with mountain gear: a series of short sequences of people struggling to put on boots, gloves, and goggles will convey more about the spirit of the place than the best-written descriptions.

In chaotic scenes, such as this school group preparing for the slopes, the old rules of composition apply: try to include elements that unify or structure the scene, and have a focal point—here it is the fully outfitted child looking into the camera.

9

Portrait clips take the viewer close to the people in the video, offering an opportunity to become involved in the action or life of the place. It gives the viewer a chance to see what the people there look like and how accepting they are of tourists.

When you present a portrait of a place, you may find that a narrative helps structure the sequencing. By placing a lunch sequence into the movie, you can visually signal to the viewer that you are at the halfway point.

8

As the autofocusing sensor examines the center of the image, the camera has focused past the faces to the background. This leaves the portraits out of focus due to insufficient depth of field. You can bring focus to the faces by panning to one of them.

10

Ski slopes are not just about skiing. For some people, the location is a pleasant place to go for walks, enjoy the views, and trudge through snow to restaurants. For long shots with small detail it is best to shoot from a tripod.

11

Not everything you video has to be stunningly beautiful—you want to show the reality of the location, too. These shots of a snow-taxi trundling about its business provide a change of pace, as well as variety in sounds.

12

Take the time to feature some of the local architecture in your portrait of a place. You can start with your hotel or chalet, but you should then go on to include any other beautiful or unusual buildings in and around the area.

13

To drive the narrative, you will need a few continuity links. If, for example, you want to feature a view of the town square, which is dominated by a clock tower, you could first insert a different viewpoint of the tower, perhaps from your hotel window.

Sporting event

The emotional distance between viewers and participants is perhaps greatest in movies of sporting events. Try to bridge that distance: enter into the mind and heart of the athlete, as Leni Riefenstahl did in her film of the Berlin Olympics. Consider the loneliness of a long-distance runner, or the cup fever of a soccer team, for example.

Perhaps you wish simply to record the scene from the point of view of the spectator: cheering on a friend, while documenting their efforts in an track meet. Your friend will necessarily only be part of a larger picture of activity, and the chances are that you will see them only for fleeting moments. So the challenge is to create a context for those brief contacts.

Before the event

The key to successful sports recording is planning and preparation. Scout the location beforehand, just as a runner or cyclist would check out a route.

When covering smaller events, contact the organizers in plenty of time to see if they will give you a pass that will allow you access to areas closed to the public. This will give you a wider choice of viewpoints and subjects. If you do get a pass, make sure you are absolutely responsible and reliable or you will make it difficult for yourself and others the following year.

During the event

The most difficult element of location filming is finding a higher-than-normal viewpoint. This means that you will have to arrive very early, before all the good vantage points are taken. Where necessary, you will have to hold your camera up high above your head and monitor the shoot via the fold-out LCD screen. It will be tempting to use the long end of your zoom for most of the time, but wherever you can, use your wide-angle attachment—that will force you to enter closer into the action.

Do not jump straight into the action—build up to it. This shot looks like a pleasant afternoon on a lake. Initially, the viewer notices the swans, but other things are happening. As the viewer investigates other parts of the image, we start to zoom in.

Unless you have shown a title sequence at the beginning, the viewer still does not know what is going on. But now we have their interest, we can cue in a recording of the announcements being made, informing the viewer that this is a triathlon.

●HINTS AND TIPS

In order to capture a sporting event on video, you will need to be fast, well-prepared, and on the ball.

● Keep an eye on the professionals: without getting in their way, learn from where they position themselves. If they run anywhere, it is for a reason: follow them.

● Memorize the running order and the layout of an event—you will not have time to refer to maps.

● Drink plenty of water: on hot days, you will need to keep hydrated. You may also have to wait a long time for athletes to arrive, so wear a hat and sunblock.

● For steadiness combined with mobility, try using a monopod rather than a tripod.

2

This may be one of the rare occasions when a long, very slow zoom is the right approach. As we pull deeper into the image, we start to make out swimmers, lots of them, in the river. The spectators on the bank unknowingly offer an amusing contrast.

3

Next, we want to be in the thick of the action, as with this close-up of swimmers coming to land. We get a sense of their numbers by holding the camera steady while they enter and exit the frame. A wild track of splashing noises can be easily added.

5

Do not spend too long on the commentator, but go back to the main sporting action. While the announcement track continues you can split-edit to another part of the race. Cut to a group just starting on a circuit. Notice the change from long view at long focal length, to an extra wide-angle view here. The shadows on the road in the last shot of the sequence hint at what may be coming up soon—because so far we have ignored the spectators.

Sporting event continued

Here a group of cyclists is returning from a circuit around town. This may be a good point to narrate a very few key facts—such as how many participants are involved, the oldest and youngest competitors, and so on—before cutting to the spectators.

Comments from expert spectators can be an amusing element of the video. Modern sunglasses are useful: asked nicely, these men agreed to being videoed close-up so I could record the reflection of the race in their glasses.

To reinforce the fact that some races are starting when others are ending, cut to the beginning of another event. Here, the next wave of swimmers jostle for position at the start. Again, vantage point is important; unfortunately, mine was not so good for this shot.

A multidiscipline event such as a triathlon offers good opportunities for cutting rapidly between races. Try some slow-motion and speeded up effects in postproduction to create a bewildering swirl of running, cycling, and swimming.

Suddenly slow the pace down again to show the exhaustion of participants. You could hold the best frame for several seconds to suggest the feeling that one cannot move again. The viewer will wonder, Is it all over? Is the video about to end?

At the end of the event, everyone else can relax in the sun and have a good stretch, but you have to keep working. Now you can obtain shots that show some of the other aspects of sports, such as the bonhomie and the physical exhaustion.

8

With the next edit, surprise the viewer with sequences on the huge support effort that makes sporting events possible at all. At a soccer match, it might be a volunteer preparing orange juice for halftime; here, an attendant is handing out cups of water.

Avoiding confusion

Shooting a sporting event can be confusing if you are not participating yourself. But the spirit of the event is always warm, and people are glad to advise you. Make sure you ask monitors or officials for advice on where to go and when.

After the event

If this year you do not get a pass, try to ensure that you do next year by sending the organizers a copy of your edited video, perhaps with a few printouts of the best frames. You may be invited to record the following year's event.

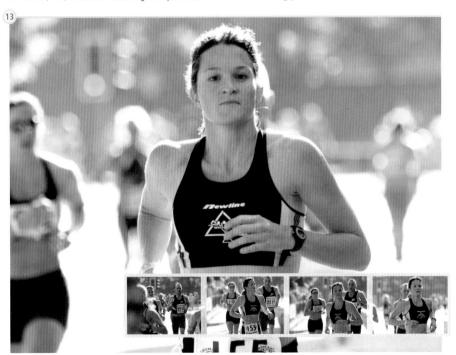

13

It is always worth saving one last surprise for the viewer: here, it is the revelation that the race is still going on. I allowed the runner to come right up to the camera, losing focus as she flashed past the camera position. This is a great last frame to

hold, showing her determined expression, before fading to white and rolling the credits. Such an ending opens the way to adding another event, perhaps a completely different one, since the whiteout can lead into any other shot that is full of light.

Family video album

The video album is the modern equivalent of the family photo album. It brings together sound, movement, and light to recreate memories and past moments in the most direct way. Of course, the video album is subject to a highly selective remembrance of the past, but it can go much further. An ongoing video album is a marvelous way to record children as they grow, preserve the memories of older family members, or make a documentary of your day-to-day life.

Preserving the past for the future

While it may seem like favoritism to concentrate on just a few members of the family, that is probably where you should start. If Dad is too busy with work commitments or the teenagers are camera-shy or think it is a silly idea, concentrate first on the most cooperative or available family members. Once you show the doubters a rough cut of what you are doing, they may well warm to the idea.

If any elderly family members have fascinating tales to tell, you could encourage them to recount some to the camera—even if you have heard the stories before, perhaps your children's children could learn something when they watch the movie in years to come. Just let the tape run, and edit out any pauses later.

If you are asked to act as videographer for another family's video, make it easy for yourself by lighting the area evenly. You can then record from many angles without having to alter the lights. For this shoot, we start off with all the family members together.

Adults are usually the most self-conscious, always aware of the camera and behaving awkwardly. However, they may not mind filling center stage when necessary for the movie, so catch a glimpse of them and move quickly back to the children.

If a child takes himself into a corner away from the bustle and activity, it may be that he simply wants to be alone. If you follow him, do so at a discreet distance using a long focal-length setting from a tripod position.

●HINTS AND TIPS

Family videos, especially those that span many years, can be difficult to plan, coordinate, and keep interesting, so bear the following points in mind:
● Keep the shots varied: even if it is just someone talking to the camera, you can shoot a close-up of the hands, mouth, or eyes while the sound rolls on.
● Use footage of as many generations as possible.
● Include your children's friends, but be sure to obtain the consent of their parents.
● Keep adding to your video album. Many families start with the birth of a baby and intend to keep shooting but lose impetus once the child starts school.

It is not long before the children run off, leaving the youngest playing with her mother. The longer your video camera runs, the more the family will become accustomed to your presence and behave naturally. Each person's character will then emerge.

You can supplement the main room lighting you have with an on-camera light. But beware of shiny surfaces behind the subjects, such as glass doors, mirrors, and windows. Here, chrome kitchen fixtures have caught a flash of light from the camera.

If there is a center of activity, such as this tunnel, then you need only set up the video camera pointing at it, resting on a tripod, and let the tape roll. You can stand behind the camera to encourage the play or simply get on with other jobs such as setting up lights elsewhere. Change camera angles, zoom setting, and framing from time to time, but otherwise you can do all the important work in the editing. Playing back some of the footage to the children may help encourage more activity.

Promoting a business

If you are known as a videomaker, your boss might turn to you when she needs a promotional video, for example, for the website or as a looped movie (one that runs continuously) for a trade fair. How do you make the most of this chance?

Work professionally

Brief, budget, plan, execute, and postproduce with the discipline of a professional videomaker. The crucial questions are: what is required, how is it to be done, how much can you spend, and when does it have to be done by? Always confirm all the details in writing with a line manager.

Budget and plan

Once you know your budget, you can plan how to spend it. Perhaps the offices need a lick of paint, the plants can be renewed, and flowers brought in. You may need to rent lights or a better camera.

What is coming up on the calendar? Not the social events, perhaps, but graduation day if you work at a school or college, the launch of a new product, or an open day for the public. These events may take up only a few seconds' screen time but are nonetheless worthy inclusions.

Satisfy the customer

The key is to ensure that the shoot captures the kind of footage wanted by the company's director. The example on these pages shows a video to promote the work of the Guitar Institute, a center for guitar study in London. The director wanted to present an up-to-date image, with a strong appeal to the young aspiring stars of tomorrow.

Consider safety

Be particularly careful if you need to involve other people in the shoot, especially if they are to enter areas to which they would normally not have access. Check with those responsible for insurance and clear all details with your safety officer.

It may seem boring, it may be conventional, but you may have to open the movie with a shot showing the front door of the business premises. However, you can still be creative by fading in the sounds of guitars and voices inside the building.

We pull back slowly to a young female student warming up with her guitar. The sunlight is very strong from the window, burning out the right-hand side of the image, but the client likes the bright, modern feel that the overexposure gives to the shot.

Another cut reveals other guitar sounds and enthusiastic players. The bright sunlight helps create an airy atmosphere but does not conform to broadcast regulations. The use of a Broadcast Legal filter in postproduction would tone down any superwhites.

The next logical step from the establishing shot is to show the first thing that a guitarist does with his or her instrument: tune up. We could have the sound of some tuning up mixed in with the general noise of the Guitar Institute starting on a typical weekday morning. The background sounds can be recorded wild and added later. Note, though, that it can be surprisingly difficult to record background that is suitably characteristic of a location and that can be listened to repeatedly.

In this scene, two tutors "widdle"——play lots of notes very rapidly. The microphone should be held close to the guitarist who dominates the shot, moving as the camera pans to the other. Next, we fade in the sounds of a class elsewhere in the building.

The change in soundtrack cues a change of pace, and we cut to a teacher seen through a window. Over the wild track of a band playing, we can have some narration explaining that we are waiting for a good moment to enter the classroom.

Promoting a business continued

Model releases

If the employees of a company are being videoed for promotional purposes for the first time, obtain model releases—after all, having their picture taken is not part of their job description. In future, it may be deemed that part of an employee's duties is to help promote the company—an element of which is to have their photograph taken for company purposes. If this is added to the job description, there may be no need for model releases each time an employee is photographed.

7

Cut to a teacher instructing her class. We knew from an earlier reconnaissance trip that this room was rather echoey. In such situations, it is best to clip a radio microphone to the subject, rather than follow her around with a boom.

9

A change of color, a snap cut, and a crash of percussion change the mood of the video. Focusing on the drummer tells the viewer about the range of musical genres taught at the Institute without having to say anything about it.

10

Here, we pull back to bring the guitarist into the shot, showing that interaction between students is almost as important as the lesson. Whatever your subject, you can increase the amount shown in the frame by using a wide-angle attachment.

11

Between the sequences of the various activities around the building, remind the viewer of the function of the organization—in this case, teaching. Here we cut to a solo player waiting for the start of her lesson.

12

The sound of a door opening, followed by a wild track of noises from other rooms, leads us to a one-to-one class. This shows the audience, without spelling it out for them, that the Institute offers individual lessons as well as classroom teaching.

8

Next we cut to some shots of various angles of the mixing desk, while the audio slowly builds with the disembodied voices of musicians chatting and preparing to play. This sequence shows that it is not necessary always to hold the camera level. While it is very disturbing for the audience to have a horizon that is constantly on the move, some variety in the angle of tilt can help add visual interest. Here the camera is tilted around the mixing console as if fascinated by all the knobs and dials.

13

Let the action develop naturally. If you try to direct people doing their normal job, they may overact and perform stiffly. Here we show a close-up of a teacher's hand as he points out a fingering position to his student.

14

We step out into the corridor and see a student walk away with her guitar. It is the girl who was tuning up earlier in the video. This type of closing shot provides a symmetry to the movie, before we fade to the end titles and show the organization's contact details.

5
Editing and postproduction

Video software principles

Your first encounter with video editing may be very daunting. Entry into the exciting world of nonlinear editing will be made easy through clear explanation of the principles, including logging, the rough cut, and edit decisions.

Editing

The techniques of nonlinear editing are examined, with their roles and purposes defined. Quick-fix spreads help you correct color and exposure, as well as offering advice on how to handle common editing problems and techniques for working with transitions and effects.

Postproduction

Including creating titles, working with sound, mastering DVDs and VCDs, and streaming to the Internet, this chapter shows you how to refine your movie in preparation for a wider audience.

Editing principles

Video editing does not have the same feel and character of film editing. Hanging lengths of film over a bin, scratching at film with a little blade, and applying dots of glue have all been replaced by the click of a mouse, and the flickering images on a little periscopic screen are now steady brilliant images on an LCD monitor.

Anybody who has ever used a computer has complained about the steep learning curve of one software application or another. Be prepared, then, for the difficulty ahead when you first tackle NLE (nonlinear editing) software of any capability. This chapter will explain the principles common to NLE applications and attempt to relate them to what you are trying to achieve artistically. These principles can then be applied to the many applications available. Examples will, of necessity, be taken from the more professional software, since they cover anything that most videomakers will attempt. But you do not have to buy such software to produce rewarding videos.

What is editing?

The following quote, from a website giving career information, is entirely true yet completely misses the point: "Film and video editors watch all the film footage. They decide which parts are not interesting and cut those parts out. They put the most interesting parts of the film back together." What it misses, of course, is just how those interesting parts are put together.

It may be tiresome to be reminded that the software should always be a servant of the creative intention, but it is a mantra worth repeating over and over again. For the software to serve you, however, you have to master it. This calls for practice, practice, and more practice. But an understanding of the basic principles will speed up the learning process.

Four-point editing

We start with a number of clips or takes: this is the raw footage that you have shot. This material may still be held on the camera's tape, or you may have already downloaded the footage on to your computer. Your movie—also called a "project" in some software—will be made up of a sequence of clips or parts of them.

The nature of nonlinear editing means that, under their largely superficial differences, all software applications operate in the same way, namely by manipulation of four points: two in the

Insert edit

The insert edit places new footage into the timeline of an existing sequence. Because the insertion does not delete or replace any material, the overall length of the sequence increases. The simplicity of the move disguises its great power to interrupt action with a visual aside or prompt, allowing you to show two things happening simultaneously but in different places, or the same thing from two different viewpoints.

New clip

Insert edit

Original sequence

New sequence extended by insertion of new clip

New sequence

clip to be inserted, two in the sequence being created. In the clip, the first point defines the start, or "in" point, while the second marks the "out" point, or the end of the clip. These points may be the actual start and end, or anything in between. The time between the in and out points defines the duration of the clip.

In the sequence, you will need to tell the software where to insert the clip: this is the in point in the sequence, while the out point is where the clip will end and another starts.

The key is to realize that when you determine or set any three of the points, the fourth is automatically determined. If you set the length of the clip, then set where to insert it in the sequence, you then know when the clip will end in the sequence. Furthermore, the sequence will get longer. On the other hand, you may set a certain length of sequence to be replaced by a clip—that is, you set the in and out points within the sequence. Now when you mark the clip's in point, its out point follows because the time between the in and out marks must equal the length previously set within the sequence. In these cases, the sequence will stay the same length.

Visualizing the edits

One way to visualize your edits is to imagine a wall of an exhibition with a row of pictures side by side. Suppose you decide you want to insert two more pictures in the middle: if you do not want to lose any pictures already hanging, you must decide where to insert these pictures, then extend the line of existing pictures by shunting them over to make room for the new ones. But suppose the length of the line of pictures is fixed: if you remove any pictures you must replace them. Or, to insert new pictures, you must remove as many as you add.

Another analogy is to view NLE as similar to word processing, in which clips are sentences, or groups of words, and a text is like the video sequence. Edits move sentences or groups of words around: some edits increase the length of the text, pushing all successive words further from the beginning. Others replace or overwrite existing words, keeping the overall length the same.

And just as with word processing—in which the real reason for knowing the keystrokes, shortcuts, and functions of the application is to be able to communicate through your writing—the reason for learning how to use NLE software is to tell a story convincingly and effectively.

Overwrite edit

You will use an overwrite edit when you need to add new material to a sequence but cannot increase its length. The most common reason for this is when you need to match the length of your movie to the length of a piece of music or other soundtrack: if the overwrite material fits between cues, you need not worry about synchronization. Often, overwrite edits use material shot at the same time as the main sequence but from a different angle.

New clip

Overwrite edit

Original sequence

New sequence

Sequence length remains unchanged

The editing process

Editing in video has many similarities to editing text. When editing text, you manipulate and order the basic elements of words and sentences, following grammatical rules, to communicate clearly and effectively. You cut out unnecessary words and rearrange them to make them flow more coherently. And you may drop in little surprises to keep the reader interested.

In video editing, you work with the basic elements of your clips—aided by the soundtrack. Just as the same sentiments expressed by a poet, novelist, or businessman will generate very different texts, so the same clips produce different results depending on the editor.

Broadly speaking, the editing process consists of the following steps:
- Putting the clips into a sequence.
- Fine-tuning the relationships between clips.
- Adjusting the sequence as needed.
- Determining the transitions between clips.
- Balancing the colors and exposure of each clip to create a unified whole.
- Working the recorded sound or music into the movie at appropriate times.

Nonlinear editing

NLE is the key to digital video editing, providing what is known in the rest of the digital world as "random access." Whereas film editing involved rolling a reel of film backward and forward to find a frame to cut up and join with another piece of film, this is now achieved in seconds and with just a few keystrokes.

Movie clips are data files on your computer and are essentially just like Word documents. You can jump to any point on a clip just as you can jump from one piece of text to another. When a movie is only on tape, you have to reel through the tape to find the start or middle of a clip. This is not only tedious, but it also wears down the tape. The nonlinear editing process is slowed down only by the time it takes your computer to find the file and display frames from it: on modern machines, scrolling through a video clip is a rapid process.

Your first edit session

For the rest of this chapter, we will assume that you have learned, from your video camera's instruction book, how to create an active connection between the camera and the computer so that the camera is recognized.

You have shot hours of material, and a little stack of tapes waits on your desk. What is the best way to start? If you have shot your movie in "run-and-gun" style—that is, without using a script—then this is a good time to visualize what story you wish to tell and how you want your movie to look. This will help speed up the process of identifying shots and sequences that work well, and spotting those that do not move the story on. If you taped by following a script, or even a list of shots, then assessing the rushes—the unedited footage—will be much easier.

If you have shot "dump-truck" style—that is, you shot just about everything that moved and many things that did not, all 'just in case'—then you have a long job ahead of you. You will need to review all the footage and log each take. Having to do this just once should cure you of shooting

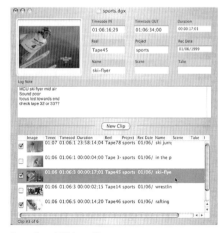

Imagine DV Log-X

This special utility offers convenient controls and handy features that speed up the logging process. The application will also control a wide range of devices—from DVCam and DVPro, to analog video machines.

dump truck ever again—or you will give the logging job to some other poor soul. Having said that, if you are making a documentary (*see pp. 190–1*), this is really the only way to work.

Logging your footage

Count on the logging process to take at least as long as the total duration of the footage you have shot, probably longer. You will need to watch the whole lot and, although you may fast-forward through some of it, you will also spend time writing up the details. The good news is that the more thoroughly you log the footage, the easier and smoother the editing process will be. The bad news is that, in truth, logging can be incredibly dull and frustrating, because all you want to do is get on with putting together the preliminary edit.

If you are using entry-level software, you may have to do the logging by hand. However, professional software enables you to log details while you review clips—in fact, it is often an integral part of the application. A less costly alternative to professional NLE software is special logging software, such as that from Imagine: TPEX

for Windows or DV Log-X for Mac. These can greatly simplify the process by offering automatic incremental counting, automatic completion of entries, and basic storyboarding. Most importantly, the logs can be exported to work with standard nonlinear editors for capturing batches of video.

Marking clips

An entire take that has no value to you can be ignored at the logging stage: simply do not log it, and avoid wasting time and space capturing it. But if only a portion of the clip is unusable, you will want to mark the start and end (in video parlance, the in and out points) of the portion you want to keep and, therefore, capture. This job is known as marking clips.

Some editing applications use buttons or keys to set the in and out points. Others use slides in the preview window. It is advisable to leave short "handles" before and after the precise in and out points—a second or two before the in and after the out. Should you mark too tightly, you leave yourself no room for maneuver—or change of mind—later, and you will need to recapture.

Logging and capture

Entry-level NLE software applications simplify the editing process by copying media files from your tape to the computer. After shooting the tape, you rewind it in the camera, and as you play back through the software, it compresses the camera's files—from the first to the last take without pause—as it copies it to the computer. Professionals will prefer to start, review, stop, replay, and rewind the tape numerous times to minimize the load of material they capture, thus taking into the computer only what they are sure they will need. However, numerous stops, starts, and rewinds will cause a great deal of wear and tear on a camera's tape mechanism and possibly on the tape, too. For proper logging, the ideal but costly solution is to use a desktop video tape recorder (VTR) controlled by the NLE or logging software via the DV connector from the computer.

```
DV NTSC 48 kHz Anamorphic
DV PAL 48 kHz
DV PAL 48 kHz Anamorphic
DV to OfflineRT NTSC (Photo JPEG)
DV to OfflineRT NTSC Anamorphic (Photo JPEG)
DV to OfflineRT PAL (Photo JPEG)
DV to OfflineRT PAL Anamorphic (Photo JPEG)
DV50 NTSC 48 kHz
DV50 NTSC 48 kHz Anamorphic
DV50 PAL 48 kHz
DV50 PAL 48 kHz Anamorphic
DVCPRO - PAL 48 kHz
DVCPRO - PAL 48 kHz Anamorphic
DVCPRO - PAL to OfflineRT PAL (Photo JPEG)
DVCPRO HD - 1080i60 48 kHz
DVCPRO HD - 720p24 48 kHz
DVCPRO HD - 720p30 48 kHz
DVCPRO HD - 720p60 48 kHz
Generic Capture Template
```

Capture-input options
This pop-up menu gives a wide range of options for decoding the video capture—effectively a format conversion. To save space and speed up editing, a good choice is Offline, which uses compressed images. After editing, the full-resolution footage can be captured.

The editing process continued

Capturing video footage

Once the logging is done, you are ready to capture the video, a process also referred to as uploading. This is the time at which the media files representing your video footage enter your computer. Either the files themselves are uploaded from camera to computer or, more usually, they enter the computer in a compressed version—for example, as QuickTime files. In the latter case, editing decisions are made using proxy files: small-size files standing in for their full-resolution counterparts. Naturally, this procedure speeds up manipulations, particularly if you create transitions. But it slows down the final stage, the render, in which the editing decisions, transitions, and any other effects of the final cut are turned into the completed movie. Even if the end product is of low resolution, the render can still take some time (*see pp. 12–13*).

Considering the edit

The material uploaded from your tapes into the NLE software forms the movie-based equivalent of the rough cut. With all the material sequenced in more or less the right order, and with all the obvious mistakes and technically faulty material omitted, you will be able to see whether you need more footage or whether you have too much. Either way, this is where the fun begins.

The next stage is to "string out," or assemble, the material with more precision and direction. Aside from the content and story, there are several other factors to consider:

- Overall length. Your budget may have allowed for only a 10-minute short, or perhaps you intend to make a feature-length movie, but start short. If you make one minute's worth of watchable video out of an hour's take, you are doing very well.
- Pace and rhythm. Will you have long periods between cuts, or will you cut and intercut many times per minute? It may seem that pace should depend on the overall length, but that is not the case. Two minutes of an intense Bergman film can feel like an hour, while an hour of Jackie Chan action can seem like 10 minutes.

- Sound and music. Keep in mind the need for a soundtrack. Do you have the recorded sounds you need to use in a particular clip? Or will you be able to dub (add on) some post-recorded sound? If not, you may have to rethink how you use the clip.
- Continuity. A movie needs continuity – that is, a logical flow between the beginning and the end. This does not mean that everything must be shown in chronological order, even in a documentary, but it does mean that changes in technical aspects such as exposure or colour should be motivated – that is, they must be justified by the action (*see p. 60*).

The timeline paradigm

The timeline is a graphical representation of the content of your movie. You read it by starting at the left and working to the right, passing from one clip to another in the same order that they will be shown in the movie. As you insert clips into the sequence, the timeline lengthens; if you change your mind and delete sequences without replacing them, the timeline shortens. The timeline is fundamental to all time-based digital media.

Poster-frame timeline

The simplest depiction for a timeline is the poster frame. In this mode, the first frame of a clip is taken, by default, to represent the whole clip. The drawback of this option is that it does not show the relative lengths or duration of the clips in the sequence.

Scalar timeline

A scalar timeline represents the duration of a clip as a proportion of the whole. Depending on the software design, one common behavior is set so that as you add clips and the sequence lengthens, the clips squeeze up to fit more into the screen.

Final Cut Pro timeline

In a professional timeline, such as in Apple Final Cut Pro HD shown here, clips can be displayed with more detail, moved with precision, and viewed at different scales, while many tracks of both video and audio can be accommodated.

Timecode

The smallest unit of video that we work with in NLE is the frame. Frames are identified by a standard code, called the SMPTE timecode, which is written as hours:minutes:seconds:frames. Thus 00:03:06:24 means 3 minutes, 6 seconds, and 24 frames from the beginning of timing. With PAL, which uses 25 fps (frames per second), the next frame will be called 00:03:07:00. Leading double zeros, e.g. for hours, may be omitted. NTSC, however, is not so simple because it uses a frame rate of 29.97 fps.

The standard way to count frames is called "drop-frame," which was constructed to prevent the accumulation of error due to counting whole frames. NTSC drop-frame mode is written with a final semicolon before the frame number—thus 00:03:06;27. Unfortunately not all NLE software programs recognize or work with SMPTE timecode. If you wish to work professionally or expect to export edit-decision lists from one machine or software to another, using standard timecode is obligatory.

Clips, graphics, still images, and sound are handled in tracks that overlay the timeline. These can be thought of as layers of material: one layer can hide another layer, or both can show through. At the same time, an audio layer can play throughout. Basic applications such as Windows Movie Maker carry two video and two audio tracks, but even mid-market NLE can handle 100 tracks of audio.

The most important feature for us is that, in all but the simplest software, the timeline can be displayed at different scales. So you can compress many minutes' worth into view across your monitor or zoom in to a few seconds' worth to pick off material frame by frame.

Timelines can be displayed in two ways. One shows the poster frames—the single frames that stand for the entire clip, usually the first—in a line; this is a useful visual reference. The other is a scalar display: the proportion of the total duration that each clip takes up is represented by the amount of space the clip takes up.

Editing decisions

The visual layout of your NLE software on screen will influence the way you edit your video and how quickly you can work. Professional software may offer as many as nine different open windows carrying information. This might be a concern to a beginner, but it is a delight to the experienced videomaker who needs quick access to a wide range of functions. At its heart, all NLE software works with a core set of three windows: one shows thumbnail pictures of the clips that are held in what is variously called a bin, album, or collection; the second is the viewer or preview window; and the third displays the timeline.

The insert edit

An empty timeline waiting for your first clip can be as intimidating as a blank page waiting for the first touch of an author's pen. But once you have dragged your first clip from your collection to the timeline, the rest is easy. Or it would be, if all we had to do was string together all the great footage we had shot. In a flurry of creative energy, you will soon have the string-out completed. But a quick review will usually indicate the need to interpose a new clip in between two already present in the sequence. This is the first basic edit manipulation—the insert edit (*see p. 142*).

In most editing software, you simply click on a clip and drag it to the timeline. The total duration of the sequence will increase by the length of the newly inserted clip. Wise editors, however, are usually aware of the need to keep the video no longer than absolutely necessary. One way to achieve this is to insert only a portion of a clip: instead of dragging in the entire clip, trim it down to what you need and insert that. When you logged and captured, you should have left handles—brief lead-ins and lead-outs—to enable you to do this. For the same reason, your shooting should have started a little before anticipated action and ended just after.

All NLE applications allow you to mark in and out points in a clip: the in point is the exact frame you start a clip or take, and the out is precisely where you want it to end. You can copy the section between two points and paste it into the timeline or drag the trimmed clip according to your software's procedures.

When you play back the sequence, do not worry at this stage if the changes are sudden or appear too abrupt. Any transitions that need fixing can be smoothed out later.

1 The string-out
Your preliminary stringing out of clips produces this sequence of a tour in the country. But upon reviewing it, you may decide that the transition from trees to a close-up is too sudden and that you need to insert another clip.

2 Insert a new clip
Find another shot of trees that is suitable and drop it in between clip 01 and clip 17. This pushes all later clips on by the duration of the new clip—11 seconds, 13 frames—lengthening the sequence by that amount.

3 Save as you go
Following each edit decision, it is a good idea to make a practice of saving the change immediately. Remember that you are not changing the actual clips themselves, only making a list of editing decisions.

Editing interfaces

These two screens display the basic three subwindows of NLE software from competing giants Apple (iMovie, *above*) and Microsoft (Movie Maker, *right*). In each case, the collection of thumbnails or clips for a project or video are put to the side of the viewer, or preview window, while the timeline runs underneath, displaying various tracks and the sequence of clips.

Refining the edit

Once you have uploaded several clips and strung them together, you will want to fine-tune the timing of your edits and refine the transitions. It may help your understanding of some edits—such as trimming, cropping, and overwrites—to see their similarity to their word-processing or image-manipulation counterparts. Here we look at the most common of the many refinements that are available in NLE software.

Trimming and cropping

These two actions are essentially the opposite of one another. Trimming removes selected frames from the middle of the clip. The clip is therefore split at that point (*see below*) and its timecode is adjusted to show a shorter time.

Conversely, a crop takes out all the frames that were not selected—usually from the beginning and end of the clip—and this, too, shortens the clip.

Of course, it is also possible to split a clip without first having to trim or crop, and that is to do so directly (*see below*).

Monitoring clip length

When you work through your clips, you will begin trimming and cropping them. Since you are not actually discarding any frames, you can subsequently refine the edits, moving the in and out points or changing the duration of a transition effect (*see pp. 156–9*). But look out for warnings that your clip is too short for all the effects you wish to implement.

Splitting clips

When clips are imported by the NLE, the breaks between one take and another are usually recognized automatically, as is the case with all basic software. Such an approach sends all of the takes on tape into the computer. Professional-grade software will expect the editor to mark clips with in and out points, so the capture takes in only what is wanted.

Whichever approach is taken, there will be times when it is useful to split a clip into smaller subclips. This makes it easier to handle long clips and helps define points at which you can intercut.

In most NLE application programs, you first place the play head—the marker that shows where in a clip a displayed frame comes from—at the point where you wish the split to be introduced. Next, call up the Split Clip command, and the program does just that.

1 Locate the split
To make this clip easier to work with, it first needs to be intercut or split, so the play head is set to an appropriate point in the clip.

Undo Move	⌘Z
Redo Split	⇧⌘Z
Cut	⌘X
Copy	⌘C
Paste	⌘V
Clear	
Select All	⌘A
Select None	⇧⌘A
Crop	⌘K
Split Video Clip at Playhead	⌘T
Create Still Frame	⇧⌘S
Special Characters...	

2 Split the clip
The command to split the clip is applied. Your application may offer a tool looking like a razor blade, which reminds us that the edit is just like cutting through a length of film.

3 See the result
The split clip is now in two parts, each with its own timecode and icons. The overall length of the two clips added together remains as before, because no transition has been applied.

Reversing direction

Some cross-fades and dissolves work better with the frames running in reverse order because the reverse movement in one clip may blend better with the forward movement of the following clip. Another thing to remember when using this effect is that no one can tell whether the original panning movement is the original (provided, of course, there are no other indicators, such as traffic or people walking). You may have panned a view from right to left but in the preceding clip you filmed someone pointing to the right. By reversing the pan, you can keep all the movement flowing in the same overall direction.

Reverse
To reverse a clip, select the clip or a part of it and call up the Reverse Clip Direction or similar command. In the example on the left, reversing the direction of facial expressions greatly changes the emotional message.

Overwrite edit

Just as you can replace a phrase in a word-processing document by selecting it and overwriting it with a new phrase, so an overwrite edit replaces an existing clip, or part of one, with another.

There are broadly two reasons for making an overwrite edit in video. The obvious one is when you find a superior clip to that in the string-out— perhaps a sharper or better exposed shot.

The less obvious reason takes us a very long way from the word-processing analogy. An overwrite edit offers a simple B-roll intercut—that is, you can interrupt a clip with an aside or flashback, then return to the clip. The key to this is to keep the audio for the main clip playing throughout—even while the intercut is shown. Typical uses of B-roll take place, for example, when an interviewee is talking about a document, and we cut to show that document, or when you have shot a sporting event and, between takes of the race, you overwrite B-roll shots of the spectators cheering.

For this to work, you have to set the software up so that the existing audio is not replaced when new material is pasted over it. Depending on the software, you may have to select "disconnect sound" or "extract audio with paste over" or similar phrases.

1 Overwriting a shot
During the course of a shot of a lizard looking around, you want to intercut to show a dangerous predator approaching. Simply select a portion of the predator's approach and overwrite—this is usually at the play head, where the frame is stopped.

2 Playing the clip
The selected area of the clip to be overwritten is shown selected—note that not all software will display this. When the sequence is played, the movie will cut straight from the lizard to the predator and back again without any transitions.

Further editing

Digital video editing software is capable of even more than we have already covered, and techniques that were a chore when working with film are now just a mouse-click away. These are not gimmicky transitions but entirely valid editing techniques. The first is a feature that would have been a boon for film editor—the ability to restore to original.

Restore clips

A key feature in NLE software, but one that will not make any real difference to your working methods, is that you do not work on the original files of your clips at all. You are manipulating proxies or smaller files that stand in for the actual files. The editing decisions you make are essentially just a list of instructions to the software. This means that when you thought you had shortened a clip, deleted sections, or split a long take into numerous smaller portions, you have not, because nothing happens to the movie itself. Therefore, you can restore the whole clip very simply, by telling the software to forget all those instructions. This can be quite a drastic command, so it is wise to make a duplicate of the edited clip—store it at the end of the film or save the first version under a different name or version number.

Stills clips

If you wish to stop one frame from a video tape, you freeze-frame it—that is, you hold the tape still while continuing to read it. With digital video you can go further: you can create stills from clips and use them to slow down the action, hold the viewer's attention on some amusing expression, or show something in detail.

Of course, each frame in a movie we watch is in fact a still image—but each one is slightly different from the last and the next. So a stills clip is one in which we simply show the same picture for as long as we wish. The stills clip is treated like any other clip: you will need to insert it in an appropriate point in the sequence.

One word of advice: the first duration you pick for the stills clip is likely to be too long—even one second is a long time in a movie, and two seconds will significantly slow down the action. In any case, you can easily change the duration, either by editing on the timeline or by directly changing the properties of the clip.

Should you wish to exploit this effect extensively, you will find that capturing images in progressive-scan mode gives better results than shooting in interlaced mode.

Restore Clip

This dialog box makes it very clear what will result from the request you have made—you are, in effect, throwing away all of the editing decisions that you have input into the software, so think twice before agreeing to Restore.

Inserting a stills clip

Here, a frame from the middle of a clip is turned into a still clip and appended to the clip collection. If you add it to the sequence it will lie between two clips, almost never where you want it. It is best to split a clip where you make the still and insert it there.

Setting stills clip duration

You can change the length of the stills clip either through the timeline-based controls or directly by entry in the Clip Info dialog box. Depending on the software, you enter actual duration in time code or number of frames. In iMovie, for instance, if you enter a number, it assumes you mean frames and calculates the duration automatically.

Slow and fast motion

One aspect of digital video that can be bettered by fairly basic film-based cameras is its inability to shoot true slow-motion sequences such as those you see in many movies to highlight an epic or heroic moment. For this to be possible, the rate of capture of frames has to be speeded up, a capability found on only the most costly of broadcast-production cameras.

We can cheat in digital video, however, by instructing the software to interpolate extra frames in between the ones shot. The greater the number of extra frames, the more slowly the movie will appear to run. The effect is not at all as smooth as true slo-mo (slow motion), but it is better than nothing. The problem with this method is that the soundtrack will also be slowed down, so you will need to extract that and replace it with something of the right duration.

The converse is to speed up the action—simply by dropping frames. The clip takes less time to run through and the action seems faster than it should be, but its comical effect limits its use.

Speeding up playback
With fast-motion playback, the action is sped up and the duration of the clip is shortened—compare this illustration with that of the normal-speed length (*below left*).

Normal playback
In this application, iMovie, a simple slider enables slow- or fast-motion playback: it is at the bottom, with hare and tortoise icons. Other software programs implement this effect in different ways—for example, via a dialog box.

Slow-motion effect
With slow motion, the clip is lengthened and the action slows down—this also lengthens the whole movie. Be aware, though, that the sound is also slowed down and will sound unnatural, so you will need to replace the soundtrack (*see pp. 166–9*).

Stills frame

Creating a stills frame is different from creating a stills clip. It is not strictly an editing move: you simply save a single frame of your movie as a separate image file, usually in JPEG format. This image can be incorporated into another movie or it can be treated like any other image file, to be emailed to friends and family or printed out to put in a photo album. The image dimensions of a nominal 640 x 480 pixels at an output resolution of 72 dpi is sufficient for a fair-quality print measuring about 100 x 125 mm (4 x 5 in). However, the way colors are processed for video is much less complete than the processing for a true digital photograph, so colors are less rich and lacking in subtle transitions.

Manipulating stills
A stills frame can be manipulated and printed like any other digital image. This frame from a beach vacation video will be sized to 72 dpi so, when printing, change the resolution to one suitable for your printer, perhaps 150 lines per inch.

Quick fix Color correction

One of the unsung heroes of the movie industry is the colorist. It is the job of this highly skilled technician to match different film stocks and correct all the color imbalances and exposure errors made by the DP (director of photography). The end result of all the colorist's work is a film that looks as if it has all been shot on one continuous roll of film, with perfectly consistent color, contrast, and exposure. In video postproduction, you will be responsible for all that.

Problem

The overall color of the movie is inconsistent from one take to another. This manifests itself as sudden changes in color cast between adjacent cuts.

Analysis

Varying color balance is due to two related factors: the white balance of the video electronics, and the prevailing color temperature of the illuminating light. If the color temperature of the light changes, the white balance of your camera may fail to keep track—either because it is unable to or because you set it manually. For example, the day may be sunny—in the sun, the overall balance is warm—but when a cloud passes over, the color temperature rises, making the tone more blue.

Solution

To avoid making excessive corrections in postproduction, it is best to set your camera's color balance manually, using a white or gray card before each take: target a neutral patch under the lighting in use and set the white point by pressing the appropriate button or menu choice (see pp. 104–5). There will still be small differences even with the most careful camerawork, so you will have to correct clips as necessary in postproduction. The key decision is which clip will act as the master, or reference, point; you then adjust everything to that color balance. This is especially important with takes of the same scene or adjacent cuts.

All NLE applications offer color-correction tools of varying power and ability. Some will apply the change to the entire clip, some only to the portions you select. The changes you ask for may need to be rendered applied to all the frames of a sequence) before they can be fully viewed in sequence.

Problem...

Before correction
These two frames, side by side from adjacent clips, were taken moments apart. In the first, a house lamp provides warm coloring; in the other, a wall lit by a skylight has a blue tone. We need to match the warm-colored clip to the cooler one.

...solution

After correction
It is a tricky adjustment to reduce the reds and yellows in the highlights, but the color match has improved. However, it now highlights a difference in contrast between the two clips—a result of the right-hand clip having been shot with a little digital zoom.

Color settings
The three-point corrector for Apple Final Cut Pro looks professional and daunting. Although it is both, it is also a powerful program capable of subtle enhancing effects as well as very large corrections—or, indeed, deliberate color changes.

Quick fix Exposure correction

The majority of exposure corrections in digital video arise from the need to compensate for the errors or "enthusiasm" of the video camera's automatic exposure systems.

Problem

The overall brightness of a clip is too dark or too light. Another variation of this problem is if an autoexposure meter reacts to changing conditions before you wish it to do so, as in the frames shown here (*see right*). A more advanced issue is whether the luminance range of the movie is broadcast legal.

Analysis

Automatic exposure systems, however clever and complicated, can do only what they have been programmed to do. Technically, they deliver the correct exposure almost all the time. But such a system has no way of knowing, for example, that it looks unnatural for a room to become suddenly darker as you pan toward a bright window. The best solution is impractical for all but costly studio-made feature films: the aperture is changed by a puller at the same time as the camera is panned. At any rate, even the most careful camera operator makes slight exposure errors, and video is intolerant of errors.

Solution

Exposure inconsistency between clips, or within one clip, has to be corrected in postproduction. All NLE software provides some degree of control for exposure and contrast. Unlike color correction, there are industry standards—at least for the whites and blacks. For home movies you do not need to concern yourself about them, but the key is to avoid whites that are too bright.

Problem...

Exposure before
Starting the pan from right to left, this hotel room and lamp start off correctly exposed. But as the window comes into shot, the bright light from the

left makes the autoexposure close down the lens aperture, making the lamp darker. Taken by itself, the image is correctly exposed, but not just after another shot has been seen.

...solution

Corrected exposure
I partially brightened the first few frames revealing the window to help maintain the exposure on the lamp—it does not matter that the window is now more

overexposed. With the next frames, we lose the lamp so the exposure can return to what was originally shot. For sequences such as this, you may have to correct a few frames at a time.

Waveform for exposure
The waveform monitor is a feature of all professional video editing software. It shows the luma (brightness) and saturation of the image scanning from left to right. Note the waveforms above the topmost line in the

monitor, indicating that the lamp in the first image is illegally bright. Notice in the corrected image (*above*) I did not allow the brightest part of the lamp to become white. In the waveform, the peaks would fall below the top line and would therefore be broadcast-legal.

Transitions

What happens between the end of one clip and the beginning of next—the move from the out point to the succeeding in point—is the region of transition. The most basic transition, arguably not a transition at all, is the cut or snap cut—a name that emphasizes its abrupt character. It is also by far the least noticeable transition available.

Transitions were originally invented to smooth the changeover point from one clip to the next. This would give the audience a chance to adjust from the mood and pace of one take before being carried to the next scene, perhaps one filled with very different emotions.

With film, the process was rather hard work, even for the simple fade, and involved laboratory or darkroom processes. With digital editing, the easy application of effects is essentially digital image manipulation applied many frames per second. In fact, the Photoshop application was invented for just this kind of task but was "hijacked" for use in digital photography.

The ease of programming digital effects has given rise to the transition becoming almost an art in itself—so it is easy to use too many in a film. But some pop videos are none the worse for being almost a catalog of transition effects.

Transition effects

Modern NLE applications come with a ready-built package of transitions, and all major software will accept plug-ins (supplements to the basic application) that extend the range. All will, or should, offer the basic three: cross-dissolve, fade in, and fade out.

Assuming you have defined the out point of one clip and the in point of another, applying transitions involves just two decisions: which transition effect to employ, and its speed—that is, how quickly the transition should run. The latter can be tricky, requiring experience and artistry. If it is too long, your editing decisions will be "spotted": the viewer becomes too aware of the effect and is distracted. If it is too short, it may fail to do the job of easing a change of mood.

For the sake of clarity, the examples shown here were created with stills clips.

Choice of transition
The choices of transitions offered will most likely be all you ever need, unless your movie requires special-effects transitions. You can always create effects in an image-manipulation application and import the images.

Maximizing performance

NLE is very demanding on hard-disk performance. Many computers have energy-saving modes that put the hard disk to sleep whenever possible or after an interval of not being accessed—this is fine for normal computing, but it can reduce the performance and possibly also compromise the quality of your digital video work. Indeed, a hard disk that is slow to wake up can crash the software or at least cause incomplete rendering (production of full-resolution transitions) or dropped frames (missing frames that cause the movie to flicker). It is advisable to turn off hard-disk sleep when working on digital video: open the Control Panel or Energy Saver dialog box and change the settings.

Cross-dissolve

In this transition, frames near the end of one clip are laid over the beginning of the next clip with the opacity dropping steadily through the duration of the transition. In this way, the underlying clip shows up more and more clearly while the overlying clip gradually disappears. The "cross" in the name refers to the fact that the effect is applied to both clips at the same time. This transition, like several others, works in two directions at once. One of the most frequently used transition effects, the cross-dissolve is regarded by many as their default transition. Remember that it has the effect of reducing the length of both clips.

Blend awareness

The cross-dissolve is a soft, safe transition effect that works with a wide range of movements from one clip to another. But take special care at that brief moment when both images are visible, right at the midpoint of the transition; it is here that you must make sure that there is no unattractive blending of images or colors.

Fade

A fade works in one direction only—actually this makes it an effect, but it is used so often at transition points that it has been adopted as a transition. A fade-in starts with a black screen, then the clip becomes brighter and brighter until it is seen at normal brightness; you use this to introduce a clip. The opposite is the fade-out, which causes the tail end of a clip to become darker and darker until it is black. There are a number of ways, technically, in which the darkening effect can be achieved, as well as factors that determine how convincing or smooth it is. This differentiates professional software from lesser products. The fade is not a cross effect because it affects only one clip at a time. You may wish to fade out the end of one clip and fade in the next. This is achieved simply by placing the two transitions end to end (see below).

Fading out and in

Fade-outs work best where the contrast is higher than usual: the lost of luminance intensifies colors and overall shape is retained, as in this singer's backlit hair. If contrast is low or colors monochromatic, loss of luma makes the image look muddy. Fade-ins work best where the contrast is normal or lower, because it is less clear what the darkness will reveal as the luma is raised. In comparison, a high-contrast subject, such as these bass guitarists, reveals itself almost immediately, appearing merely dark but not mysterious.

Fade-in and fade-out bars

This timeline shows the fade-out and fade-in transitions. The triangles within the bars are pointing in opposite directions, indicating that these clips have opposite effects.

Transitions continued

Using transitions

Depending on the type of transition you use, you may find that it alters the total sequence length. This is because of the need to overlap an end section and a start section equal to the duration of the sequence. For example, a 4-second cross-dissolve or wipe needs to overlap 4 seconds of the end of the first clip and 4 seconds of the start of the next. Therefore, the total running time lost from the sequence is 8 seconds.

Once a transition has been rendered, it is essentially a clip, meaning that it can subsequently be edited just like any other clip, together with any associated audio track. It follows, then, that the speed of a rendered transition can also be altered, by adjusting the playback speed.

Transitions can also be used on stills clips or images, but, as with all transitions, the changes may need to be fully computed—that is, rendered—before they can viewed.

Washes

The opposite of a fade (in cinema, at least) is a wash. Luminance is raised in a wash-out, so that the image becomes brighter and weaker in colors until pure white is reached. It is a deceptive transition in that it is very simple technically but its emotional impact on the viewer can be very strong indeed, especially if the following bright white is held for a few seconds. The wash-in is trickier to use, unless it follows a wash-out. This is because entering a clip from pure white after a cut or a fade is visually jarring. Consequently, washes, like fades, are often used in pairs.

Clip duration
An effect applied to only one clip at a time does not impact on its duration. This clip was originally 5 seconds long; after the application of a 2-second wash-in, the total clip duration is still 5 seconds, including the 2-second transition effect.

Effect-led transition
Exposure-based effects were originally exploited for their special effects rather than used as transitions. Washes and fades—deliberately increasing or decreasing exposure—were popular in the days of film because they were easily

done in-camera. The effect makes it seem as though a spotlight has turned at the camera and then has swung away. Here the wash is used as a transition—from the singer washing to white, then washing back again, this time to reveal the band.

 The clip before that title or transition is too short; it must be at least 03:14.

Render bar
The thin red line under the transition (the green lozenge) is not as long as the transition: this means that the render—calculating the transition—is still in progress. If you attempt a preview, you will see a warning or a partly black screen.

Short Clip warning
If a clip is too short in duration to accommodate a chosen transition, you will see a warning such as this. Increase the clip duration by combining other clips or slowing down the playback, as long as it does not interfere with the audio track.

Wipes

Wipes are favorites for moving between parallel storylines—a domestic example might be the dog racing around the garden while Dad reads the paper. In a wipe, the start of the next clip pushes the last seconds of the first clip aside, in the same way as wiping a misted window reveals the snowy world outside. You can set the wipe's direction and pace.

Close/open and warps

Variants of the basic wipe abound: essentially a wipe is a moving mask that reveals the underlying layer (next clip) as it changes in size, shape, or position, simultaneously hiding the preceding clip. Any shape or distortion of mask gives a new way of wiping. The Circle Closing transition is one of the next generation of wipes.

Radial wipe
The radial wipe in this NLE software reveals the underlying next clip with a clockwise rotation, similar to that seen on a ship's radar system in movies. Depending on your software, you may be offered a choice of directions. Because this type of transition renders both clips at once, it reduces the overall length of the sequence.

Circle Closing wipe
Cropping a circular shape from the outside is an effective wipe in scenes that are busy with movement, such as this one shot at a rock concert. The juxtapositions do not look elegant, but they do not need to be—it is the sense of moving in and out of the action that is required. Some versions offer a soft margin to the circle, which is preferable to a hard outline.

Scaling

Scaling down a preceding clip so that it becomes progressively smaller, revealing more and more of the next clip, is a more complicated variant of the wipe. It works best when shifting between very different material. In this example, the two guitarists simply disappear into an abstract, out-of-focus shot of the concert lights.

Scaling to nothing
The sequence above shows the most basic scale-down effect: the leading clip shrinks in size, progressively revealing the successor clip. Of course, there are many other ways of scaling down: further examples include incorporating movement across the frame, scaling in combination with fades, and so on.

Titles and credits

Digital technology has made the application of text onto movies, or titling, a much easier job than it was in the past. Titling was once a labor-intensive, skilled job. One method was to film, frame by frame, plastic letters on black, then double-expose it on to the scene that is to carry the text; another was to split beams of light to combine a projected image with the text. But what has been gained in convenience is at the expense of control—you may be limited to the effects built into your software. And, of course, you will need a good design eye to produce an interesting use of text that is appropriate to the film.

Length and mood

Title sequences are often the last thing considered in moviemaking, but the name of the movie and much of the information you have to place in the credits may have been decided long before you even started shooting.

Sometimes, the most straightforward method of titling is the most effective—titles can be text on a blank background, for example. This simple, easy, no-nonsense approach is like the curtain rising in a theater: after little ceremony, we move straight into the action.

A more involved title sequence, in which text is imaginatively woven with some scene-setting footage, may introduce a movie that is more leisurely, one that allows itself time to develop mood and atmosphere. The length of title sequence should be proportional to the movie's overall length—very brief indeed for a short that lasts less than 10 minutes in duration.

Fonts and frills

The choice of font—the design and look of the letter forms that make up the words—is as important as the background against which they are read by the viewer. It is a cliché—but no less effective for it—that blocky fonts, with strokes the same width throughout, suggest modernity or industrial processes, handwriting can suggest informality or youth, and a Gothic font is often used to introduce an element of horror.

Titles effects

Numerous effects that animate titles are available even in the most basic software. Yet the simplest effects—those that fade in and out—are often the most effective. Depending on your software, once you choose the effect, you may have control over the speed and timing, the length of a pause if any, as well as the size and color of the text. Another level of control is available through altering the speed at which the title clip itself plays: you may want to slow down the playback of the background footage to make it last longer, or you can run titles over a still.

Coordination with action

The best titles work to tell a story as a lead into the larger story. Here, we see the words appear one by one, in time with the sun bursting from behind the cloud. As the sun breaks through, the last word appears, providing an effective cue to the next scene.

Cross through centre

In the cross-through-center title effect, letters appear jumbled up, converge into a mass, and then finally separate out to reveal the title. Used in this sequence—a prosaic pan across a small garden—it suggests that perhaps some mystery or puzzle is about to unfold.

Zooming titles

A dull stretch of urban development can be transformed into a low-key drama by titles that appear to zoom on to the screen from a distance. Once the title sequence is over, the action should begin immediately.

Zooming and fading

A zooming-in effect works well when set against another movement, as here, with the flight of a gull. The inexpert tracking of the flight, which causes the gull to move around within the frame, has been put to use to interact with the title. The final frame shows the title fading away, cueing a dissolve or fade.

When you create titles for your movies, you have to put on yet another hat—that of designer. A careful choice of typeface and effects helps set the scene and shape the viewer's expectations.

● Titles do not have to be on the first frame of the movie—they can follow an introductory clip.

● Do not forget to acknowledge and thank everyone who has helped you make the movie, including the coffee makers and bottle washers!

● Avoid excessive use of special effects with text—they may distract from the viewer's enjoyment of the rest of your movie.

● If there is a lot to read, allow a generous pause time for your viewer to do the reading.

● Awkward cuts or problems in continuity may sometimes be solved by using titles—but if you use one as a section title, you may need to use at least one more.

Setting the scene
Although generally speaking you should try to avoid busy backgrounds for titles, they can sometimes work with clever use of fonts and colors. This cast list, presented on the inside of the windshield of a bus, indicates some information to the viewer about the setting of the opening scene.

Using effects

Digital video effects are also known as filters, which tells you that any filters that you may know about from digital photography could, in theory, be found here. The differences are that the filter is applied over a period of time, and the strength of the effect can vary over the duration of a clip.

You need to place a clip on to the timeline before you can apply filters, although, depending on the software, you may be able to preview an effect in other ways. It is best if a small preview window is available, since the effect can be shown in real time. This is important because the majority of filter effects need a good deal of computing power and time to render a full-size viewing.

Choosing effects

The best way to choose an effect is to allow it to choose you. Some—such as a stream of electricity appearing to come from a subject, or a star in orbit trailing stardust—are good for amusement value but cannot be used often. Others—such as those that adjust colors, brightness, and contrast—will be used time and again; the differences between effect and postproduction tool are blurred here.

Another group of filters simulates old processes or their low quality, such as one that simulates aged film. Why would anyone spend a small fortune on the latest equipment and edit on computer only to recreate the poor colors and jerky frame projection of amateur cine films? Because it looks great, and when used with suitable subject matter, the effect is surprisingly convincing.

Applying effects

Once you have placed a clip on the timeline, you can then apply an effect. Depending on which application you use, you may have some control over the strength of the effect once you have

Original

Effects time control
Controls timing the effect set how long after the clip commences the effect should reach full strength, and how long before the end of the clip you would like the effect to start to diminish. Long intervals give smooth, steady transitions. A zero setting at the in point starts the effect at full strength immediately; at the out point, a zero setting keeps the effect to the very end.

Hue shift

Changing the colors
A shift in hue, shown here, can be used to create amusing effects or to give advance notice of a change in place or mood. At the same time, colors can be made more or less vivid, and overall lightness can also be adjusted.

Effects control
Simple sliders allow you to adjust the strength and type of effect. However, the lack of a box to allow you to enter a precise numerical setting will make it difficult to replicate exactly an effect proven to work on another clip.

selected it. You should always be able to control the timing of the effect: one selector determines how long into the clip it takes for the effect to reach full strength—it may be immediate or slow-building; the other control sets the removal of the effect—a zero setting keeps it in for the duration of the clip. Some effects take a certain path—as is the case with Star Dust—while others have a direction—such as Lens Flare: you need separate directional or positional controls for these effects.

Mirror

Variety of effects

The effects that can be found in NLE software and as additions to applications or as stand-alone programs are numerous and varied. It is possible to group them by function, which can also help match their capabilities with your editing and project needs.

Effects such as Aged Film, Sepia (an overall low-contrast brown tone), and Monochrome imitate the look of early film. These effects tend to be applied to the whole of a clip or sequence, rather than being introduced gradually.

Effects that adjust colors, brightness, contrast, and sharpness as special effects differ from postproduction by degree. If you exaggerate a color change, you are applying a special effect, not a postproduction color-balance adjustment. Used in this way, effects are often best introduced and removed gradually.

Changing shape and content

A different group of effects alters the geometry of the image but does not change the overall tone or color. The letterbox- or 16:9-adjusting filters, for instance, simply change the shape of the frames—either by shading off the top and bottom or by distorting the image. Mirror and N-Square also introduce geometrical effects: one mirroring half of the image, and the other repeating it.

Added effects filters introduce entirely new elements into the clip, not based on anything in the clip at all. In this group we find Rain, simulating a heavy rainfall, as well as fun but limited effects such as Star Dust and Electricity.

N-Square

Mirror and N-Square effects

Visually interesting effects come from the filter that creates a perfect mirror image of one half of your footage (*top*), while a slider adjustment allows you to choose the number of times the image is repeated (*above*). With moving subjects, these effects can be mesmerizing, and both are well suited to music-video work and artistic projects.

Effects menu

Because the effects are listed in alphabetical order, it is easy to find the one you want—if you know its name. However, if you are searching for an effect based on the function it performs, it is likely to be more difficult. The best way to discover what an effect can do is by trial and error.

Aged Film

Original

Sepia

Strong color cast

Old processes

The Aged Film look (*top*) all but destroys your precious video footage in the name of art: it introduces grain, lowers the contrast and saturation, throws in scratches, and makes the frame jump around. The Sepia effect (*above*) is far gentler and is very effective, provided it is not overused. Both are often seen in TV commercials.

Heavy color cast

●HINTS AND TIPS

The best way to learn about effects is to try them all out on different kinds of clips. Also, remember:

● If your software does not allow you to apply more than one effect on your clip, even after rendering, try exporting the clip as a full-resolution movie. Then reimport it as a clip carrying the first effect. You should now be able to overlay a second effect.

● Transitions and titles can be added to the effects clip.

● If you do apply multiple effects but later change your mind, deleting an effect simply deletes one item in the edit-decision list. Delete them one by one, in the reverse order to that in which they were applied.

● Effects usually require a great deal of computing power, so shut down any unnecessary applications.

Adjust Colors

A soft touch here will correct color casts and improve exposure if necessary. But a heavier effect is also useful—here to introduce strongly graphic looks (*center and above*) that could pave the way for a transition to a modern restaurant interior or an art exhibition. This promises to be far more interesting than the safe and predictable ferry ride of the original clip (*top*).

Original

Soft glow
At times, the crisp, sharp image is not the most appropriate. For this sunny, happy seaside clip, a soft-glow effect blurs both colors and details to dreamy effect.

High contrast

Star Dust
Not all filters are designed for serious work. Effects such as stardust glittering across the frame to suggest a magical feel may charm younger audiences.

Extreme contrast

Brightness/Contrast
As with color adjustments, a gentle touch on the brightness or contrast filter can greatly alter the look of your movie. An extreme-contrast image (*above*) can look attractive on the monitor screen but may not work well on a domestic screen because the white areas are uncomfortably bright and the black areas are not quite black.

Electricity
Another example of a fun effect is the electric spark, which has its uses for comedy movies or horror films. Both Electricity and Star Dust (*center*) require heavy processing to render.

Editing the soundtrack

A videomaker's increasing command of the medium is reflected in an increased appreciation of the importance of the soundtrack. When you are starting out, recording sound using the camera's own built-in microphone is not only the most convenient option, it is also the one with the fewest technical difficulties. But as you become more ambitious, you will want to graduate to a mounted microphone; from there the complications increase, but the quality of the sound you record will improve. Here, we explain the basic editing controls for a soundtrack recorded together with the video footage.

Setting levels

Different NLE applications implement the setting of levels in different ways, but this is essentially an audio-control exercise. A pair of separate, good-quality loudspeakers for monitoring is an essential purchase: the tiny speakers inside your computer are woefully inadequate for the task of sound monitoring, and the small units on your desk are not much better. Neither will give you the dynamic range you need.

With the monitor speakers and output levels set to normal, you can play back your video and evaluate by ear whether the sound level is correct. Of course, sound professionals will use specialized meters with what is essentially a calibrated system to obtain broadcast-quality sound. With equipment designed for amateur or consumer use, sound levels are recorded at what is technically too low a level for broadcast, but it is still adequate for domestic purposes.

Time-based adjustments

With the most basic entry-level NLE software, you cannot even adjust the volume. But at the next level of NLE you can, and just as you can gradually introduce and trail off a visual effect, so you can fade sound in and out. In software such as Apple iMovie, introducing a fade is as simple as clicking on the volume indicator on the timeline and dragging the line up or down to increase or reduce audio levels. The position of the transition corresponds to the position on the timeline, so you can synchronize changes with what is happening on screen.

Levels meter
A display such as this is good for an objective monitoring of audio levels: it is graduated in decibels and gives a constant readout of the state of the audio. The two green lines indicate that the audio is present on both right and left channels.

Waveform diagrams
One of the joys of digital video is the way it increases your awareness of the world of sound. A fascinating exercise consists of relating the waveforms to the sounds you hear. In this highly magnified display, the black bar represents the duration of one frame of NTSC video.

No volume
With the Edit Volume control not activated, the timeline for the clip simply shows the length of the clip and its poster frame (the first frame)—there is no "levels line."

Edit levels
With the Edit Volume control activated, the purple levels line appears throughout the length of the clip. It is located through the middle, indicating its default volume setting.

Low levels
If the volume is adjusted down, the levels line sinks toward the bottom of the display; and if the volume is increased, the line naturally moves toward the top.

Examples shown here are taken from iMovie, the audio-control interface of which is particularly easy to understand.

Editing on the timeline

To select an item in order to make changes to the soundtrack, you need to place it on the timeline. Once this is done, you can set the overall volume or introduce gradual changes, known as fades. In addition, the audio channel can be extracted and worked with independently of the video. This enables you to combine your footage with audio from other sources or move the audio to a different part of the video.

Fades

The gradual rise of a soundtrack to silence, or its fall to silence, is a staple of sound editing. NLE software programs implement this in different ways, but the easiest method is to manipulate the line that represents audio level, either directly on the timeline or in a separate window. The angle of the slope of the line indicates how rapid the change is. It can be quite sudden—like when a door opens on to a busy street—or very leisurely, a slow rise in volume that is barely noticeable until it reaches normal levels—such as the sound of a motorcycle approaching from a distance. The colorful term for this effect is "sneaking in." But the scale or magnification of the timeline can be changed, and this changes the slope.

Cross-fades

The audio cross-fade is a transition similar to a cross-dissolve in video: as one track diminishes to nothing, the other track rises from nothing to normal volume. Although this may sound like just another gimmick, it is actually the most natural way for the soundtrack to follow the visual transition occurring in the movie.

For example, as you walk from the street into the house, the movie cross-dissolves from scenes of the street to children playing in the garden. The soundtrack follows suit: from street noises of traffic and so on, you cross-fade to the sounds of

children at play. For this transition, you work with two separate audio tracks that are "unlinked" from the video. Unlinking enables the audio transition to follow a rate of transition different to that of the movie.

Extracted audio combined
In this diagram, the audio for the clip (in the top line) is reduced for a few seconds, then raised again. At the same time, the audio in the separate soundtrack (in purple) is raised from zero (fade-in), then lowered back to zero (fade-out).

1 Set fade-in
Here, the sound is set to fade in from its low level at a certain point. One click on the timeline defines the in point for the rise in audio level. Click again on the levels line and drag it up to raise the level and program in a gradual fade-in. Note: the labels for the tracks have been removed to facilitate international editions of this book.

2 Set fade-out
Setting the fade-out is achieved in a similar way to setting the fade-in: click first to define the start of the fade-out, then again and drag down to define both the speed of the fade-out (the steeper the slope, the quicker the fade) and its out point.

Editing the soundtrack continued

Extracting audio

So far, the soundtrack has been treated as part of the video: starting and ending at the same time, synchronized to it. A key step to editing soundtracks on video is to separate the two, a process called "extracting audio." By default, once extracted, the audio remains synchronized to the video, but it is possible to unlock or unlink it. Then the audio clip becomes a data file in its own right, a separate entity that can be split, cropped, have parts extracted and pasted elsewhere, exported, and even used in another video.

It follows that you may be able to combine several audio tracks. Entry-level NLE software may allow you to work with one or two tracks, but professional programs can handle up to 100 audio tracks.

Eliminating unwanted noises

It is impossible when shooting on location to avoid unwanted noises. The easiest to deal with are short, sharp, percussive sounds—high-level peaks—such as doors slamming, dogs barking, or a car horn sounding. It is much harder to deal with noises of longer duration, especially if they are of a low frequency. Sounds such as the roar of an aircraft overhead, an emergency siren, or a burglar alarm going off mean that you will have to shoot another take or record the material separately in postproduction.

To eliminate short, sharp noises, try copying a clip of room or ambient tone and dropping it over the undesirable piece of audio on a separate track.

You may need to reduce the level of the track carrying the noise at the point it starts, then raise it again: remember that fades can be very rapid.

Back-timing

An effective editing technique is to synchronize a climax or turning point in the visual action with appropriate music. The technique is called "back-timing," after the method employed in the days of film: given the climax of a piece of music and knowing its duration, the operator timed the film backward to work out in which frame the music should start.

And that is exactly how it is done in digital editing, except it is much easier: you import the music track and slide it underneath, making the movie and music coincide at a chosen point. With a careful choice of music, you can make it sound as if it had been written, arranged, and performed especially for your movie.

Split edit

Perfect synchronization is often essential—for example, when you can see the subject speaking. However, it is not the only way to edit sound; indeed, a little off-timing can be highly effective.

Two audio tracks
Relatively simple NLE applications such as iMovie allow you to work with two audio tracks (the bottom two). For many purposes, that is all you will need, and it saves the complications of working with multiple tracks and mixing them.

Synchronizing sound
For extra precision in the synchronizing of sound and video, it is easiest to locate the peak in the sound with visual markers, as seen above: the music builds rhythmically to a peak, followed by silence. This makes it easier to synchronize with the video climax.

In a split edit, the audio transition takes place just before or after the action: the deliberate "mistiming" can create tension and expectation in the audience with very little effort.

The split edit is used most effectively in highly charged dialog: as the hero speaks, the camera cuts to the heroine listening while he is still speaking, then we hear the heroine reply. The visual transition takes place before the change in audio: we see the reaction that the speech is having while the hero is still talking.

Nearer to home, imagine that you are videoing an elderly relative talking about their favorite record and the memories it evokes. You fade in the music for a few seconds, keeping the camera on your relative's face as you watch them recall the music. Only then do you cut to a close-up of the old record spinning on the record player. The change in audio track precedes video, and the effect is much stronger than if you had synchronized the two.

Recording a voice-over

Entry-level NLE programs such as Windows Movie Maker or Apple iMovie make it easy to record a voice-over track for your movie. You attach a microphone to the computer, set the recording mode, ensure you are at the beginning of your movie, then speak. Keep your eye on the level meter to ensure you are speaking at normal levels, not too quietly or too loudly—you may need to practice this beforehand to get it right. Of course, the voice-over track should be recorded as an audio clip in its own right—so that you can add location sound or ambient noise if you wish—but one that is synchronized with your movie.

●HINTS AND TIPS

There are some simple rules to observe when working with sound to ensure the best working practices.

● When monitoring audio levels, use a reference point of—12 decibels (dB) maximum for the majority of situations; decrease it to—18 dB to –20 dB if you expect some loud noises.

● Work in a sampling-rate environment of 48 KHz (16 bit) if possible—that is, shoot your digital video with the audio sampling rate set to 48 KHz.

● Do not mix sampling rates (see below): if necessary, change the sampling rate to 48 KHz before working on the files. Never mix sampling rates within a sequence created from mixed sources—for example, digital video and CDs: some systems will not work at all with mismatches; even if they do, mismatches could cause problems further into production.

● Log audio clips as you would video clips if you use material from CDs, the Internet, or other sources. This will allow you to keep track of your material. By default, extracted audio takes on the same name as its parent clip.

Quality of sound

The quality of digital sound varies with the sampling rate—that is, how many times per second a sound is measured to digitize it—as well as the highest frequency that can, in theory, be recorded. For the highest audible frequencies, 48,000 samples per second must be taken. The setting for sampling rates in your sound card or camera, or when importing video, will need be matched throughout.

Sampling rate	Highest frequency	Format/use
48,000	24 KHz	DAT (digital audio tape), hi-fi
41,000	20 KHz	Audio CD, non-Web cross-platform
32,000	16 KHz	Audio CD, Web cross-platform
11,025	5.5 KHz	Analog broadcast
8,000	4 KHz	Voice

Creating your own DVDs

The invention of the DVD format and its associated technologies has led to the fastest take-up of any new technology of all time. However, the tremendous opportunity it provides to aspiring moviemakers has taken a few years to be realized. Creating a DVD was once a costly industrial exercise. Now, due to a liberalization of DVD standards, DVD burners in every new personal computer, and, above all, inexpensive—even free—authoring software, the time is ripe for a total upheaval in movie distribution. And if your computer does not have its own DVD writer, you can purchase an external writer for little more than a CD writer.

Authoring software

The software applications currently available cater to all levels of requirements—from making a simple DVD carrying just your movie, to creating a professional-level DVD complete with chapters, menus, multiangle viewing options, stills images, music, and interactive elements. (*See pp. 36–7 for details of DVD authoring software.*)

After you have spent innumerable hours—by turns frustrated, exhilarated, and exhausted—working on your movie and you are happy with the end result and have backed it up, you are ready to burn your DVD. Here we describe the basic steps that are common to all authoring software.

Adding chapters

Chapters are the episodes or acts of a movie. It is customary to add chapter markers at natural turning points or cuts in the movie—a major change of scene or pace, or a big development in plot. Chapters enable your viewers to return to a part of the film they like without scrolling through (as is the case with tape). If you are creating your movie in NLE software that is able to create chapters compliant with DVD standards, then the time to identify the chapter points is when the movie is complete. If not, you should be able to add chapters when you bring your film into the DVD-authoring software. In any case, you should give your chapters descriptive names, such as "Prelude" or "Amy meets Bill."

Poster frames
Some DVD-authoring applications allow you to choose the poster frame to use on a button. Here, in iDVD, you select a still image by unchecking the Movie dialog box, then move the slider until the frame you want is in view.

Chapter markers
By default, chapter markers are placed at the beginning of edits or clips, but they can also be placed anywhere the play head is located. The poster frame is available for the DVD to use to identify the chapter and you can give your chapters either descriptive names or simply numbers, as shown left.

Encoding

The next step—irrespective of what you wish to do with your movie—is to encode it into a format suitable for its destination. This is not as simple as it sounds since there are numerous possibilities. For DVDs, the choice is straightforward: encode your movie as MPEG-2; but within that, there are several choices, so let your software choose the basic default settings to begin with—usually MPEG-2 with VBR (variable bit rate, which compresses the data more efficiently). If you encounter problems with viewing your movie—slightly inaccurate image proportions perhaps, then it could be the encoding. You may have to upgrade to a more sophisticated encoder, such as Discreet Cleaner or Compressor, rather than what is built into your NLE software.

When encoding to MPEG-2 with VBR, you should count on about 4 GB for 60 minutes of video—it may be more or less, according to the nature of the film. Long, slow takes of solitary figures in the desert in the style of *Lawrence of Arabia* will compress efficiently, but jerky footage shot at night—such as the type used in *The Blair Witch Project*—will require a far greater data capacity. If your movie is very long, you can encode as MPEG-1, but the quality will drop to that of VHS tape.

Current Settings

DV NTSC 48 kHz
DV NTSC 48 kHz – 23.98
DV NTSC 48 kHz – 24
DV NTSC 48 kHz Anamorphic
DV PAL 48 kHz
DV PAL 48 kHz – 23.98
DV PAL 48 kHz – 24
DV PAL 48 kHz – 24 @ 25
DV PAL 48 kHz Anamorphic
DV50 NTSC 48 kHz
DV50 NTSC 48 kHz – 23.98
DV50 NTSC 48 kHz Anamorphic
DV50 PAL 48 kHz
DV50 PAL 48 kHz Anamorphic
DVCPRO – PAL 48 kHz
DVCPRO – PAL 48 kHz Anamorphic
DVCPRO – PAL 48 kHz Superwhite
DVCPRO HD – 1080i60
DVCPRO HD – 720p24
DVCPRO HD – 720p30
DVCPRO HD – 720p60
OfflineRT HD (Photo JPEG) – 23.98
OfflineRT HD (Photo JPEG) – 24
OfflineRT HD (Photo JPEG) – 25
OfflineRT HD (Photo JPEG) – 29.97
OfflineRT HD (Photo JPEG) – 30
OfflineRT NTSC (Photo JPEG)
OfflineRT NTSC (Photo JPEG) – 23.98
OfflineRT NTSC (Photo JPEG) – 24
OfflineRT NTSC Anamorphic (Photo JPEG)
OfflineRT PAL (Photo JPEG)
OfflineRT PAL Anamorphic (Photo JPEG)
Uncompressed 10-bit NTSC 48 kHz
Uncompressed 10-bit PAL 48 kHz
Uncompressed 8-bit NTSC 48 kHz
Uncompressed 8-bit PAL 48 kHz
✓ Custom...

Export formats
A full range of export formats is a bewildering sight (*left*): it shows just how many options professionals have to contend with. If in doubt, let your software make the decision for you.

Digital video in multimedia

If you are authoring multimedia discs, you may want to run video within a multimedia presentation. Macromedia Director is a leading application that is able to import digital video in QuickTime, QuickTime VR, AVI, and some MPEG formats, provided these are imported as QuickTime. Digital video movies are always linked—that is, the original video file must be available to the Director projector, preferably within the same folder as all the other material. Since the frames of the video are not the same as those in a Director "movie," the video will run normally. Embedding a video in this way allows the multimedia programmer to use your video as if it were a graphic or image that can be navigated to or called up. Beware, however, of a movie's propensity to increase the size of your presentation file.

Regional codes for DVD playback

Also known as country codes or zone locks, regional codes are recorded on a DVD in order to limit the disc's playability to the areas in which it is sold. Therefore, a Zone 2 disc—sold in Japan and Europe—may not work in a Zone 4 player—that is, machines in Australasia and South America. Discs without locks (also called Zone 0 discs) can be played on any player. Many players—so-called multiregion models—can play discs from any region. In fact, the majority of players are able to play any disc but are locked electronically to certain regions: it is possible to bypass these locks, but it may not be legal to do so. DVDs that you create do not need to carry zone locks, unless you wish to limit their use, which may be an issue if the content of your DVD may cause offence in certain regions.

Creating your own DVDs continued

Designing the interface

The crucial factor offered by DVD authoring is the ability, for the first time ever, to set a mood, or "environment," for the movie. The concept of interface design is similar to creating a website, in that you create a visual environment to set the scene, provide titles to inform, and offer buttons with which to enter the movie. And, similarly to web design, DVD files must conform to strict rules about file types and location.

The intricacies of interface design are outside the scope of this book. However, help is at hand, since all but the top professional applications offer collections of templates that you can adapt to your own needs. You can change the wording, of course, but you can also select the typeface, as well as its size and color. You will also be given a small choice of button shapes, which can be labeled. The buttons will be linked with your chapters, so that viewers can use the buttons to navigate their way through the movie.

Preview

Before committing a movie to DVD, which takes time and is not yet a cheap medium, it is a good idea to preview what it will look like. You can catch problems like dropped frames, clips that for some reason were not rendered fully, and other mishaps.

In addition, you can import images from your digital photography collection to serve as backgrounds—indeed, you could even use stills from your movie. Note that TV pixels are usually not square, whereas (generally) they are in digital photography. So be aware that there may be small shifts in the shape of your images. This disparity is recognized in applications such as Photoshop CS that compensate for nonsquare pixels.

Menu template choice

The choice of menu template styles gets wider with each new software release. You can choose from a variety of backgrounds that resemble, for example, a picture postcard, a birthday card, or an old book. Here (*top left*), a cool, modern design is suitable for urban settings; a swathe of bright red cloth (*top right*) bridges old and new, mirroring the movie, about a modern college. The old-style projector (*bottom left*) displays a scene from the movie with an aged film effect; a clean, modern look with paintbrush strokes (*bottom right*) offers yet another solution.

Button shapes

Templates for button shapes save you from having to design your own. The labels for the buttons can be customized, and some will either show a poster frame or run a sample of the movie within the button. It is also possible to change the button size.

Creating Video CDs

Even if you do not have a DVD writer, you are likely to own a CD burner because they are more or less a standard feature on modern computers. If that is the case, you can distribute your movies on CD. The quality obtainable is not as high as on DVD, nor is the data capacity—which may have an impact on the length of movies you make. More importantly perhaps, CDs are much less costly than DVDs. There are two CD formats currently used: VCD and SVCD.

VCD format

Video CD uses standard compact discs to hold video that is compressed to the MPEG-1 format. Images measure 352 x 240 pixels in NTSC, and 352 x 288 pixels in PAL—the reduction in image size is effectively a file compression, and it reduces file sizes very effectively. The compression is "lossy," however—which means that data is lost in the process and cannot be recovered.

The use of MPEG-1 means that VCD movies can be played on DVD players, as well as in computers with suitable software. Note, however, that while good quality CD-R discs are easily read by any DVD or CD player, even high-quality CD-RW media (CD-rewritable) are known to present problems for some CD players. A full 700 MB CD of MPEG-1 data works out as around 60 minutes of video with basic stereo sound (two-channels of audio), not surround sound (more than two channels of audio).

SVCD format

Super Video CD, also known as Chaoji VCD, is a format invented by the China Recording Standards Committee in an attempt to counter the dominance of DVD, allowing digital movies to be viewed by a greater number of people than that able to invest in new technology. SVCD is in widespread use in Asia and is spreading globally. It offers higher video quality than VCD, being based on the higher-specification MPEG-2 format. However, this means that they can only hold a movie of about 34 minutes in length.

Another reason for the higher quality, as well as a commensurate increase in the amount of data they hold, is that the image dimensions are larger than on VCD: 480 x 480 pixels for NTSC, and 576 x 480 pixels for PAL. While SVCDs can be played in a computer's DVD or CD drive, they may not be compatible with all set-top DVD players.

Making a VCD

VCDs are easier to make than DVDs because they offer fewer functions; therefore, you have fewer decisions to make. They do not have chapters, so they are best suited for movies intended to be watched in one sitting. In software such as Windows Movie Maker, you simply click in the Disc option to call up the dialog box, where you select the VCD format, before clicking to create the disc. Ensure that your CD burner is up and running and that you have a blank CD inserted.

VCD burning
Making a Video CD is as easy as dragging the movie file into software such as Roxio Toast, choosing Video, then Video CD, and clicking OK. Note that files are treated like any files on a CD, and further files may be written at a later date up to the capacity of the CD.

Quick fix Reproduction problems

Once your movie leaves the confines of your desktop, it runs the risk of being lost in incompatible formats, strict broadcast limits, and conflicting systems. Two of the most important problems are considered here. Even though you may not be ready to broadcast, it is good practice to keep to broadcast-legal limits.

Problem

You send your movie to a TV network or professional and they send it right back. They have not watched it, but they say it has "not passed QC [quality control]" or that it is not "broadcast-legal."

Analysis

In analog video, which currently also includes broadcast television, the signals carrying the video and timing or synchronization are combined. If the video signal is too strong (for example, if the whites are too bright) or the ratio between the signal and the synchronization exceeds a certain limit (for example, 10:4) then the electronics that draw the screen image may not function correctly, hence the term "broadcast-safe." Colors that are too saturated or strong are also a problem. Another broadcast requirement is that movies use 4:2:2 color space, but it is not necessary to make this conversion for home use.

Solution

The best solution is to avoid the problem when the image is acquired. First, reduce the lighting contrast to within a 5-stop range. Second, measure and set the camera exposure carefully. If your camera offers a zebra-stripe display, this will indicate if any parts of your scene are superwhite (too bright). Professional NLE applications offer a postproduction broadcast-legal filter.

NLE range check

A range-check view shows that the luminance is too high (red stripes) at over 100 percent, while the green stripes show luma values at 90–100 percent: this clip is not broadcast-legal. The range check view is useful when making corrections in NLE to ensure you stay within standard limits.

Superwhites in shot

In this shot (*above*), the white shirt of the man in shadows is within limits, but the shirt of the man in the sun is well beyond limits—it is superwhite, with no detail or color, just a very high video signal.

Zebra stripes

This simulation shows what a zebra pattern looks like in the video monitor (some cameras display vertical bars). Zebra stripes flash or blink to show the areas of the image that are above 100 or 75 IRE—whatever limits you set in the camera.

Problem

Images that look fine on your computer monitor look terrible—or merely differently colored—on another monitor. The reproduction of hues is not reliable, and the contrast varies.

Analysis

All monitors reproduce the same signal in different ways unless they are carefully adjusted to a standard—that is, calibrated. Domestic monitors will vary a great deal and there is nothing you can do about them.

Solution

You should assess your images on a screen that bears some approximation to an industry standard, ideally a professional video monitor. You also need to calibrate your production monitor. Professional monitors offer a number of advantages over normal, domestic TV sets. Apart from costly features such as the ability to change scan rates and format, the main advantage of a production monitor is the Blue Only mode. Selecting this sends the blue signal to all three monitor electron guns, which gives you a black-and-white picture built up from the blue channel. This enables you to judge the channel that is typically the one giving highest levels of noise. In addition, the Blue Only mode is needed when calibrating the monitor.

Call up the SMPTE bars (or whichever standard is appropriate) and switch to Blue Only, or observe the screen through a dark-blue filter—for example, a Wratten 47B. Using Hue and Luma controls, adjust the Chroma and Hue (or Phase) controls until the four large bright bars match the small rectangles at their base. Then adjust the brightness so that the middle of the small vertical bars under the third dark bar just reaches black. Finally, the contrast control should be adjusted if necessary.

SMPTE bars
These bars are among the most widely used of standard signals or test patterns for assessing both acquisition and display devices.

Note that there are precise standards for each bar: if the pattern is not accurately generated, it cannot be accurately displayed.

SMPTE Blue Only
The Blue Only view of the SMPTE bars is shown here as it might look before calibration. The small, squat rectangles under some of the bright bars are distinguishable but should blend with their corresponding large bar. The small thin rectangles under the third dark bar are distinguishable where the middle should blend with the large bar.

SMPTE Blue Only: bars correct
This is what the Blue Only view should look like after correction: all the long bars are uninterrupted by any change of luma, while the small vertical bar under the third dark bar is just visible. Finally, the small white square in the bottom row appears white but not blindingly. (Compare with the image above.)

Streaming to the Internet

It is remarkable that anyone with Internet access anywhere in the world can look at web pages created elsewhere. It is even more amazing that we can also watch movies online, thanks to video streaming, in which a server computer sends compressed video files over the Internet. These files can be viewed while downloading—the key point being that the viewer does not need to have downloaded the entire file before starting to watch the movie. A simple analogy would be someone drinking from a glass while it is still being filled up.

Basic decisions

Digital video requires very large amounts of data to be processed without interruption. To stream video successfully, you must match the viewing size and the compression levels you will accept with the capacity, or bandwidth, available to your viewer. For viewers connected to the Internet by modem, you should not stream—that is, send a line of data—at more than 36 Kbps (kilobits per second). Those on broadband or ADSL connections can handle 256 Kbps or more. The wide difference between these rates means that you may want to provide two movies, each optimized for a different connection.

The format for video stream will naturally be influenced by the computer you use. If you work on the Windows platform, you work around

Serving video

The special demands of video call for a number of special arrangements at the server that distributes the video to viewers. If you wish to put streaming video on your website, it is necessary to check that the company hosting your site, which may be your Internet service provider, is able to handle video. If your hosting company can handle video, then all you have to do is upload your video to your website in the usual way, providing a download link on your site for visitors to click. However, video streaming may be a special facility for which you need to pay extra. Depending on the streaming rates you use, different formats are preferred: Windows Media and QuickTime run best at rates up to 512 Kbps. Consult your hosting company for the latest recommendations. Also keep in mind that video streaming pushes out a lot of data, so you may exceed your account's limits on bandwidth.

Windows Media Technologies—a set of different software for creating, editing, and reformatting content. The core is the ASF (Advanced Streaming Format), to which other file formats such as WAV, AVI, MPEG and MP3 can be easily converted. Movies are watched using Windows Media Player. Apple Mac users will center their work around QuickTime, using software such

Choosing picture size

For the slowest modem downloads (28 Kbps), you can only stream audio: video can be streamed at about 1 fps (frame per second) for a picture measuring 160 x 120 pixels. At 128 Kbps and in good conditions, a picture of 320 x 240 pixels can be streamed at 15 fps: the result is jerky but better than nothing. At 512 Kbps, you should be able to reach 25 fps with a 320 x 240 pixel image, and this will run smoothly most of the time, with the occasional stammer or hesitation. It follows that streaming video is made possible by high-speed connections, such as ADSL.

160 x 120 pixels

Educational previews
You can learn so much from even the trailers of blockbusters or independent films, such as this one for *Spider-Man 2*. Trailers often show the best bits of the movie. Once streamed to you, a frame-by-frame analysis is possible and highly educational. You will see that even the big studios do not get everything perfect all the time.

as iMovie, and watch movies in QuickTime Player. QuickTime movies are compatible with Windows Media Player and can be watched on Windows machines.

Watching movies online

Thanks to the wide acceptance of QuickTime and now Windows Media Player, there is a very large quantity of material available on the Internet. For better-quality viewing, you can install Real Player (or RealOne for Mac OS); this software must be paid for, but the fee also gives you access to many mainstream movies as well as radio. However, unless you have the very fastest line, even quite small movies will take some time to get started. The reward for your patience, though, is the chance to watch movies that never make it to distribution to movie theaters. You can also analyze the movies and learn useful techniques in your own home.

There are numerous web sources for movies: a search using the key words "online movies" will bring up hundreds of thousands of matches. Although the quality is variable, it is worth exploring a good number. Their offerings range from Hollywood blockbusters to 60-second independent shorts and animations; you can use these movies as learning tools or simply for inspiration. If you pay subscriptions you may be relieved of advertisements and be able to download better-quality video streams.

320 x 240 pixels

640 x 480 pixels

6
Going further
with DV

Movie genres

Your progress from making home movies to productions aimed
at audiences beyond the family can be rapid and painless.
This chapter demonstrates how your videomaking skills
can be developed and taken further. Various types of movie
are discussed, and attention is paid to structure and story.

Developing ideas

Before you can make a movie, you first need to have an idea.
Whether it is simple or complex, this is the seed from which
the project will grow. Here we look at ways of bringing out the
full potential of your idea before the shooting begins.

Writing screenplays

Practical hints for scriptwriting and creating screenplays
are outlined, as are some of the different ways of creating
storyboards. A quick-fix section offers help for problems
commonly encountered with location work.

Approaches

With a handful of short films on your DVDs, and after hundreds of hours spent at the computer following days of setting up and filming, your thoughts will turn to greater things. It is likely you already know what you want to do. Film styles, much like other modes of creative activity, tend to choose you rather than give you the choice.

Being different

The futures of moviemakers are no longer held solely in the hands of movie magnates. The boundaries and limits that were formerly fiercely constrained by the need for technical resources of an industrial scale have now been swept away. Working with video, you can shoot hundreds of hours of footage without having to remortgage the house, and the cost of editing that box load (no longer a truckload) of tapes is only that of your time. So if you want to do it—whatever "it" may be—you probably can.

One concern of novice moviemakers is the "groove problem"—the notion that once you have made a success of working in a particular genre or style, you will be pigeonholed. Certainly it is easier once you have made, for instance, a successful pop video to continue making them. You have a track record, and you have a great first item for your showreel. It is then easier to get work of the same type.

But directors can and do cross genres. For example, although Steven Spielberg is often associated with action-adventure movies, his oeuvre also includes a thriller about a deranged trucker (*Duel*) and a tearjerker about a soft-hearted alien (*ET: The Extra-Terrestrial*). And Lars von Trier, one of the founders of the Dogme movement vowing chastity from special effects and artificial lighting (*see p. 90*), has made one movie using a bank of 100 cameras (*Dancer in the Dark*) and another using 800 lights (*Dogville*). So make whatever you want, however you want.

Hollywood goes digital

Robert Rodriguez (*From Dusk Till Dawn, The Faculty, Once Upon a Time in Mexico* [above]) is one of the growing band of directors forsaking film for high-definition video. He was introduced to HD video by George Lucas, who used it for his *Star Wars* prequels. Rodriguez is also credited with being part of the movement that persuaded film festivals to accept entries made on video.

Movie genres

As cinema has evolved, so the styles or modes of film proliferated: documentary, narrative feature, B-movie, art-house, and others. There is now even a semiofficial list of 22 recognized genres within feature films—ranging from romantic comedy and thriller to psychodrama and period adaptation. Broadly speaking, though, the trend is now an erosion of any clarity that may have existed in the boundaries between these ways of making movies. For example, a biopic (from "biographical picture") about a comic-book author can exploit special effects to recreate or simulate the world of its subject (as in *American Splendor*), while a romantic feature film may use documentary footage to locate the time and place of the main character (as in *Forrest Gump*).

All of this means that your movie's content or story comes first; leave it up to others to decide which genre your work fits into. In practical terms, the point is that you can create a movie in any style within an affordable budget. But first, you need an idea that grabs you—one that will push you along the road to the complete movie (*see pp. 194–5*); and next comes the writing of the screenplay (*see below*).

Documentary goes mainstream
The Wim Wenders film *The Buena Vista Social Club* was the first to show that documentaries could hit the mainstream moviegoing market. It was shot entirely on digital video.

The essential screenplay

At the heart of your movie planning is the screenplay. It is a narrative that maps the movie's journey from one scene to the next, describing location, lighting, props, camera angles, and moves, as well as providing the dialog (if any) and directions for any actors involved. When you are starting out and learning the craft, it is best to begin with a modest 10-minute short. There will be plenty of time later to progress on to a 100-minute all-action feature or to attempt a screenplay based on a classic novel. If your movie has no dialog, then you could consider shooting it without a screenplay. But not only do you miss out on the fun of tackling one, you also miss out on the advantages—every one of which will improve your movie. Some of the numerous benefits of working from a screenplay include:

● You know what you are doing, and why. This means you waste less time, effort, and tape.
● Anyone helping you will know what you are doing and why at any point in the proceedings.
● Scripted dialog can be improved upon while shooting or used as a basis for ad libs or improvisation.

● You can budget around a screenplay far better than you can from just a list of locations or items.
● A screenplay is more directed than a shot list, encouraging a disciplined approach to shooting, which in turn will aid efficient editing.
● A screenplay forces you to visualize the effects of changes of scene and pace, as well as of camera angles and fields of view. For more on storyboarding, see pp. 200–1.
● A screenplay enables you to plan for the editing and postproduction processes.
● You can plan for all requirements such as lighting, props, and sound more easily.
● A screenplay will help you when it comes to scouting for locations.
● You can plan a shooting schedule that is economical, rather than shooting the action in the order it occurs within your movie.
● The screenplay offers a springboard for improvisation if the creative spirit descends upon you.
For more on screenwriting, see pp. 198–9.

Types of movie

Taking your moviemaking further often goes hand in hand with the move from the family context into the public arena. At this stage, you must raise the standard of both the content and presentation of your work, as well as taking on more responsibilities. The types of movie that you make then become like career decisions—a dynamic compromise between what you would like to achieve, what suits your temperament and skills, and what is possible given your resources and location. In that sense, what you record is an output determined in part by the programming of your personality. For example, if you do not enjoy popular music, it will not cross your mind to shoot pop videos, however much you recognize the pop video as a vibrant, energetic genre that has been hugely inventive with video effects.

Motivating idea

Whatever you decide to do, you will find it helpful to define your movie in one fairly short sentence. Call it the theme, its thesis, or even the mission statement, but it is important to sum up your movie succinctly. The best place to learn how to write such a sentence is to read the blurb on the back of commercial DVD and VHS movies. In the movie industry, these are written after the film is made, but you have to do it the other way around: before you do anything else, write that sentence.

Documentary

Movies based on reporting real events or people's lives seem to promise to write themselves, but you must do a great deal of research beforehand. It is entirely possible to do everything yourself: produce, record sound and vision, and direct. This is hard work, but it is also the least expensive way possible. You could even find a subject no farther away than your street. All you have to do is talk to people, ask around, and research. The frail old man next door could turn out to have been a war reporter; and he may still have a head full of memories and an attic full of news clippings and photographs. Of course, more ambitious subjects are also possible (*see pp. 188–91*).

Artistic projects

You can take any aspect of your visual or aural world and turn it into a subject—the only limits are your courage, personal perspective, and commitment. The budget can be minimal, and you can take all the time you like, allowing the ideas to develop organically. Furthermore, you can work on several ideas at once, which makes the most of your taping excursions. For example, I am fascinated by lights and the way the camera appears to represent reality but actually records only what it is designed and built to do. My current project works with the artificial lights of

Documentary-making
As free-form or as tightly controlled as you wish, documentaries can be made anywhere, at anytime, and with the smallest of budgets and the most basic of equipment. They offer an excellent training ground for feature-length movies.

Artistic creations
In some respects, artistic videos need more discipline than other forms precisely because they can be formless and lack the usual forces that drive them to completion. However, they suit low budgets, and technical quality is not the highest priority.

the city seen in an equally artificial way by the camera. With such a subject, you can even make a virtue of the variable picture quality obtained from consumer digital video cameras.

Music videos

Digital video techniques mesh so well with popular music that they could have been invented for it. Music videos are always short, there is an inexhaustible supply of music for you to work with, and there are numerous unknown musicians only too eager to have their work creatively and imaginatively interpreted. Better still, this is a genre in which anything goes.

Short movies

Working on a short movie is similar to writing a short story: not only do you have to set the scene very quickly, but at almost the same time you must also take the viewer into the action. On the other hand, you do not have to develop a long story line. For example, the short could be about what a child gets up to on the long walk home after school; for a subject such as this, you do not even need any dialog, just ambient sound. Furthermore, you can shoot straight—as if working with film—or use every trick in the digital video book. Making shorts is, of course, the best possible training for moving on to feature-length work.

Making shorts
Short movies can be treated as an art form in their own right or may be considered as the building blocks for a longer project. The haunting mood of this short—*Breathe*, directed by Samantha Harrie—is tangible in just a single frame.

Hybrid

These categories are far from rigid. In fact, they are only highlights in a continuum of approaches ranging from one that intervenes as little as possible—the "pure" documentary—to one in which every single element is contrived and constructed—the fantasy-world feature. A documentary about a psychic can exploit digital video effects in order visually to "enter" the psychic's mind, while a fictional feature can use documentary techniques of mobile camerawork, available light, and amateur actors to make it seem like a documentary or a true story.

Shooting music videos
Perhaps the fastest-growing art form in history, the music video has become so dominant in just a few frenetic years that there are entire broadcast stations around the globe delivering nothing else. Unique in being driven by their soundtracks, music videos have been a wellspring of adventurous filmmaking, often thanks to generous budgets and the need to make an immediate impact. But memorable music videos can also be made for almost no financial outlay.

Building blocks

There are numerous variants of the answer that goes along the lines of, "It starts somewhere, something happens, and then it ends." The question is, of course, "What is a movie?"

But the truth is that it is hard to find a movie in which the basic structure is not one in which, first, a scene is set: where we are, what period of history or future it is, and who the characters are and the state of their lives. Then something happens to upset the peace or status, forcing the characters to respond, from which we learn what they are "made of." Or it may not be so dramatic: this phase of the movie may explore the details, flashback to explain why things are the way they are, and so on. This leads eventually to the resolution or, in the case of a documentary, a pulling together of all the strands to lead to a conclusion or the need to investigate further.

Defining the structure

Even experimental moviemakers cannot escape this basic structure: their attempts to break away from it—using flashbacks and parallel stories—serve only to reinforce its fundamental nature. And it is a structure common not only to movies, but to plays, novels, and longer poems; it even extends to the design and layout of art exhibitions and, of course, also applies to extended pieces of music. In fact, it is helpful to use the terms from sonata form (a structure that dominated classical European music for centuries). The first part is called the exposition; then comes the development section; and the end is the recapitulation—a reminder of the beginning. If you bring any favorite movie to mind, the basic structure will most likely be just that: exposition, to story development, to recapitulation.

Despite the structure, moviemaking has an infinite capacity for creative solutions. This is the point at which the structural elements, or building blocks, that have been considered elsewhere in the book all come together.

Camera angles

As every shot requires you to position the camera so every shot is a creative opportunity. It is all too easy to leave the camera on a tripod that is set at a convenient height. The importance of camera angle is well illustrated by the example of the great director Orson Welles: during the making of *Citizen Kane*, he insisted on a hole being dug in a factory floor to get the camera low enough.

Now that even high-end video cameras are being designed to be shoulder-mounted or handheld, there is no excuse for not taking the camera off its support and working with fluid camera movements. Also, Steadicams (which dampen or limit small movements), cranes, and mounted booms are relatively inexpensive to rent and easy to use with digital video cameras because they do not need to be as heavily constructed as those used in the motion-picture industry. Another crucial advantage is that a video feed can easily be taken from the camera to a small screen mounted at the base of the support, so recording is easily monitored. And, of course, modern cameras are easily controlled by infrared remote devices.

Composition

From every camera position there are dozens of different potential compositions at a given focal length. And when you multiply that number of compositions by the number of available focal lengths, you will see the huge opportunity for creativity. Unlike a photographer, who only has to compose one image at a time, you have to compose for the entire take, combining camera tracking movements as well as the movements of

Placing the horizon
This composition from the independent short *Al Sur del Desierto* by Galel Maidana shows how a low viewpoint gives dominance to the figure, while the pile of sticks creates a dynamic diagonal line.

your actors. For many years, the nearly square TV format has restricted the creative possibilities for composition—after all, widescreen cinema was invented in the 1950s—but the arrival of the 16:9 widescreen TV format is changing all of that. It means that digital video may return to the compositional flexibility offered by widescreen—placing actors at opposite ends of the frame or filling the entire span with chaotic action, a technique so effectively used in the *Star Wars* and *Lord of the Rings* movies.

Finding an angle
There are dozens of different angles on, say, a conversation under the parasols—from overhead (*left*), through all the intermediate steps, to tabletop level or even below. As a cinematographer, you have to find them all, evaluate them, and use them.

Getting close
Video can transform the experience of an ordinary and overgrown yard. Simply by running the camera close to the ground and pushing aside the flowers on the way (*right*), you will bring prominence to things usually beyond the viewer's confines.

Building blocks continued

Close-ups

As the great cinematographer Joseph V. Mascelli put it, close-ups are among the most powerful storytelling devices available to the moviemaker. Shot and timed carefully, close-ups—and extreme close-ups in particular—add visual clarity and emotional impact to the storytelling.

Watch any episode of the TV show *CSI: Crime Scene Investigation* for one masterclass after another in the art of the close-up. Notice the ease with which scenes in this series move effortlessly between cut-in close-ups—in which a larger scene is cropped to a magnified view of a portion—and cutaway close-ups. This is where we get near to an object that may be under discussion but was not visible in the preceding scene. Such an object may be seen at different angles: a tiny bit of evidence picked up by the scientist, or presented objectively, to display its features.

Another kind of close-up takes the camera into the personal space of the speaker, pulling the viewer right up to the speaker, perhaps cropping down to only the lips moving; this so-called subjective close-up is also much used in episodes of *CSI*.

Continuity

Good continuity while shooting your movie will smooth and power the editing process, whereas shooting errors in continuity will add difficulties to the job of editing (*see pp. 60–1*).

The core concept in movie continuity is that everything counts—even details that escape the conscious notice of the viewer. Anything that disturbs the flow of narrative or upsets the logic of movement through time and space can distract the viewer from the world you have created. Clean clothes after a street brawl, a change of tie during the course of a conversation, a crooked picture on the wall that rights itself between scenes—these discontinuities are small, easily missed details: subliminally noticeable and a sign of low standards on the part of the moviemaker.

Your movie could suffer from lack of continuity in space. A screenplay may call for different locations, and a documentary may sometimes move around, possibly between continents. Even a vacation video that starts in England and ends up in Honolulu has a space continuity problem to solve: you need a transition shot that takes your viewer from an overcast daily commute to the bright Pacific sun. A short clip of the plane taking off will do nicely—a technique used in countless movies. Without that clue, the jump is too big to understand. And if the move is from one foggy city to another, such a clue is even more important.

Time continuities are obvious, but they are easily lost because it is necessary to record footage in separate takes over the course of several days and at different times of the day. You can lose time continuity simply by forgetting about a clock or wristwatch that is in shot, or that a meal served piping hot in one take is stone cold by the time you adjust the lights to shoot a different angle.

Finally, continuity also depends on technically assured camerawork and is a matter of smoothing out or eliminating any differences in white

Dreary day
In the prelude to a vacation movie, you can make the coming contrast clear by setting the pre-vacation scene. Here is a dreary commute to work on a cloudy day.

Flight transition
The transition from an overcast day at home can be made quickly and simply with a short sequence of the trip. Even a short clip of the plane's touchdown may suffice.

Tropical paradise
From the touchdown clip, you can slip straight to the tropical sunset—there is no need to shoot collecting the luggage, traveling to the hotel, and getting unpacked unless you really want to. A movie narrative gains its strength and impetus from what you leave out, not from what you put in.

balance, exposure, chrominance, and luminance between takes. (*For more information on these subjects, see pp. 60–1*).

Discontinuities can be intentional, of course, designed to confuse the audience. Such "mistakes" can be seen in *A Clockwork Orange* and in battle scenes such as those in *Gladiator*: the flash of a blade may lead you to expect the next blow to come from the left, but instead it comes from the right.

A switch from color to monochrome can be used to set emotional stages. The emotive power of glimpses of color in the otherwise monochrome *Schindler's List* is well exploited.

Editing
The final decisions about the pace and rhythm of a movie are made at the editing stage. There is only one way to learn how to edit and that is to do it—either with your own material or in tutorials. The overall length may be set by external factors—such as a distributor's accountants—rather than by the director. For example, distribution reels for 35 mm movies (called "release prints") are a maximum of 20 minutes long, so no one wants a 63-minute movie, which needs four reels but uses only three minutes of the last one. An extra three minutes of cuts are likely to be requested.

Documentaries

The central concern in making a documentary is honesty. That does not refer to the way the content is presented; instead, it is to do with whether, in all honesty, you think you can stay the course—long, arduous, fickle in its reward, if not downright thankless—of making a documentary. And you will not get rich either: it is a safe bet that no one has bought a ranch in Montana or a palace in Monaco on the proceeds of documentaries. Very, very few documentaries achieve the high profiles of movies such as *Bowling for Columbine* or *The Buena Vista Social Club*.

The power of obsession

For ambitious documentaries, you need an idea that will carry you through the long haul. Maybe you are fascinated by a never-visited tribe deep in the Amazon, or you would like to document the matriarchal societies of the Himalayan foothills, but you will need to be obsessed by the idea to get you even close to the shooting stage.

Central hypothesis

There is a vital difference between pursuing a subject for a documentary and propounding or arguing for a position, while using the same material. Regardless of how you may feel about the objectivity or subjectivity of the form, a central hypothesis at the outset will make your job easier. It helps shape both the research and the direction of the film, as well as ensuring that you create a narrative that moves at a good pace, rather than a bland presentation of facts.

For example, imagine that you enjoy world music and your research has led you to discover that some wonderful fiddle or violin players have emerged in a very unlikely spot, a Himalayan kingdom. This is exciting because the location promises to be highly photogenic, the subject is unusual—there is a good chance it will attract the attention of a program commissioner—and the soundtrack will be great.

But the movie lacks a focus or direction: it is not saying much beyond "Did you know they play violin in the Himalayas?" But your research also uncovers the fact that certain groups regard the music as a threat to the country's culture. And the differences are drawn along racial as well as religious lines. The story then comes alive, taking on a dimension beyond mere musical curiosity. The struggles of the musicians becomes symbolic of the tensions between the nation's divided communities—fiddle-playing becomes political. And there you have it—a working hypothesis.

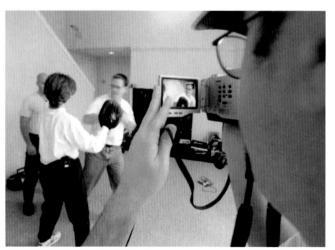

Keeping mobile
Documentary moviemaking is by nature mobile—taping a kick-boxing lesson (*left*), you too may need to move quickly. But a camera that is too mobile produces video that is tiring to watch, so a balance needs to be struck.

Taping interviews
Video is invaluable as an adjunct to other methods of research or survey work— for example, to provide visual records of the course of an interview (*right*) or for selecting presenters for the documentary.

The steps to take

It cannot be emphasized enough that the keys to documentary-making, as in all moviemaking, are research and planning. It is wise to corroborate the story—that is, ask an independent source about the facts you are investigating—even if you are confident your source is reliable. Trawl the Internet, but be aware that not all information on the web is reliable, so visit official sites wherever possible. University libraries can be helpful if you are pursuing genuine research provided you can obtain a reference from a recognized academic—and you will probably find, somewhere in the world, an academic or journalist who happens to be an expert on your subject and is only too willing to help. Exploit your network of friends and contacts, too: you may well know someone who knows someone who knows what you need.

Planning

One factor that distinguishes documentary planning from that for other types of movie is that your freedoms of movement can be highly restricted. You may have a very tight time frame to work in: a gathering of hill tribes may take place only very four years; or next year's Navruz (Islamic New Year) will be at the right time of the

● **HINTS AND TIPS**

A successful documentary is one in which the passion of its maker is tangible. But there are also practical considerations to bear in mind.

● Work within the fields of your expertise.
● Exploit connections with key locals; network with everyone you can.
● When working abroad, identify an honest, effective local fixer.
● Look after any crew, especially local crew if working abroad.
● An exploratory trip to check out locations and the story will be worthwhile, if time and the budget permit.
● Create a cast list of people you interview and give them roles—hero, hero's helper, the enemy, innocent bystander. You are filming a drama based on real life.

year to film in the desert. If only for this reason alone, one of the most important strategies is to have a number of projects at different stages of research and development at any one time. You can work on a project for years, hear nothing but stubborn silence from the embassy about your visas, then suddenly you are given four weeks' notice to pack your bags and go, now or never, as once happened to me.

Documentaries continued

The timeline

Given the dependence of a documentary on timing, or perhaps simply to ensure that its subject is still topical by the time you are ready to offer the movie, it is wise to create a timeline that stretches backward from the end of the postproduction and edit (*see opposite*). How long will it take to edit the movie—will you try to do it yourself (cheap but hard work) or hire a professional (quicker but costly)? How long will the shoot last? How will you prepare the team? How much time will be needed for research? For an ambitious, "professional" documentary you are not likely to have much spare time out of two years—if everything is counted in, and assuming that you are generously funded.

If the timing of the shoot itself is critical, the need for accurate planning is even more important. Precise schedules offer another advantage: your crew knows exactly what is required of them, and when. For example, no one can plan if you ask them to be available "early next spring"; it is much easier to commit oneself to "the first week of March."

Being disciplined

The arrival of digital video has created a new danger for documentary-making. The temptation is to shoot vast amounts of material that will take months just to log and review. Cinematographers had to be selective when they worked with precious and extremely costly film. Even 16 mm film is a precious commodity compared to the costliest DV tape: 1 hour costs, on average, $30 with DV, but it would require 1,600 ft (488 m) of 16 mm film (running at a slow 18 fps), costing around $800, not including processing.

The discipline needed for working a dual system (separate recording of sound and video) will help slow down the trigger happy. Another way to discipline the shooting is to stick to a script or shot list: anything not strictly necessary should not be shot. But few will have the courage to see this policy through (and quite rightly; one of the joys of documentary-making is responding swiftly and with agility to changing situations).

Daily review

The daily review is the analysis of the progress made each day, and it can prevent you from becoming too distracted. One benefit of working in digital video is the availability of daily rushes—something that in the past only a large Hollywood studio was able to provide for its directors.

In the end, you can upload the shoot on to a laptop computer supplemented with external hard-disk drive and review the day's take. You will quickly see what is superfluous to the story and which new avenues you could investigate. However, it is not best practice to take a partially used tape out of the camera for review. One solution is to start every day with a new tape—this is also a good practice for logging purposes. Besides, you have now backed up the shoot. The downside of the ease with which rushes can be reviewed is that the working day can become very

Working a dual system

Recording sound separately from the video—for example, using a boom mic connected to a dedicated sound recorder—ensures high-quality sound and is known as working a dual system. But if sound is also recorded from a microphone on the camera, as shown here, you obtain a backup for the sound. Another advantage of the backup is that, in postproduction, it makes it easier to synchronize the wild soundtrack with the video, making the use of a clapperboard not absolutely necessary.

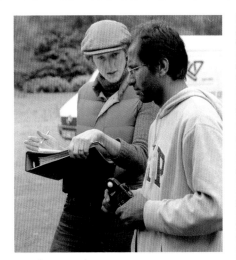

Keeping notes
It is ironic that such a visual and auditory medium relies so heavily on keeping written notes. Keep a record of everything you record, or editing will be harder work than necessary.

Documentary-making is technically driven despite a shooting style that is less formal than that used when making feature-length movies.

● If possible, record dual system—sound on the video as well as in a separate recorder. Not only is sound superior, you will also have a backup.

● Use a time-of-day timecode to aid synchronization in postproduction.

● Use a new tape at the start of each day. Do not have a tape that covers two days or you will cause confusion with timecodes.

● Keep a meticulous and comprehensive log of every take—both sound and video.

● Assign somebody to take production stills and portraits during the shoot.

● Make a note of the names of everyone you record.

● Avoid reviewing the tape in camera as you shoot and do not remove the tape until the end. These steps will avoid breaking or confusing timecodes.

long indeed, and after a hard day's shooting, the last thing a camera operator wants to do is sit in front of a video screen for the whole evening.

Obtaining releases

You may think that because your documentary is intended to promote good causes you do not need to obtain model or personal releases. But you would be wrong—litigation is a worldwide pastime. It will be difficult to achieve in practice, but try to obtain a signature against a written personal release for everyone who is interviewed on camera. To be on the safe side, you could even record them signing the document. To seal the release, some payment, of at least $1, should be made. Most people are willing to participate, especially if they feel they are taking part in a worthwhile cause, and they will be only too glad to be paid even a nominal sum.

If someone refuses to give consent, you must decide whether to use the footage or not. It is customary to seek a release following the interview.

Using a timeline

A successful moviemaker has to be strong on organization and scheduling; being a passionate creative is not enough. A timeline (measured in months before delivery) is an invaluable aid to ensuring minimal loss of time and reduced costs. Use this example as a guide, putting in your own timings.

Sample timeline	
Start research	24 months
Start on script and scenarios	18 months
Obtain financing	12 months
Elaborate research: make contacts, obtain permits	6 months
Recruit production team	3½ months
Book tickets and rent equipment	3 months
Shoot	2½ months
Postproduction (log, edit, record narration)	2 months

Short movies and features

The capacity for movies to contain many layers of meaning and the moviemaker's ability to manipulate the passage of time means that the short is an art form in its own right. It needs only the spark of your imagination for it to come alive.

Choosing a subject

You can make an interesting short about anything. To some, this states the obvious; to others, it seems an unlikely assertion. If this notion seems risible to you, perhaps moviemaking is not in your blood.

A man wakes up to an alarm clock and makes breakfast. This may not seem the most promising of scenarios, but it is one of the most intriguing parts of *The Ipcress File*, a virtuoso catalog of film techniques in a few minutes. Two men playing chess. Sounds slow and dreary? In the hands of Ingmar Bergman, this scene of *The Seventh Seal* is an allegory on the meaning of life and death.

You do not need to come up with a brilliant or original idea. Few stories are new, but there are still infinite ways in which they can be told.

Scale of project

Your creativity does not need to be limited by a small budget or few resources. The following is a list of summaries of short movies:

● An after-dinner game of Truth or Dare becomes addictive, with tragic consequences.
● A couple finds a briefcase—what is in it?
● A long, tedious day is spent filling in a job application form.
● A commuter finds himself alone on a station platform and performs a strange dance.

The dinner-party short needed a cast of just five people, the briefcase story needed only two, and the other two each required a single actor. The short movie about filling in the application form did not even need a script—the actor was alone and said nothing—yet it is engagingly funny and sad at the same time.

Awareness of timescale

If a week is a long time in politics, one minute of a movie can sometimes feel like an hour. If you are accustomed to the leisurely development pace found in a two-hour feature-length film, it is a very instructive exercise to watch a few shorts lasting just one or two minutes. As you watch them, keep in mind that it takes a long time to shoot a minute. I have personally watched a crew of seven plus one actor spend six hours shooting a total of four minutes of film, which will end up lasting just 20 seconds in the final cut.

Learning by example

An important development for the aspiring movie-maker is to change your focus on movies from that of the moviegoer to that of the movemaker. Initially, it may not be a change that you like. Instead of being caught up in the drama and emotions of the moment while watching a thriller, for example, you have to concentrate on the details. You will register and recognize shots: an extreme close-up of an eye, followed by a snap-zoom to an interior establishing shot of a dark room, then back to the eye, and so on. But this change in the focus of your attention and your growing skill in analyzing cinematic technique is the start of your education as a screenwriter or director.

● Watch and rewatch movies that you admire. Try to work out why you like them, why the directors did what they did, and how they did it. Is the impact created by the editing or the camerawork—or both?
● Try watching movies without sound as well as with. A good soundtrack controls both the emotional and the visual experiences.
● Watch TV documentaries even if you want to shoot features—you can learn how editing makes the best of limited material.
● Read screenplays of your favorite movies.
● Watch the filmmaking documentaries found on DVDs.
● Trawl the Internet for movie shorts and independent films to download and study.

Keeping the movie simple

Invisible Light is a short feature movie that demonstrates how effective moviemaking does not need intricate plots, large budgets, or elaborate sets. The movie stars two women, one of whom (Choi Yoon Sun as Gah-in) is in the throes of an affair with a married man. On her return from studying abroad, her affair and estrangement from her culture sends her into depression and despair. The second woman (Lee Sun-jin as Do-hee) is the wife of the man having an affair with Gah-in, and she is pregnant with another man's child. The anxieties of the women and their relationships with men allow the writer and director Gina Kim, with cinematographers Peter Gray and Benito Strangio, to work almost entirely close-up with available locations.

Color design
Using available locations with minimal alteration calls for careful design: the green apple brings some color variety.

Wide angle
To depict Gah-in's eating disorder, director Kim uses a wide-angle view. This helps signify isolation and loneliness.

Color palette
A change in the color palette of a scene can be an effective way to indicate a change of location.

Long focal length
A longer focal length and a more distant view turns the viewer into a spectator, creating separation from the action.

Working with animals
The decision to include animals in your movie should never be taken lightly. Here it worked out just fine.

Evening light
Working at sunset is recommended for experienced crews only. Instead, you can simulate sunset light with filters.

Extreme close-ups
They may offer a good solution to location problems, but extreme close-ups are a test for both the lighting (the luminance range must be very carefully controlled to avoid "hot" highlights on the skin) and the camera operator (depth of field is very limited). It is also difficult for the cast and behind-the-scenes crew: because the viewer is so close to the subject, errors in makeup become very visible, and any awkwardness in the acting can be embarrassing.

Developing an idea

While no one can help you have an idea, you can be guided through the processes of turning inspiration into script, and screenplay into movie. Here are some pointers that are more practical than inspirational, but they should not be ignored—at least not until you have gained in experience and the ability to attract financing.

Showing the story

Primarily, video is a visual medium, and it is at its strongest when it shows the viewer something, and not when it tells by using words. A sequence with voice-over is little more than radio with pictures. But action—someone looking around to identify the source of a sudden noise, two people tentatively kissing, or a cyclist wobbling along a lake shore—grabs attention and involves the viewer, perhaps even provoking an emotional response. A common mistake is to write emotion into the scenes: emotion arises from within the action first and dialog second.

Choosing an indoor setting

Write indoor scenes whenever possible. That way, you are not at the mercy of the weather, local officialdom and police, or curious bystanders. Sound recording is infinitely easier, too, with far fewer erratic and unpredictable noises to cope with. It is easier to keep equipment safe and secure, and catering may be easier to arrange.

Using one location

A clever low-budget trick is to set your story in one location. It involves less moving around and less setting-up time. Keeping production simple means fewer distractions for the cast, who spend less time getting bored and cooling down emotionally—a common problem for nonprofessional actors.

Shooting at dawn and dusk

One of the main problems with shooting at dawn is the likelihood that preparation will take place in the dark (*see Night shots, bottom right*). Another issue, though—this time common to shooting at both dawn and dusk—is that there is only a short amount of shooting time available before the light changes, especially when working in the tropics or at the equator. If you need another take, you will have to wait an entire day, with no guarantee that the weather will be the same—and, therefore, no assurance as to whether you can use what you have already shot.

Recording at dawn
At either end of the day, videomaking is a hostage to fortune and the weather. It is no coincidence that the biggest film studios are in the Sunshine State.

Minimizing location work
Why rent a hotel room when you can beg or borrow a friend's apartment? Make the best use of it that you can, even if it means painting it and repainting it back afterward.

Keeping characters to a minimum
The simple reality is that the fewer participants your movie needs, the more likely it is to be made. For a budget movie, one actor is enough and two are ample. When writing about a dinner party, do you really need six people? Three people may be all you need. Try to avoid using extras, too.

Keeping dialog to a minimum
Your first draft of dialog is sure to be too long. Use action to move the story on, and set the scene with camerawork, not words. Outside of film noir, a voice-over is often an admission of defeat.

Asking for feedback
Finally, perhaps the hardest act of all: show early drafts to someone you trust—meaning someone you trust to be critical and to tell you the truth. It is too much to hope that they are experienced script readers, but at least they might have some knowledge of movies (*see also pp. 198–9*).

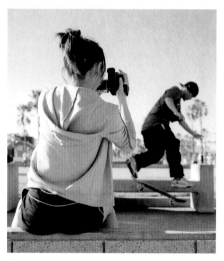

Shooting tests
The low cost of digital video means you can shoot tests and try out ideas thoroughly—as in this skateboard-stunts project—before any fully produced action is recorded.

Night shots

While special effects such as earthquakes, low-lying mist, tornadoes, and even torrential rain are costly to create, night shots may seem within reach of your microscopically small budget. Consider the problems, however. Night shots require much more time to produce: studio lighting setups to simulate night time need much more attention to detail than daylight setups. No one can see what they are doing, so even finding equipment takes much longer than usual. And much greater care is needed to ensure safe operation. As an alternative, day-for-night lighting may be considered. With this method, you use camera lens iris control to underexpose heavily while leaving ambient light levels high enough to work in. On location, working at night means working unsocial hours, possibly causing a nuisance and disturbance with lights and noise. These factors aside, asking any cast or crew members (if you have them) to work unsocial hours is likely to mean paying them more money or an overtime rate.

Registering your ownership

One of the fears, and a very reasonable one, is that someone will think your story idea is so good that they will commission a well-known screenwriter to write it. Once you get over the compliment that is being paid, you will want to sue. To get off first base you need to prove that not only were you truly the author of the story but that you wrote it first. In countries such as the United States where there is a formal mechanism to register, it is prudent to take advantage of it. The cost is relatively low and the forms are easy to fill in. In countries that do not have a formal mechanism, such as the UK, you can make arrangements with a lawyer to deposit your screenplay, marked with the date of completion, as proof of ownership. A worthwhile further precaution is to send in scripts for review by registered mail; some people send a copy to themselves and leave the postmark-dated envelope sealed on receipt.

Quick fix Location problems

The theory is that with proper planning you will not encounter problems. Naturally, life is more complicated than that, and problems will arise even after the most thorough preparation. Part of the challenge of videomaking is in the solving of such problems. Entire books are filled with the experiences of moviemakers using their infinite resources and sagacity to overcome obstacles. Here are a few common difficulties.

Problem

The location you have chosen seemed big enough at the time, but when you arrive with the crew it seems too small, with hardly any space in which to work.

Tight corners
The clutter that accompanies any video production and shoot can make the most spacious location seem cramped. Crew must be given the time to work steadily and carefully.

Analysis

It is quite possible there is adequate space: you just need to make use of it efficiently. Before you fire the location scout, see if you can adapt the storyboard or composition to exploit the space. And unpack your equipment neatly.

Solution

Survey the space and work out how best to use it—preferably before you move in—and how camera angles or wide-angle lenses can make the space appear larger than it is. The bulkiest items are usually the lights, so see if it is possible to light the room from outside—outside the room or even from outside the building. Or reduce the number of lights you need: try bouncing off walls, for example. To improve or ensure neutral colors, hang white paper or cloths over the walls (*but see Beware the heat, p. 203*). If you need to remove furniture that is not in shot, do it before the gear is brought in. Dispense with a bulky tripod and support the camera on furniture or beanbags.

Problem

You have taken over a person's home, and they start to become nervous when you begin to unload your truckload of gear and busload of crew. You are in danger of being asked to leave.

Analysis

You have failed to prepare them properly. And the amount of crew members and equipment may be unnerving them.

Solution

If it is too late to prepare the home owners properly, you should at least have prepared the crew. If the house is carpeted, provide everyone with slip-on covers for their shoes: this shows the owners that you care about their home. Tell the crew to wear only sneakers or soft-soled shoes: high heels are absolutely forbidden. Take bubble wrap or old blankets on which to place heavy boxes of lights and equipment—this will protect furniture and polished floors. Starting by tiptoeing around the property will give the owners confidence in your professionalism.

Preparation
If you have constructed a set in someone's living accommodation, care of the property shares top priority together with safety and care of your props and equipment. Large lights may draw high current loads, so protect domestic circuitry.

Problem

You will have to film in challenging conditions—extreme cold or wet, or extremely hot and dusty.

Analysis

Working in challenging environments is worth an entire book, but planning and preparation make it possible to work almost anywhere. The main problem with cold is keeping the batteries going and preventing condensation from entering the camera. The main problem with wet is keeping condensation out of all of the electrical connections and preventing the tapes from getting damp. Dust attacks the delicate video mechanisms, but also covers the optics, degrading image quality.

Solution

Professional cameras are extremely sturdy and capable of working in very tough conditions. If you rent equipment, ensure that the rental company knows what you intend to do: they will give you advice on how to look after the gear. Amateur cameras are not built so robustly, in order to save weight and cost. Keep spare batteries warm, close to your body in cold weather; do not breathe near the camera when reloading cassettes. In damp or wet conditions, keep the camera and tapes in a waterproof

case with plenty of silica gel (which absorbs water vapor). Consider using a waterproof cover (*see p. 25*). In dusty conditions, use a waterproof case for storage or a waterproof cover, avoid changing tapes outdoors, and keep the optics free of dust with a rubber blower, which puffs air to dislodge dust.

Cold conditions
The moviemaker's camera is vulnerable in very cold conditions because the equipment is reliant on electrical power. Wrapping the camera in a protective blimp or padded cover can help protect it from cold, even if that gets in the way of the controls.

Problem

You are commissioned to video an event, such as a wedding, and find you are not the only one doing so. The others keep getting in your way.

Analysis

Now that videomaking is so much part of the culture of major life events, any family member could be wishing to video—not to mention the photographers present. And some of them may consider themselves the most important videographer or photographer present.

Solution

The best way to avoid conflict is to agree from the outset to help each other do your jobs, but also establish who has the primary position. The professionals—those who are being paid for their work—should have the best positions and be allowed to shoot before anyone else

But as soon as they have their shot, they should move aside for the others. And everyone should try not to step into another's line of sight.

Working at odds
With three videomakers and two photographers covering a Hindu wedding, it can be difficult keeping out of each other's way. If the video-camera operator shines his light into your shot, you can be sure you are an equally unwelcome part of his

Writing the screenplay

On these pages we consider the fairly formal requirements of a screenplay. One might suspect that authors who write about how to write successful screenplays are rather like financial advisers writing about how to make money: if they really knew how to do it, they would be doing it! More often than not, the rewards for doing the real thing are greater than those for writing about it, but fortunately, there are numerous excellent books (many written by successful screenwriters) to show you how to construct a story.

Defining script and screenplay

First, let us dispose of a confusion—one that even many dictionaries perpetuate. The difference between a script and a screenplay is that the script is contained within the screenplay. The script is the text of what actors or narrators say—essentially the words of the dialog—perhaps supported by indications about the style of delivery or cues as to when to begin speaking.

The screenplay includes all of the above and more: directions—intended primarily for the crew—such as the slugline (interior or exterior scene and location), lighting indications, timings,

and action to take place. Clearly scripts and screenplays are linked to one another, but they are not the same thing.

The format

The beginner screenwriter will be told that the screenplay should be written to follow certain formulaic rules of formatting. There is, of course, no single standard, even within Hollywood, though each studio may operate their own. The point of the format is to enable rapid assessment of the screenplay as to its length, complexity of production, and pace. (It is useful to note that one page of correctly formatted screenplay equates to about one minute of screen time.) If your screenplay's formatting is not in the right style, an agent or production company may not even look at it. If you know who you wish to submit to, you should ask them for their formatting rules or a sheet on their house styles.

The elements

Broadly speaking, all screenplays will consist of several distinct elements. One of the purposes of formatting is to separate these elements so that

Making changes

During production, hundreds of conversations can take place over the screenplay, which is continually crossed out and rewritten as filming progresses. The important thing is to ensure that all cast and crew members always have the latest versions of any rewritten pages.

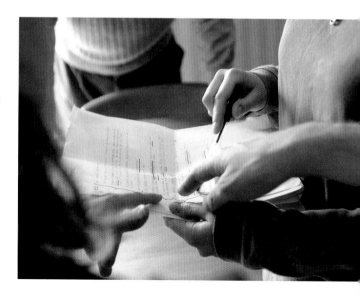

director, cast, and crew can locate them quickly, by position as well as by content. Following is a list of some of the key elements found in a screenplay.

● Action describes what is happening on screen, the scene's visual content. This example is from the shocking prologue of *Un Chien Andalou*, written by director Luis Buñuel and artist Salvador Dalí.

"A man is sharpening a razor by the balcony. The man looks at the sky through the window-panes and sees ... A light cloud moving toward the full moon. Then a young woman's head, her eyes wide open. A razor blade moves toward one of the eyes."

● The slugline or scene heading locates the scene and is always in upper-case type. Begin with INT. and EXT. for interior and exterior, followed by the location, and the time of day if relevant.

EXT. FOREST—NIGHT.

● For the script, we need the character name (again in upper-case type) and what they say, the dialog. A character may be a computer screen, with its display as the "dialog".

SCREEN
Do you want to know what the Matrix is, Neo?

● The use of an adverb in parentheses indicates to the actor how to deliver the dialog, where it may not be obvious from the words themselves.

MAXIMUS
(quietly)
A people should know when they are conquered.

● The shot indicates a shift of focus or zoom within a scene toward a person or a thing.

MAXIMUS gazes down at the German position.

Or it can indicate an actor's point of view (POV).

TRINITY'S POV: the world appears to spin.

● Transitions indicate how one shot or scene moves to the next. Generally you do not need to indicate them since it is obvious that one scene cuts to another. If a dissolve or fade is needed, the editor or director will use it.

● Finally, you will need the housekeeping features, such as act and scene numbers—the greatest variation in formatting is to be found here, with some numbering scenes cumulatively, others only within each act. Some screenwriting books even advise you to omit the numbering, since that will be done after the screenplay has been bought. Another housekeeping feature is the cast list: if several members of the cast are in shot, they are listed at the beginning of the scene.

Within this basic framework, there are also some fairly standard notions about how to show dialog interrupted by action, addition of titles, or anything superimposed over the scene.

When the thespians take over

The screen- or scriptwriter cannot be too protective of his or her work. Once the actors start speaking the lines, they are sure to come up with suggestions for changes that will improve the dialog and possibly even change some parts of the script. The wise director and writer will listen to them: if the actors feel uncomfortable with their words, it is likely that the audience will too. Actors who understand their characters often like to add to the script: the poignant last words of replicant Roy (Rutger Hauer) in *Blade Runner* were written by the actor during a rest break.

Working with the words
Actors prefer to love their lines—then they are more likely to be convincing and do not feel they have to act. And it is wise to be guided by their stage experience.

Storyboarding

When a screenplay is accepted, the words need to be turned into visuals—the storyboard—that show the framing and composition at the start of each shot, and perhaps intermediate and end positions as well if the shot tracks and zooms during the take. The process focuses the mind on to the actuality of the scene, forcing you to think about the numerous details that need to be decided. For a low-budget production, a storyboard may seem unnecessary, but having it on paper acts as a quick reminder.

You do not need to be artistic. Storyboards can be very simple, with stick figures for the characters, lines to indicate the room, and labels for camera positions. You could depict a scene with an overview of the room showing camera and actor positions and arrows to show movement.

Another approach is to use software such as FrameForge 3D Studio, which gives you a library of objects so you can build your virtual set. You can set up different camera positions around the set then zoom, pan, dolly, and crane, with all the monitors updating automatically. It is also possible to change the position, scale, and orientation of each object individually.

Calculating duration

One thing that a storyboard does not include is any way of representing duration. If that is a problem for you, a timeline in addition to the storyboard images can be useful. Try stringing the

storyboard pictures over a timeline marked out at one-minute intervals, for example, with enough space to allow for three or four pictures.

Suppose your main character is having lunch and is daydreaming: you might start with an extreme close-up of him eating the last of his pizza, then another close-up of him emptying his wine glass. Pull out to show that he is in a restaurant. He sits back—cut to an extreme close-up as his eyes become heavy, with other diners out of focus in the background—and he lets out a deep

The basic concept
A storyboard is like a cartoon version of your film: each frame summarizes the action and also suggests camera angles and lighting, with notes under each frame on pacing or effects.

Basic line or stick-figure sketch

Full graphic sketch

Final scene from movie

Storyboard styles
You do not have to be a great artist to create effective storyboards: a simple stick figure, even more simple than that shown above, can indicate camera angle and closeness of shot. A more elaborate drawing (*center*) indicates details of the set

and the lighting effect required. The actual shoot (*right*) need not follow the drawings exactly (unless stunts are called for, in which case safety may depend on accuracy). Here the DP has used a wider angle than that shown in the storyboard.

Storyboarding software

In FrameForge 3D Studio you can add characters or objects into locations you design, define camera positions and zoom settings, and create snapshots to build a storyboard.

breath. Pan away to the door: a beautiful girl walks in and over to his table. She sits across from him and takes off her jacket—her eyes fixed steadily on him… This could all happen in less than a minute of the movie, or it could take five minutes or more. A timeline helps you plan the pace of the action.

Other methods

The storyboard is not the only way to represent the video prior to shooting. One option is not to preconceive it at all. You may be good at inspiring amateur actors but not very good on camera angles: leave that job to the camera operator or

director of photography. An experienced DP should be able to work out (and perhaps sketch out) how a scene should look after reading the screenplay.

Another approach is to abbreviate the storyboard, including only the key moments, allowing the detail to be filled in during production. This approach is generally acceptable only if you are directing a very small team.

Where the narrative is not necessarily linear—as it may be in a documentary—a storyboard might not be the most appropriate model. You could try the "dartboard model." In the center, the bull's-eye, you sketch out the key shots: the climactic encounter, or the historical footage that is central to your video. Around that, encircling the central shots, you place the next most important shots: the face-to-face interviews, or the pictures that provide the facts and establish the context. In the next circle, you place the lesser shots: the establishing pan, the sequence connecting one location with another, and so on. This gives you an overview of the project and may help reveal weaknesses—too many talking heads, perhaps, or that you need some landscapes to vary the pace.

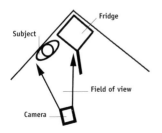

Sketching the set

Another way to storyboard is production oriented. You show the position of the camera, its view, and the positions of props, and then provide a lighting diagram. This can help with planning the management of the set and with shooting the sequence.

Crossing the line

The viewers of your video see only what you frame for them. Suppose you record a two-shot, a couple talking together. You can walk all around them and easily locate the viewer in relation to them. On one side the woman is to your left, on the other she is on your right, and at another she is in front of you. But if you were to video from each of the positions and intercut between them it will look as though the woman keeps swapping sides. That is because the viewer does not have the benefit of seeing the transitions between positions. Camera operators talk about never "crossing the line": takes should always be on the same side of an imaginary line joining the two subjects. This is also known as the 180-degree rule: if two consecutive camera angles are greater than 180 degrees apart, the actors appear to swap places.

Working safely

Although everything to do with working safely involves using common sense, that quality is the first to go once you enter complicated, fast-moving situations. Furthermore, common sense cannot be relied on when a long shoot makes everyone tired and emotional. The substitute, then, is discipline applied to a few simple rules that all crew must respect and be familiar with.

Sharing responsibility

The first and most important rule is that everyone on set is responsible for the safety of everyone else. In particular, the crew has an absolute responsibility to ensure total safety for the members of the cast. Actors cannot be expected to watch out for lights and microphone booms and trailing cords—certainly not while they are on the set. Once off set, of course, they have to take care of their head, arms, and feet, just like everyone else.

Defining the area

On larger-budget productions, a set manager will be responsible for making sure that the set functions safely and that all operations proceed smoothly, ensuring that nothing impedes the flow of moviemaking. Working with smaller budgets, and therefore with people taking on multiple roles, it is still useful to appoint a person—the continuity boy or girl, or the director's assistant—to check that there is a clear demarcation between the set and the production clutter, and that nothing is on the set that should not be. Shooting can proceed only when he or she gives the all clear. A toolbox left in the set area may not only ruin a take—it could also cause an actor to trip over.

Working on location, it is even more important to define the set area and to work neatly, mainly because it is very easy to lose small items in unfamiliar surroundings. If working outdoors, use brightly colored tape to enclose the area, so that members of the public do not wander into view. Use warning cones next to piles of cables, electrical boxes, and supports of heavy lights to keep people from venturing too close.

Keeping the electrics neat

Cabling and cords for lights and sound can be a real problem for any production that uses more than a single camera and sound recorder. Props may have to be powered too.

With planning, it should be possible to position the cords so they cause the least obstruction to the traffic of cast and crew. If necessary, cables should be enclosed in tunnels so that they are kept neat and can be stepped on without damage being caused.

Tangled wires

With separate items of equipment needing to be powered and wires going to and from mixers, a dangerous tangle will soon develop unless cables are continually neatened up. In this shot, power cables are perilously close to the tracks in the lower left of the picture, and there is even one lying across the track, where it could easily be damaged. The cables also lie across a busy route for crew. Some, but not all, of the potential problems were dealt with soon after this shot was taken.

Rules for safe working practices

Freelance workers in the film industry enjoy the discipline of the medium in which everything is subservient to getting the footage "into the can." But some people on the set may not be very experienced, especially on a small-budget production. So it is useful to set some rules at the beginning of a shoot and make sure that everyone is conversant with them.

● Everyone must know where the first-aid kit is located and who the nominated first aider is.

● Before a take, everyone turns off their cell phones or pagers or leaves the set: only the first aider may keep their phone on, set to silent alert.

● Anyone has a right to stop a take if they believe a dangerous situation is developing.

● Running on set is forbidden.

● Only gaffers and the best boy are allowed to touch high-power electrical equipment.

● Only nominated crew are allowed up on platforms, ladders, or cranes.

Public safety
Working in public areas calls for extra caution and care: while concentrating on making the video, the crew must also be aware of danger from curious or unobservant members of the public. This camera operator is using headphones that allow her to listen to the soundtrack without cutting out ambient noise.

Cables should also be kept well away from tracking (portable rails on which a truck or dolly rides). An experienced gaffer should be called in to check the safety of all but the simplest lighting setups.

Beware the heat

Luminaires used in film and video production generate wonderful floods of light but also tremendous heat. If they are placed too close to objects, they can melt, scorch, or even set light to them as heat comes out of the lamp both from the front and around the housing. Keep lamps well away from wallpaper, paintings, plastic items, and furniture. If you attach gels (transparent colored sheets) over the lamps, ensure they are heat-resistant and that the air can circulate freely around the luminaire. The gaffer or best boy should constantly monitor for overheating. Lamps should be turned off or to "trickle current" whenever they are not needed.

Shooting safely

The word "safety" is also used in conjunction with ensuring that the editor has plenty of footage to work with. Tape is not as precious as film, so it is no longer necessary to shout "Cut!" the precise second that a scene has been shot in order to save on costs. Filming should continue for several seconds after the scene is acted through, for a number of reasons:

● Handles—a few seconds before and after the clip—may be needed for fades and other transitions.

● Echoes can be allowed to die away naturally. This helps with the audio editing later and will help create a more natural sound .

● Actors' expressions and gestures may suddenly become more natural once they think shooting is over. A few seconds of footage of natural gestures or uninhibited laughter, for example, can come in handy during the editing stage.

Glossary

16:9 Ratio of width:height of a widescreen TV screen.

180° rule Camerawork and editing indication to avoid consecutive positions or cuts in a scene that point in directions greater than 180° apart.

1080i High-definition format using 1,080 active lines with interlaced scanning.

24p 24 frames per second progressive scan: a video simulation of cine film.

25i 25 frames per second interlaced, of PAL/SECAM standard.

25p 25 frames per second progressive scan.

3:2 Ratio for pull-down to convert 24 fps film to 30 fps: the first frame is held for three video fields, the next for two fields, and so on.

30° rule Rule of thumb that the camera angle on a subject should change by at least 30° between cuts.

30i 30 frames per second interlaced, of NTSC standard.

30p 30 frames per second progressive scan.

4:2:0 Sampling program in which one chrominance channel is sampled at half the rate of the luminance channel, and the remaining channel is sampled at less than a quarter of the luminance channel.

4:2:2 Sampling program in which the two chrominance channels are sampled at half the rate of the luminance channel.

4:3 Nominal ratio of width:height of a standard domestic TV screen.

480p Format using 480 lines per progressive scan frame. Also a mode of watching HDTV (high-definition television) on standard-definition sets.

720p High-definition format using 720 active lines with progressive scanning.

A

A/B-roll Editing technique using two analog players.

accessory shoe Open slot on top of a camera into which a light or microphone may be attached; also called hot shoe.

action safe area Central 95 percent of active picture area that can be seen on a video screen.

active picture area The portion of a TV picture that contains the image, excluding portions carrying synchronization signals.

acquire To transfer movie clips from camera or player to computer for NLE (nonlinear editing). Also used to mean filming or recording transmitted video.

AFM Audio Frequency Modulation: method of processing high-fidelity audio signals.

A-frame The first and only film frame captured complete on adjacent video fields.

AGC Automatic Gain Control: electronics that monitor the strength of an incoming signal and maintain correct levels.

AIFF Audio Interchange File Format: uncompressed file format for audio; widely used for digitally sampled recordings.

aliased Stepped or jagged appearance of lines or borders caused by a low resolution of video chip.

ambient noise Background noise such as the sound of wind, traffic, and so on.

A-mode Editing method that uses scenes or takes in the order they were shot: usually applied to working with film reels.

analog An effect, representation, or record that is proportionate to another physical property or change.

anamorphic Optical effect or design that squeezes a wide view into a narrow format.

angle The same scene and action filmed from different viewpoints or perspectives.

animation In digital video, the process of changing features, such as color and text, over time.

aperture Lens setting that controls the amount of light entering the lens. A large aperture (say, f/2) lets in more light than a small aperture (f/22). Also, anachronistically, known as f-stop.

APS Automatic Picture Search: facility built into digital video cameras that enables the beginning of a clip to be located.

artifact Visible or audible feature that was not present in the original or is a distortion of the original, such as flickering, ghosting, or streaking.

aspect ratio Ratio of a frame's width to its height. Also picture ratio. Usually 4:3 (or 1.33:1) or widescreen of 16:9 (or 1.78:1).

authoring Process of creating DVD programs, including the designing of interface, collecting the materials, organizing into chapters, adding extra content, and writing to disc.

autoexposure Camera-controlled settings aimed at giving correct exposure.

auto-iris Automatically controlled iris diaphragm or lens aperture used in digital video cameras as one of the controls for exposure.

autoplay Feature of players or software to play a DVD or VCD on insertion.

AVI Audio-Video Interleaved: codec and protocol for sound and video promoted by Microsoft.

Glossary continued

B

backlight switch Control that increases exposure to compensate for strong lighting coming from behind the subject.

balance Comparison of the volume of the channels of stereo or multiphonic sound.

balanced Said of a cable or connector that has three lines to separate the signals from power.

bandwidth Measure of the amount of information needed by a system in order to handle a stream of video or sound signals.

bars and tone Broad patches of colors and an audio tone used to calibrate audio and video signals.

batch capture Using software to capture all the marked clips from a tape in one pass, rather than one clip at a time.

best boy Assistant to the gaffer.

Betacam Tape format widely used in broadcast video, particularly as Betacam SP and Digital Betacam.

Betamax Analog video format withdrawn in 2002; recognized by professionals as superior to VHS, its rival format for the domestic user.

B-frame Bidirectional predictive: a type of frame used in MPEG coding based on both preceding and following frames.

bin In nonlinear editing, a folder containing and organizing working digital video clips. Named after the cloth basket over which strips of film were hung.

black level Measure of the black portion of a video signal: 7.5 IRE for NTSC, 0 IRE for PAL.

black striping Recording blank footage on tape prior to shooting in order to lay a timecode.

blooming Effects visible when phosphors on a TV monitor are excited to too high a level—details soften, contrast is distorted, blacks are poor, and midtones are inaccurate.

blue screen Evenly colored blue background against which a subject is filmed to provide footage for chromakey work. Also synonymous with chromakey.

BNC Connector type used in electronics: features a coaxial cable with a central pin with rotating metal collar for locking.

Book A, Book B, and so on Standards defining DVDs: Book A: the physical format; B: DVD-Video format; C: DVD-Audio format; D: DVD-R format; E: DVD-RAM format.

boom Long pole used to extend the reach of a microphone, especially to hold it out of shot, above the action.

broadcast-legal Video images that comply with broadcast standards for brightness range and color.

broadcast quality Video signal that meets the appropriate national broadcasting standards—for example, FCC or EBU.

B-roll Footage used to intercut into primary sequence or soundtrack—for example, to illustrate an interviewee's comment. Also footage used to provide cutaways.

burning Process of creating a CD by writing data to the disc.

bus-powered Equipment that needs only one cable, which carries both data and power.

button On screen, an area of projected image that is active and can be clicked on with a pointer or cursor to start an action such as play or fast-forward.

C

cable basher Person responsible for ensuring cables and trailing leads do not "bash" into equipment or personnel.

camcorder CAMera-reCORDER: the combination of video camera with a device to record the video.

capstan Part of a tape player that spins and—pressed against the pinch roller—draws the tape through the machine.

capture Process of making a video or digital-image recording. Also, process of recording one source of video on to another, such as from analog to digital.

cardioid Type of microphone that accepts sound from a wide angle, including a little from behind.

cassette Housing for tape consisting of a plastic shell and reels for tape; may contain a microchip for memory and a switch to prevent recording.

CCD Charge-Coupled Device: semiconductor sensor used to capture light and form the video image; may be single, covered with a filter pattern, or used in a set of three.

CCIR 601 A standard or protocol for digitizing video; also known as D1.

cell Unit of video of any length on a DVD; used for organizing or grouping content.

channel Set of data or signals relating to a specific range or measure—for example, the left and right channels in stereo sound or the luminance or chrominance channels of video.

chapters Sections or bookmarked parts of a DVD program that allow the user to navigate through the movie, jumping from one section to any other.

chroma Color information data, measured independently of light levels.

chromakey Replacement of areas of the same color with image from another video. The subject is shot against a uniform blue- or green-screen background (hence the alternative name of "blue screen") in preparation for replacement during compositing.

chrominance Measure of the depth or richness of color.

clamp White or black clamp: adjustment to luminance levels to bring them into legal or standard limits.

clapperboard Small sign with a hinged arm that can be closed quickly to make a loud noise to aid synchronization of soundtrack and movie. Usually written on to indicate scene, take number, and time.

clip A single take or section of a movie consisting of an unbroken sequence of frames.

coaxial Type of cable or socket in which a central conductor core is surrounded by insulation material. Often abbreviated to co-ax.

codec COmpression/DECompression: routines that code and decode signals from video or sound.

cold Negative polarity in an interconnect or circuit.

color correction Use of filters or postproduction techniques to alter white balance, in order to produce true neutral colors.

color space Method or model for describing the way color is processed in the camera; may refer also to compression of color signal.

color temperature Measure of the color of illumination of a scene.

comb filter Electronic filter that alternately accepts and cuts out certain frequencies, and which, when matched to signals carried at different frequencies, separates the information. Used to decode composite video signals.

combo drive Drive that is capable of reading both DVD-ROM or DVD-RW and CDs, as well as writing CD-R media.

component video Video signal transmission using three components: luminance, luminance minus red (Pr), and luminance minus blue (Pb)—for example, in DVD video. Provides superior quality to composite video.

composite video Video signal transmission that combines the chrominance and luminance channels. The receiving equipment must separate the signals using a notch or comb filter.

compositing Blend or superimposition of two or more different images to create a new but visually coherent image.

compression Process of reducing the file size of a video or music recording.

contrast Measure of the difference between the brightest part of a scene, or the brightest that can be recorded, and the darkest part of a scene, or the darkest that can be recorded.

crew Personnel preparing for or producing a movie, as opposed to the talent.

cross-dissolve Transition in which the end of a clip fades to nothing while, at the same time, the next clip starts from invisible to become fully visible.

cross-fade Transition between two audio clips: as the first fades to nothing, the next rises to normal levels.

CRT Cathode Ray Tube: type of monitor or display using a large glass tube with electronics at one end and a phosphor-coated viewing area at the other.

cue Fast-forward movement or search of tape with display of picture. Also, event or word used to signal another event, such as the start of actor's speech.

cukie Cucoloris: mask with cutouts used with a light source to project shadows. Also known as gobo.

cut Simple, immediate transition or change from one video clip to another, or from one sound source to another.

cutaway Movie clip that interrupts a sequence in order to, for example, illustrate an item mentioned by interviewee. Also used to conceal editing problems.

D

DAT Digital audio tape.

data rate Speed at which data can be transferred from a source; usually measured in Mb/s or Mbps (megabits—not megabytes—per second).

dB Decibel: measure of ratio of power between two signals. 3dB is and sounds like a doubling in power, -3dB is a halving of power.

de-interlace Process of preparing video signals for use on, for example, computer screens. A de-interlace filter converts two interlaced frames to create a single still image.

depth of field Measure of zone or distance in front of and behind zone of best focus over which a subject appears acceptably sharp. Appears much greater than with still images because of movement.

device control Feature of digital video camera that allows it to be controlled by NLE (nonlinear

Glossary continued

editing) software in computer when connected by FireWire/i.Link/IEEE 1394.

digital zoom Increase of the apparent magnification of an image through software processing; there is no actual increase in magnification.

disc key Data passed between DVD and DVD player to allow decryption of the disc.

dissolve Fading or diminution of a signal while another rises to replace the fading signal.

Dogme, Dogme 95, or Dogma Style of movie production using handheld camera, available light, no effects or exaggeration, and minimal postproduction work.

Dolby Digital Method of coding sound that is internationally accepted. Compression method for NTSC discs.

Dolby Surround Method of encoding surround sound (three-dimensional) in a stereo signal.

dolly Movement of the camera position in toward a scene or out from it along camera-lens axis.

down-mix Combine several audio channels into two stereo channels.

DP Director of photography: person in charge of camera positions, moves, and settings.

drop-frame timecode NTSC protocol that drops two frame numbers a minute, except for tens of minutes, to compensate for the noninteger frame rate.

drum Cylinder around which the tape is wound during recording or playback for reading data on tape.

Dutch angle Camera position in which the camera is held at an obvious angle to the horizontal.

DVCam Professional digital video format: records 8-bit images, 5:1 compressed, with 4:1:1 color sampling.

DVCPro Standard definition used in broadcasting, running DV format at twice the consumer format speed; records 8-bit images, 5:1 compressed, with 4:1:1 color sampling. Also known as D-7.

DVD Digital Versatile Disc: method of storing data using microscopic changes into two or more layers in a CD-like disc. Depending on format, 4.7 GB capacities and higher are available.

DVD-Audio Sound-only version of DVD.

DVD-Video File format, based on MPEG-2, for video used in DVD, currently offers widest compatibilities. DVD-Video (fast editable) is a variant usable on DVD-RW or DVD+RW discs.

DV Stream Raw video format used for recording video image, prior to processing such as compression or gamma.

E

EDL Text file annotating the edits making up a sequence, based on timecodes of clips. It enables projects to be moved between different NLE systems and to coordinate large editing projects.

encoding Conversion of analog video or sound signals into a compressed digital form.

establishing shot A take that sets the scene, describing the context in which action is to take place.

export Software feature that allows a movie to be converted into different file formats.

eyeline Axis extending from imaginary line between two actors' eyes.

F

fade Effect that gradually turns the picture to a plain background—for example, fade to black means the image becomes darker and darker.

fader Sliding controls in audio mixing that alter balance of tracks.

field Half of an interlaced frame, containing either all the even-numbered or all the odd-numbered scan lines making up the image.

FireWire Name used by Apple Computer Inc for IEEE 1394 connectors. See also i.Link.

foley Sound effects created and recorded separately from the video for use in a movie, often synchronized to the action—such as a door closing, for example.

format Rules or protocol controlling the way data is coded and organized in a recording.

fps Frames per second: rate at which cinematographic film is recorded or displayed.

frame One portion of a sequence of pictures that makes up the movie, shown at varying rates according to the video standard. May be interlaced or progressive scan.

freeze A single frame of a movie displayed on screen for a period of time.

f/stop See aperture.

G

gaffer Electrician or lighting technician on a movie set.

gain In video: measure of level of white. In audio: measure of loudness level.

gamma Curve that defines contrast characteristics of a frame. Its shape may be varied to simulate, for example, the "film look."

GB Gigabyte: one decimal million bytes (in some cases may equal one binary million).

generators Clips synthesized by software from existing frames to be used as backgrounds, titles, or composited elements.

genlock GENerator LOCKing: a system of devices that enable a TV monitor to accept two signals at a time in order, for example, to combine graphics with a video image. Also, circuitry or signals that lock video and audio tracks together.

gobo A mask with shapes cut out of it for use with a light source to project shadows for lighting effects. Also known as cukie or cucoloris. Also, any device used to shield a microphone from extraneous noise.

H

handles Spare frames at the beginning and end of clips to allow adjustment in timecodes.

head Start or beginning of a clip or take. Also, component of recorder that writes data to the tape or reads from it.

HDMI High-Definition Multimedia Interface: a digital interface between audio and video sources and an audio or TV receiver.

HDTV High-Definition Television: any format that offers higher definition than the current standard.

Hi8 Analogue recording format using 8 mm tape, with resolution of 400 lines.

histogram Software display of distribution of luminance values in a frame.

hot Positive polarity in an interconnect or circuit.

I

IEEE Institute of Electrical and Electronic Engineers: international organization setting standards for the electronics industry.

i.Link Name used by Sony Corp for IEEE 1394 connectors. Also known as FireWire.

image stabilization Electronic or optical technology designed to compensate for camera shake. Elements in the lens may move, or the sensor itself is moved.

incoming Side of a clip that is on the B-side of a cut or the right hand of a transition: the next in time.

in point Start of a clip or sequence defined by an edit.

insert edit An edit in which material is added into an existing sequence. No material is removed, therefore the timeline is increased.

interlaced video Video signal made up of two fields of alternate scanning lines.

IRE International Radio Engineers—usually refers to light intensity scale: 100 is pure white, 0 is black.

J

jog Viewing a clip one frame at a time, backward or forward.

JPEG Joint Photographic Experts Group: organization setting standards for compressed formats for images. JPEG 2000 is a complex form of image compression.

jump cut Editing that produces a sudden or abrupt change of subject, scale, or tone between two shots—usually from the same camera position. May also refer to an abrupt change with no attempt to maintain continuity.

K

key color Color that is to be removed with a composited image during chromakeying—usually blue or green to provide the best contrast with skin.

key frame Frame or graphic that is used as basis or target for a transition or animation. Also the control that uses two defined key frames in order to calculate the transition from one (the basis) to the other (the target).

keying Process of removing a key color with a mask, prior to compositing.

key light Light source providing the main, usually brightest, illumination on a subject.

kicker Lamp placed on the same side as the fill lamp, used to emphasize detail or facial contours.

knee Point on the tone-characteristic curve that can be adjusted to change tone reproduction .

L

Laser Disc Disc similar to a DVD but 12 in (30 cm) in diameter, for storing a movie in analog form.

lav Short for lavalier-type microphone, which is worn on around the neck on a chain or string.

legal Video signal that meets broadcast standards.

letterbox Shape of broadcast or projected feature film whose picture ratio is greater than that of the screen format; top and bottom of the screen are left blank.

linear editing Editing system using tape or film that must be spooled or wound past successive clips in order to access a specific clip. Antonym of nonlinear editing.

line level Low signal carrying data between components in an audio system30 cmfor example, from mixer to recorder. Known as +4dBu.

log List of entries about each movie clip detailing name, scene, grade or quality, duration, and so on.

Glossary continued

long shot Composition in which people or objects are seen from a distance; often an establishing shot.

loop Short recording of a sound that plays continuously without break—for example, a drum beat, water flowing, or a piece of music.

LP Long Play: when video tape is run at a slower speed to increase recording time, but at lower quality.

luma Colloquial form of luminance; may be used to refer to video gain.

luma key Filter used to select or mask off a certain brightness value, usually based on the brightest or darkest part of the frame.

luminance Measure of the amount of light emitted or reflected from a subject.

M

master clip Footage of a take as originally shot, from which portions may be taken for editing.

match-frame edit Process of synchronizing a video frame with a sound cue.

medium close-up Framing that takes in a person from the head to below and just wider than the shoulders.

medium shot Framing that takes in a person from the head to below the knees.

MicroDV Micro digital video: format for video making use of very small cassette tapes.

MiniDV Mini digital video: format for video using small tapes holding 60 minutes of movie at standard-play speed.

MOS Video recording made without sound; often cited as deriving from German director Erich von Stroheim's instruction to shoot "mit out sound."

motion path Route of an animation or changes of shape, based on position of key frames within the TV format.

MP3 MPEG-1, Layer 3: audio compression component of MPEG-1, widely used for music. Note: not supported in DVD-Video or DVD-Audio.

MPEG Motion Picture Experts Group: organization setting standards for movie picture compression formats.

multicast Streaming video to many users from a single server.

N

native System that uses files or data in their original form without, for example, converting or compressing it for faster handling in off-line editing.

nighttime mode Feature of Dolby Digital that allows movies to be listened to at low volume without impairing audibility of speech. On digital video cameras, a feature that allows recording in absence of visible light, using infrared light.

NLE Nonlinear editing: editing based on an ability to access any part of any clip directly without having to pass any other clip. Based on random access of digitally stored movies.

noise Unwanted elements in a signal: in audio, heard as hiss or crackle; in video, seen as flecks of light or odd colors.

noninterlaced video Representation of video used on computer screens where there is no need to interlace the frames. Also known as progressive scan.

nonsquare pixel Broadcast pixels are not square: NTSC pixels are narrower than square, while PAL pixels are wider.

NTSC Color broadcast encoding standard used mainly in North America and Japan, with a nominal resolution of 525 lines and frame rate of 30 fps.

O

off-line clips Movie footage that is registered in a log but not held on computer hard disk.

off-line editing Use of smaller compressed or proxy files during editing, to lower the workload on the computer.

one-chip Digital video camera using a single CCD chip as a sensor, as opposed to triple-sensor or triple-chip cameras.

one-shot Short soundtrack of a single event, such as a door slamming, or a door bell ringing.

opacity Measure of how much can be see through a layer or image.

OTS Over the shoulder: framing a shot so that part of the back of a person's head is visible, framing a second person who faces the camera.

out point End or stopping point of a clip in an edit.

overblack titles Titles placed over a solid color (not only black) instead of over an image or sequence.

overlay Superimposition of an image or text on to video footage.

overscan The excess of scanning lines of a video image, such that it is larger than a TV screen. It allows for differences in TV sets or may contain information.

overwrite edit An edit in which a clip is replaced by another of equal length, so the sequence duration is not changed.

P

PAL Phase Alternating Line: color broadcast encoding standard used in most areas of world, except for North America and Japan.

pan Distribution of sound between the left- and right-hand channels, determining stereo sound position or movement of mono sound between channels. Also, a camera movement that follows action—usually in a horizontal plane—from a fixed position.

pan and scan Simulation of panning movement after video has been shot by cropping to a small portion, then moving across the view with successive frames.

pan/tilt Horizontal and vertical movements, respectively, of the camera, around an axis vertical to the camera-lens axis.

parade scope Type of wave-form monitor that separates red, blue, and green into separate displays.

part of title Technical term for chapter or section of a DVD title.

PCM Pulse Code Modulation: format of digital serial signal used in CD sound encoding.

pedestal Black level: for PAL it is set at 0 IRE; for NTSC, 7.5 IRE.

phantom power Provision of power to microphone by applying a voltage to the wires carrying the audio signal – for example, two pins of XLR carry the same voltage, usually 48v.

pink noise Uniform or steady level of audible noise.

PIP Picture-in-picture: placement of a stills picture or video within the frame of the full-frame picture or video through the use of masks.

pixel Picture element: the smallest element of a digital image; may be square or slightly rectangular. *See also* nonsquare pixel.

plate Image that replaces the key color during compositing.

plug-and-play Collaboration between computer operating system and hardware intended to make it easy to use new equipment. No software installation is needed, so you simply plug in the equipment to use it (in theory).

preproduction Moviemaking phase prior to shooting. Includes research, scriptwriting, building talent and crew, storyboarding, set design, and production or location permits.

point source A source of light that appears to be emitted from a small point.

port Input or output socket built into equipment to accept appropriate connector.

poster frame Single frame taken from a clip to stand for or represent the clip.

postproduction Moviemaking phase following shooting. Includes capture and log, editing, special effects, sound editing, rendering, and outputting.

practicals Lighting that can be seen in shot: may not be used actually to illuminate the scene—for example, candles to set period or atmosphere.

preroll Blank tape for 2–3 seconds before recording on the tape commences; needed for timecode accuracy.

production stills Photography of movie being made, including key moments from the action and behind-the-scenes documentation.

progressive scan Recording an entire frame at a time; used to create the "film look."

prosumer Equipment capable of professional or near-professional quality results, but designed mainly for use by experienced amateur.

pull-down Slowing down of frame rates to enable one format to be rendered in another, in ratio 3:2 for 24 fps to 30 fps.

Q R

QuickTime Application for viewing multimedia. Also standards created by Apple Computer Inc. for integrating video and sound into applications.

rack focus Using change of focus of lens during a take without change in camera position to direct viewer's attention. Requires digital video cameras with a manual focus control.

rendering Process of turning editing decisions and applied transitions into the final video, including any changes to the format and levels of compression.

resolution Measure of detail visible: in video, usually measured on the horizontal axis for a distance equal to the height of the picture.

rim Lamp placed behind subject's head that is used to highlight or rim light the hair (or outline of the head if the subject lacks hair).

ripple edit An edit affecting a selected range of clips in such a way that a trim of one affects the others.

roll edit An edit affecting two clips that share an edit point.

rostrum camera Setup or rig used to simulate movement in and around a two-dimensional subject, in order to animate a print.

rotoscope Process of creating an animated matte or mask that indicates the shape of an object or actor at each frame of a sequence for compositing.

Glossary continued

rough cut Edit of clips into the scripted or storyboarded order but not refined as to timing and synchronization with sound.

RT Real time: effect, transition, or other change that can playback on screen immediately, as opposed to needing time to render.

S

safe title area Central part of the picture that will not be clipped or cropped by any screen it is viewed on. Usually some 80 percent of the total image area. Also called title safe area.

sample rate Usually applied to audio: the rate at which sound is analyzed during digitization: for CDs, the rate is 44.1 KHz; for digital audio, it is 48 KHz.

scanning In video, the movement of the electron beam across the face of a CRT monitor screen.

SCART Syndicat des Constructeurs d'Appareils Radiorécepteurs et Téléviseurs: type of multiple-pin connector used between TV and VCR.

scratch disk Hard disk reserved for working files during NLE (nonlinear editing): it must turn at at least 7,200 rpm, have ample capacity, and not be set to power down when not used.

scrim Semitransparent fabric used for lighting effects: appearing opaque when lit from in front and translucent when lit from behind.

scrub Viewing a clip by manipulating the play head—that is, at a variable speed.

SECAM Sequential Color with Memory: color broadcast encoding standard used in Europe, with frame rate of 25 fps and 720 x 546 pixel dimensions over 625 lines.

second unit Camera crew that shoots action from a different position compared to the main or first unit, to give vast increase in editing freedom.

sector Physical group of data recorded: on a DVD, a sector contains 38,688 bits of channel data and 2,048 bytes of user information.

sequence Short for a sequence of edited cuts.

set-top player DVD or other player designed to work with a domestic TV set.

shotgun Type of microphone with a long barrel to accept sound from narrow angle.

shuttle Viewing a clip backward or forward at variable speed.

slate See clapperboard.

slip edit Editing decision in which a clip within a sequence is changed by moving the edit points

so that the duration of the whole sequence is maintained.

slugline Scene heading in a screenplay indicating location of action, time of day, and possibly production information, too.

SMPTE/EBU timecode Format for timecode in the form hours:minutes:seconds:frame number. The maximum frame number for PAL is 24; for NTSC, it is 29.

sound report Annotation of recorded sound, listing each different take with settings.

SP Standard Play: recording or replaying a videotape at normal speed.

spark Electrician in the production team. Also called a sparkie.

sprite Graphic that can move, following set rules, within another graphic.

stereo Stereophony or stereophonic: sound reproduction that aims to give impression of depth and distance.

stop-frame animation A movie shot one frame at a time, with small changes to positions of models made from, for example, clay or Lego pieces.

straight cut Changing directly from one clip or take to another without any transition effect.

streaming video Video broadcast over the Internet in which the recipient can view the start of video while the rest is being loaded.

subsample To take fewer measurements when digitizing, in order to reduce flow of data.

superwhite Brightness level of video higher than 100 IRE; a white higher than the legal level.

surround sound Sound or entertainment system that uses more than the two channels of stereo sound with the intention of creating a three-dimensional sound stage.

SVCD Super Video CD: format originated in China and used in Far East, based on MPEG-2, offering quality level between those of VCD and DVD.

S-VHS Version of VHS offering higher resolution—400 lines rather than 240 lines.

S-Video Super-Video: a signal transmission protocol for video that separates the luminance and chrominance channels. Also known as Y/C.

swish pan Rapid panning movement that blurs the image.

sync, or synch To synchronize—that is, to ensure than two events occur simultaneously or that signals run at the same time.

T

take To shoot or record a movie. Also, one of possibly many attempts at shooting a scene.

talent Actors or extras taking part in a movie; as opposed to the crew.

telecine Device for transferring a cinematographic film to a video format.

tilt Movement of the camera upward or downward, rotating around an axis at right angles to the camera-lens axis.

timecode Reference data stored with each frame, displaying cumulatively in the format hours:minutes: seconds:frame number. *See* SMPTE/EBU.

titles Text and pictures at the start or end of a movie to introduces the film and/or list credits.

title safe area *See* safe title area.

track Element or component of information, such as alternative languages or subtitles for a DVD movie.

tracking Following the action, keeping the camera at a constant distance from the action in a movement at right angles to the camera-lens axis.

trimming Process of removing excess movie clips during the editing process by deleting frames.

triple-sensor Set of three CCD sensor chips used to capture red, green, and blue separations of the image; the best solution where highest image quality is needed. Also called triple-chip.

twitter Flickering of horizontally oriented detail due to interference with interlacing lines.

two-shot Framing that shows both parties in a conversation or interview.

U V

unicast Streaming video to a single user from a server.

VBI Vertical Blanking Interval: that portion of a TV signal that is left clear—blanked of picture—in order to allow screen redraw. Now used for captions and other data.

VCD Video CD: video format that uses MPEG compression to record to ordinary CDs, delivering quality similar to VHS.

VCR Video cassette recorder: recording and playback device for video, generally reserved for analog devices. The most common format is VHS.

VHS Video Home Services: obsolescent analog video format used for recording TV broadcasts for later playback and (less so now) video film rentals.

video capture card Special circuit boards equipped with processors and memory designed to convert analog video to digital. It slots into an expansion bay on a computer.

voice-over Recording of narration or spoken text made separately from movie footage that runs along with the moving images.

VR Virtual Reality: images designed to involve the viewer or audience in the action or to place them within a virtual space that represents a real or invented space.

W

wave-form monitor Graphic display of distribution of brightness and saturation in a frame.

webcam Digital camera attached to a computer to allow other computers to view images from the camera through an Internet connection.

white level Brightest permissible image: it should be lower than the maximum for the monitor screen.

widescreen Format whose width-to-height ratio is nominally 16:9.

wide shot Framing that shows a wide-angle view of the scene, to take in as much as possible—often used as an establishing shot.

wild track Sound recording made separately from the video; sound recording not synchronized to action.

windjammer Fluffy or furry cover for a microphone, designed to reduce wind noise.

wipe Transition in which the first clip is erased or wiped like a windscreen blade to reveal the next clip.

X Y Z

XLR Ground Left Right: type of connector and cable providing balanced audio lines.

Y Symbol for luminance; a channel of Y/C video.

Y/C Video signal transmission that separates the Y (luminance) channel and the C (chrominance) channels. Also known as S-Video.

YCrCB Color space defined by three axes of luminance (Y) and color difference signals, the red and blue.

zebra pattern Display available in high-quality cameras shown as alternating black and white stripes that appear in bright areas. Used to discover illegal video levels.

zoom ratio Ratio between longest and shortest focal length of a zoom lens; may include optical and digital zoom lengths.

www.resources

GENERAL DIGITAL VIDEO

www.moviemaker.com
One of the best sites for the aspiring moviemaker, distinguished by first-rate writing throughout—a must-visit and must-bookmark site for regular doses of inspiration.

www.creativecow.net
A lively site highly populated with discussion groups, reviews, tutorials, and feature articles on just about anything to do with creative visual and time-based digital media. Well worth bookmarking, but be warned: you could spend a lot of time browsing.

www.videohelp.com
Appropriately named treasure trove of data, how-to articles, and explanatory guides. Worth bookmarking.

www.labdv.com
Excellent site with a wide range of information, from the introductory to the highly technical, on many aspects of digital video.

www.practicaldv.com
Modest portal offering a helpful range of short articles as well as information including lists of film courses in North America and the UK.

www.camcorderinfo.com
News, reviews, and features on many video cameras, as well as many user groups and technique guides.

www.dv.com
Free registration is needed before you can access useful parts of this site, but there is a fair range of information aimed largely at the experienced videographer.

www.atomiclearning.com
Paying subscribers have access to an enormous amount of tutorials, but a good number of tasters are available for free.

www.kenstone.net
Kenneth Stone offers helpful advice and information on many aspects of digital video; strong on Final Cut Pro.

www.videonetwork.org
This site is part of an initiative supporting the making of video for positive change and includes independent, activist, and experimental videomakers. Lots of useful, practical advice.

FILM AND FESTIVALS

www.imdb.com
The Internet Movie Database is a superb resource on films with extensive filmographies of directors, writers, history, and news—plenty to keep film lovers happy for hours. Add to your Favorites.

www.res.com
For listings of digital film festivals and screenings. Also some streaming content and reviews.

www.filmunderground.com
www.24fps.com
These linked sites provide information, contacts, help, and advice for the independent moviemaker, with upcoming projects and forums.

www.filmfestivalrotterdam.com
Active site with library of numerous stills from movies featured in the Rotterdam Film Festival.

www.britfilms.com
A portal to all things to do with British moviemaking. Includes an excellent directory of links to film festivals around the world.

www.advancedmovingimage.com
Reviews of creative use of moving-image media; being developed but worth keeping an eye on.

CAREERS AND BUSINESS

www.videouniversity.com
Study courses and tips for those wishing to turn their digital video skills to business use, with useful links and information.

www.khake.com
The Vocational Information Center's site offers advice about careers: click on "Photography and Film" and "Visual Arts."

COPYRIGHT

http://fairuse.stanford.edu
Excellent coverage of fair-use issues from the viewpoint of US law; also wider intellectual-property matters.

www.dfc.org
The Digital Futures Coalition runs a lively site useful for keeping up with the copyright issues of the day and access to key documents.

TV HISTORY

www.tvhistory.tv
Comprehensive and fascinating history of television, with thousands of sets illustrated and useful links.

DVDs AND VCDs

www.dvddemystified.com
A useful set of frequently asked questions (and answers) covering all aspects of DVD authoring and use, with links to technical sources.

www.dvdrhelp.com
Highly informative site with a great deal of practical information, downloads, and a user forum, including DVD hacks.

www.labdv.com
Technical resources with links on DVD and Super VCD.

MICROPHONES, RECORDING, AND INTERCONNECTS

www.ramelectronics.net
Essentially a reference for modern interconnects, with useful data and some links to help, installation instructions, and technical background.

www.sounddevices.com
The technical documents provided on the Sound Devices site provide clear and concise information on sound recording, microphones, and interconnects.

www.kenstone.net
Practical advice on location sound recording and other aspects of digital sound.

NEWS REPORTING AND TV

www.reporterworld.com
Handy site offering an interesting mix of clothes and equipment for field use, books, films, advice, and useful links, including government sites.

http://SYPHAonline.com
Comprehensive guide to software and equipment for the professional videomaker.

www.broadcastvideo.com
Marketplace for equipment and freelancer listings throughout the world. Good range of links.

www.broadcast.net
Portal for the broadcast TV industry: information, standards, links to manufacturers and suppliers.

SCRIPTWRITING

www.moviescriptsandscreenplays.com
Extensive links to numerous sites offering new and classic scripts, as well as advice and help.

www.writemovies.com
Portal for movie news, contests, and a treasure trove of scripts—a must-bookmark site for the film lover.

www.screenstyle.com
Portal for buying books and software on scriptwriting, with lots of advice and help.

www.iscriptdb.com
Portal to film-scripts database.

SOFTWARE AND EQUIPMENT RESOURCES
Nonlinear editing

Adobe Editing and effects software.
   www.adobe.com

Apple Editing, effects, and titling software ranging from amateur to professional.
   www.apple.com

Avid Industry-standard software.
   www.avid.com

Canopus Editing, conversion, and encoding software; some accessories.
   www.canopuscorp.com

MacXware Media Edit Pro software for video editing with picture-in-picture abilities and painting effects.
   www.macxware.com

Roxio Basic editing software; leading burning software.
   www.roxio.com

Sony Editing and media-related software, including Vegas.
   http://mediasoftware.sonypictures.com/

Strata Basic editing software.
   www.strata.com

Ulead Intermediate-level editing and DVD-creation software.
   www.ulead.com

www.resources continued

Screenwriting
Final Draft Applications for screenwriting and audio-visual scripts; for Apple and Windows.
www.finaldraft.com
Movie Magic Screenwriter Applications for creative writing, including screenplays.
www.screenplay.com
Sophocles Screenwriting software designed to improve story navigation; Windows only.
www.sophocles.net
Media Services Portal to a very wide range of software for the media industry.
www.media-services.com
Scriptware Popular screenwriting software.
www.scriptware.com

VIDEO SOURCES
www.artbeats.com
Stock footage: valuable to see what professionals make of very short clips.
www.dvworldclips.com
Video clips from around the world.
www.gotfootage.com
Broad range of material for download.
www.filmdisc.com
High-quality, royalty-free clips.

ROYALTY-FREE MUSIC AND SOUND EFFECTS
www.shockwave-sound.com
Royalty-free music, sound effects, and loops.
www.chrisworthproductions.com
Royalty-free music, some full-length.

EFFECTS
Digital Juice Supplier of royalty-free graphical content for video: transitions, effects, animated overlays for PIP, still images, and more.
www.digitaljuice.com
Moving Picture Effective tools for the digital equivalent of rostrum camera work, and animating images over video.
www.stagetools.com
Pixélan Supplier of plug-ins for "organic" transitions and effects working in NLE applications from Final Cut Pro to Movie Maker.
www.pixelan.com

Stupendous Comprehensive range of iMovie plug-ins, with an extensive amount of film-look effects.
www.stupendous-software.com
Virtix Plug-in effects for Final Cut, iMovie, and After Effects.
www.virtix.com

UTILITIES
Encoding
www.discreet.com
Range of postproduction software, some industry-leading, running on a variety of platforms.
www.pixeltools.com
Expert-1 is an encoder for MPEG that promises superior quality to real-time encoders. Offers good levels of control; Windows NT or Silicon Graphics.

Color correction and look
www.redgiantsoftware.com
Plug-ins to standard software to change the look of video.
www.synthetic-ap.com
Utilities for color correction, calibration, and color bars, tone generation, and other postproduction work.

Logging software
www.imagineproducts.com
Software for speeding up the logging-in process: HD Log-X for Mac OS X, TEPX for Windows, and other management utilities.

PREPRODUCTION TOOLS
Scriptwriting
www.finaldraft.com
www.scriptware.com
Specialized software facilitating the formatting of scripts, screenplays, and production schedules. Also, budgeting, legal forms, and more.
www.movietools.com
Home site of *The Guerilla Film Makers Movie Blueprint*: free screenplay software and inexpensive software for producers.

EQUIPMENT MANUFACTURERS

ABC Products Camera stabilizers, mounts, and balance accessories.
www.abc-products.de

Apple Computers and accessories.
www.apple.com

Audio-Technica Microphone systems and audio accessories.
www.audio-technica.com

Avid Industry-leading NLE software and systems.
www.avid.com

Azden Microphone systems and audio accessories.
www.azdencorp.com

Canon Video cameras and professional lenses for video.
www.canon.com

Dedo Light Highest-quality compact lighting units.
www.dedolight.com

DHA Lighting Gobos, projection equipment, lighting effects.
www.dhalighting.com

Flarebuster Accessory holder, anchored to a hot shoe, for shade or reflector.
www.flarebuster.com

Gitzo Tripods and related accessories.
www.gitzo.com

Hitachi AV equipment, including monitors, recorders, and camcorders.
www.hitachi.com

Hollywood Lite Stabilizers and vests for camera-operators.
www.hollywoodlite.com

JVC Range of video equipment, from consumer to professional, plus wide range of electronic equipment.
www.jvc.com

KonicaMinolta Exposure and color-temperature meters.
www.konicaminolta.com

Lee Filters Comprehensive range of color and effects filters for lamps (in foils and rolls) and for camera lenses.
www.leefilters.com

Manfrotto Tripods, accessories, and background supports.
www.manfrotto.com

Miglia Interface and conversion products, expansion cards, and mass storage.
www.miglia.com

PAG Batteries for professional systems, portable/on-camera lighting.
www.paguk.com

Panasonic Video equipment, from consumer to professional, plus a wide range of electronic equipment.
www.panasonic.com

Pinnacle Video cards, software from amateur to professional and broadcast.
www.pinnaclesys.com

P+S Technik Professional accessories for video cameras, including 35 mm simulation.
www.pstechnik.de

Sachtler Tripods, stabilizing systems, and lighting.
www.sachtler.com

Samsung Digital video cameras, digital cameras, and other electronic goods.
www.samsung.com

Sanyo Amateur video equipment plus wide range of electronic products.
www.sanyo.com

Sennheiser Microphones, headphones, and other audio equipment.
www.sennheiser.com

Sony Range of video equipment, from consumer to professional, plus electronic equipment.
www.sony.com

Steadicam Industry-standard camera stabilization from the most sophisticated to affordable lightweight models.
www.steadicam.com

ViewCast Video capture cards, streaming, and codec solutions.
www.viewcast.com

Wacom Graphics tablets covering all requirements.
www.wacom.com

Further reading

The outstanding publisher for cinematography and video is Focal Press. If you wish to tackle more advanced video practice, its catalog will include at least one title that you will find invaluable. The American Society of Cinematographers also publishes some of the industry's "bibles," which you will sooner or later find indispensable.

303 Digital Filmmaking Solutions
Chuck Gloman; McGraw-Hill, New York; 007141651-X
Claiming to "solve any shoot or edit problem in 10 minutes" is overhyping it, but this book contains substantial nuggets of advice and information. An entertaining read. Worth skimming through.

Clearance and Copyright
Michael Donaldson; Silman-James Press, Los Angeles; 187950572X
Excellent and surprisingly readable coverage of main practical intellectual-property issues for the moviemaker. Dips into related issues such as errors and omissions insurance, hiring your own composer, and copyright on the Internet. The many useful forms and precedents are alone well worth the cost of the book. Intended for the US market but useful to anyone in the business. Recommended.

Content Rights for Creative Professionals
Arnold Lutzker; Focal Press, Oxford; 0240804848
Solid coverage of copyright and trademark law, as well as rights management in media, film, and the Internet. Also discusses competition and antitrust issues, patents, and a broad-brush view of international perspectives. Worthwhile as reference, with CD containing legislative documents or links to them, as well as valuable legal precedent forms.

Capture, Create and Share Digital Movies
Gateway Press, Poway, California; 1577292847
Comprehensive introduction to digital video, featuring different software solutions; fully illustrated and with step-by-step instructions. Windows only.

Digital Moviemaking
Scott Billups; Michael Weise Productions, Studio City; 094118809
Pithy, down-to-earth advice and even provocative

at times, the text is peppered with many asides contributed from the industry. These demonstrate the author's extensive range of contacts—always a sure sign of a successful moviemaker. Very helpful on the technical background, but liable to be dated as technology advances.

Digital Video in Easy Steps
Nick Vandome; Computer Step, Southam, UK; 1840782153
Lively, highly illustrated, and an easy read suitable for beginners. It covers many of the basics in simple language, but there is a lack of in-depth information.

Directing the Documentary
Michael Rabiger; Focal Press, Oxford; 0240806085
A classic text, now into its fourth edition, this book is not only packed with sound advice it also exudes the kind of thoughtful wisdom that can be garnered only from a moviemaker with an extensive filmography. The latest editions are not greatly enhanced by its coverage of new forms of pseudo-documentary such as reality TV. However, this is essential reading for the aspiring documentary-maker.

End of Celluloid, The
Matt Hanson; Rotovision, Switzerland; 2880467837
This is a lively, kaleidoscopic survey of modern trends in the world of the moving image, taking in animation as well as videomaking and cinema, from art-house to epic features. Illustrated with stills from numerous productions.

Exploring Careers in Video and Digital Video
Paul L Allman; Rosen Publishing, New York; 082392542
Wide-reaching advice on careers and training requirements, drawn from personal experience, with range of largely US-based references. Useful for entry-level strategies.

Filmmaker's Handbook, The
Steven Ascher and Edward Pincus; Plume, New York; 0452279577
This book deserves its reputation as the best single-volume reference to moviemaking for both film and video. Strong on the technicalities with less

emphasis on the creative and business side, but if you can afford only one (weighty) volume on film and video, this is highly recommended.

Five C's of Cinematography, The
Joseph V. Mascelli; Silman-James Press, Los Angeles; 187950541X
Classic text that has stood the test of time and fashion, fully illustrated with stills from classic Hollywood films. Each essay on camera angles, continuity, cutting, close-ups, and composition is worth a book from lesser authorities. A must-have for the aspiring moviemaker.

Guerilla Film Makers Movie Blueprint, The
Chris Jones; Continuum, London-New York; 0826414532
Idiosyncratic, lively, and practical volume covering the whole business of independent moviemaking. Making a virtue of leaving nothing unsaid, it covers everything from how to format screenplays, to making arrangements for catering, and the all-important questions of marketing and distribution. Highly recommended.

How Video Works
Diana Weynand and Marcus Weise; Focal Press, Oxford; 024080614X
Technical text suitable for those wishing to enter the engineering or camera-operation side of the digital video industry. Despite its deceptively low-key title, it is an update of a standard textbook for the industry and a must-have for the digital video camera operator.

Introduction to Digital Video, An
John Watkinson; Focal Press, Oxford; 0240516370
Despite the title, this book is a technical, thorough account of the fundamentals of digital video second only to the industry standard *The Art of Digital Video*. It ranges from color theory and video principles to discussions of conversion, compression, coding, interfaces, and output.

Jerry Hofmann on Final Cut Pro 4
Jerry Hofmann; New Riders, Indianapolis; 0735712816
Even if you use other software, there are so many insights and clear explanations of features and functions found in all NLE applications that any video editor can learn from this book. Essential reading for users of Final Cut Pro; others should borrow the book and at least read the introductory paragraphs for each chapter.

Practical DV Filmmaking
Russell Evans; Focal Press, Oxford; 0240516575
The approach here is very "film school," with a list of must-see movies and complete with a short chapter on film theory, but it is none the worse for that. A number of practical projects are scattered throughout the patchily illustrated text. Written in a teacherly style; recommended to those who can learn by reading.

Producing Great Sound for Digital Video
Jay Rose; CMP Books, San Francisco; 1578202086
Comprehensive, thorough manual for working with sound, though some of the technical information is hard to follow. Clearly built on a lifetime of practical experience working with sound.

Real World Digital Video
Pete Shaner and Gerald Everett Jones; Peachpit Press, Berkeley; 0321127293
Condensed, practical, and down-to-earth coverage of the entire process, slanted toward intermediate and advanced-level worker. Recognizes and treats in a very evenhanded way the scripted and improvisational styles of moviemaking. At times it confuses itself by trying to cover too much, but it is still highly recommended.

Video Manual
Michael Grotticelli; ASC Press, Hollywood; 0935578145
A superbly concise guide to video. Although intended for professional moviemakers, if you want a small book you can carry around with you, to learn from every page, this should be it. From a fascinating history of television, through lighting basics to recommendations for tape storage, this book covers it all.

Index

Index continued